Trial After Triumph

East Asia After the Cold War

Trial After Triumph

East Asia After the Cold War

By W. E. Odom

With Contributions By
Andy Yan
and Perry Wood

Hudson Institute
Indianapolis, Indiana

Hudson Institute
Indianapolis, Indiana

Library of Congress Cataloging-in-Publication Data

Odom, William E.
    Trial after triumph: East Asia after the Cold War / by W.E. Odom;
with contributions by Andy Yan and Perry Wood.
    p. cm.
    ISBN 1-55813-042-X
    1. East Asia—Foreign relations.   I. Yan, Andy, 1957-
    II. Wood, Perry.   III. Title.
    DS518.1.03 1992
    327.5—dc20   92-6495
                     CIP

Copyright © 1992 Hudson Institute, Inc.

All rights reserved. No part of this publication may be reproduced, by any process or technique, without the express written consent of the publisher, except in the case of brief quotations embodied in critical articles and reviews.

Printed in the United States of America

This book may be ordered from:
Hudson Institute
Herman Kahn Center
P.O. Box 26-919
Indianapolis, Indiana 46226
(317) 545-1000

CONTENTS

Acknowledgments *VII*

Preface *IX*

Chapter 1 *1*
The Strategic Equilibrium in Northeast Asia: Stable or Transitory?

Chapter 2 *7*
Changing Soviet Strategy Toward Northeast Asia

Chapter 3 *31*
China's Strategic Role in Northeast Asia in the Post-Cold War Era
By Andrew Y. Yan

Chapter 4 *56*
Japan's Strategic Role in Northeast Asia in the Post-Cold War Era
By Andrew Y. Yan

Chapter 5 *83*
The Strategic Equilibrium on the Korean Peninsula in the 1990s
By Perry Wood

Chapter 6 *113*
Conclusions

Bibliography *139*

Index *147*

ACKNOWLEDGMENTS

Although I conceived and structured the study on which this book is based, I was fortunate to have available the expertise of Hudson associates who have far deeper knowledge of the region. Perry Wood is one of the few American scholars who have studied Korea in depth. He lent his expertise to this volume and quietly suffered the weight of my heavy hand as it forced him to simplify and condense his essay. He has a great deal more to say about political change in Korea, but I believe that he has produced here an excellent overview for the non-expert who is interested in the large strategic perspective but needs to depend on specialists for an understanding of individual countries.

Andy Yan, a Ph.D. candidate at Princeton University, grew up in China and acquired some first-hand experience with policy planning at the upper levels of the Chinese government. He is therefore able to provide a genuinely Sinocentric view of China's strategy. Also, his mastery of Japanese has allowed him to gain some insights into the special character of Japanese policymaking. For specialists, his chapters on China and Japan might not break much new ground, but they effectively situate the Chinese and Japanese perspectives in the overall equation of regional politics. Like Perry Wood, he has been highly cooperative in following my overall scheme for the study.

My own interest in and knowledge of East Asia derive from two sources. First, I have long studied Soviet political, military, and economic affairs. Second, my duties as a serving military officer in the 1970s and '80s required me to gain a global understanding of U.S. military and security affairs, for which I have had to pay significant attention to East Asia. I have had the privilege of several visits there and many professional ties with military and government officials in Japan, South Korea, and, to a much lesser extent, China. This background hardly qualifies me as a regional expert, but that might be an advantage: lacking some of the baggage of a regional expert I might stumble into something important yet too obvious to merit their emphasis. At the very least, I hope that by clearly expressing any misconceptions I might have, I will provoke some lucid and corrective reactions.

W.E. Odom
Washington, D.C.
February 1992

PREFACE

To many observers, the end of the Cold War presages the spread of democratic capitalism throughout the world. Indeed, some analysts have looked at recent events and have seen a new world, the end of nationalism, and even the start of a millennium of world peace. The collapse of Communism, however, has yet to fulfill that promise, as evidenced most clearly by ethnic struggles in Yugoslavia and the former Soviet Union. As the world scene changes, a sensible strategy for international relations requires valid, up-to-date information, especially regarding regions vital to the increasingly interdependent world economy. Europe, of course, remains central to the global marketplace. Hudson studies of NATO and military issues regarding the former Soviet Union and Eastern Europe are exploring this sphere of activity.

An equally important pillar, however, is East Asia. And just as discussions of European politics tend to focus on northern Europe, the heart of this region is northeast Asia. That area is in flux, and establishing a new security equilibrium there is no less important than in Europe. Understanding the political dynamics of Northeast Asia, however, requires knowledge of the goals and strategies of the nations it comprises.

Although many books and articles have been published on parts of northeast Asia, none have taken the region as a whole and considered the impact on it of the end of the Cold War. In *Trial After Triumph: East Asia After the Cold War*, Hudson Senior Fellow William E. Odom analyzes the strategy of each Northeast Asian nation in general and specifically toward each other nation in the region. He examines Japan, the two Koreas, China, and Russia, and the major outside power with a presence in the region: the United States. The book provides an overview of current issues and conflicts in the region in light of each nation's perceptions and overall strategy. Finally, the book lays out some possible scenarios for the future of the region and analyzes the likely results of the U.S.'s possible policy choices.

If this book has a central message, it is that Chinese domestic politics and Japanese trade policies are not the proper focus for U.S. strategy toward the region. In fact, the obsession with those issues discourages a thorough understanding of the forces of change in East Asia and the opportunities for the United States to affect them favorably, both for its own interests and those of the regional states. Left to themselves, the East Asian states will probably not be able to weather peacefully the destabilizing impact of the end of the Cold War. With the help of the United States, however, they can. Some of those states seem to understand this reality better than the United States does. *Trial After Triumph: East Asia After the Cold War* lays out the facts and options for American policymakers.

The many generous contributors to Hudson Institute have helped make this book possible. Although they bear no responsibility for its conclusions, Hudson Institute gratefully acknowledges their assistance.

Leslie Lenkowsky
President
Hudson Institute

CHAPTER 1

The Strategic Equilibrium in Northeast Asia: Stable or Transitory?

During the first decade of the Cold War, the United States laid the cornerstones of the Western security order. The North Atlantic Treaty Organization was the first; security arrangements with Japan, Taiwan, and Korea became the second. A number of other regional structures—CENTO, SEATO, ANZUS, ASEAN, and the OAS—occupied places in the security structure, but the first two were the cornerstones. The nuclear deterrent forces of the U.S. also served as a key part of the structure, but as historians review the Cold War from greater distances in time, nuclear forces are likely to be seen as secondary to the European and Northeast Asian alliances in maintaining the East-West balance.

These two regions possessed most of the world's developed industrial capacity and the best-educated work force outside of North America. Combined with the capabilities of North America, they overwhelmed the potential power—economic and military—of the Soviet bloc. In hindsight it is clear that the Soviet image of a two-camp struggle, socialist versus capitalist, was remarkably one-sided. Only the factor of politics—that is, political leadership—was actually in question. In the struggle during and after the Russian Revolution, Lenin's Bolsheviks had employed their leadership edge to succeed against a phalanx of opposition parties which held the loyalties of a large majority of the people. His successors strived to repeat this feat on an international scale. By 1948, Stalin had expanded Soviet hegemony considerably beyond the territories consolidated by Lenin, partly through his political skill with the Communist Party but more importantly through greatly increased Soviet military power.

In the long run, Western political leadership proved far more resourceful and skillful at managing coalitions of states than did the Soviet leadership. The Soviet bloc first fractured in Eastern Europe in 1948, when Tito refused to march to Stalin's drum. Somewhat later, the Chinese and Albanians followed his example. Hungary in 1956, Czechoslovakia in 1968, and Poland in 1980 tried to escape Soviet hegemony but were forcibly restrained by military intervention or, as in Poland, the threat of it. Under Gorbachev's leadership we witnessed the first serious attempt by Moscow to put the East-West competition aside and fundamentally restructure East-West relations. Gorbachev presented a dramatically different challenge to Western political leaders in general and the United States in particular. Without the Soviet threat, how can the old Western alliance system be maintained? Should it be maintained? Will the new world economic order—which grew up under the Western security umbrella—continue to prosper if the security relationships are completely broken?

Neorealist international relations theorists—most conspicuously John Mearsheimer of the University of Chicago[1]—follow the logic of Kenneth Waltz's "third image" for explaining the dynamics among states; they predict that the end of the Cold War, with its competition between two hegemonies, will bring to Europe chaos, disorder, and possibly even war.[2] The bipolar structure of the Cold War tended to strengthen regional organizations and alliances at the expense of latitude in policy action for individual states. Many old quarrels and issues were thus repressed by the overriding concerns of regional security.

Others—Stanley Hoffmann of Harvard, for example—do not agree.[3] They reject the notion that domestic political factors are secondary to the dynamics of interstate factors. Again, to put it in Waltz's alternative theories on the causes of war, "first" and "second" image considerations will be the critical determinants. They see the changed nature of domestic factors, international economic relations, and the role of leaders as shaping a future of Europe quite different from that envisioned by the neorealists.

A similar debate has not yet emerged over the future of Northeast Asia. Perhaps this is merely a reflection of America's Eurocentric view of international affairs. Other reasons, however, are also to be found. Gorbachev's new foreign policy wrought more dramatic changes in Europe than in Asia. Moreover, Europe has been divided into two major blocs, NATO and the WTO; Northeast Asia, by contrast, is multisided in its potential and actual conflicts. The East-West alignment has been less rigid there: China, for example, has been playing both sides for almost two decades. At the same time, there are parallels: a divided Korea had its counterpart in a divided Germany; Korea's neighbors maintained a quiet satisfaction with its division; the military confrontation in Korea had its analogy with the European "central front"; and in both regions a prosperous economic community on one side faced destitute economies on the other. The analogies can be overdrawn, of course, but they are sufficient to raise many of the same questions about the impact of the end of the Cold War on Northeast Asia as have been raised about Europe.

The purpose of this study is to examine the strategic equilibrium that has prevailed for nearly two decades in Northeast Asia, searching for developments and forces that threaten it. To put the aim of the analysis as a question, is the regional strategic equilibrium likely to prove transitory or enduring in the 1990s? Also, how do we explain a yes or a no answer?

The Strategic Equilibrium in Northeast Asia: Stable or Transitory?

It is critical, of course, to understand why and how the equilibrium in Northeast Asia came about in the first place. That knowledge can provide a basis for anticipating what could disturb the equilibrium, and what kinds of change might exceed what can be managed politically. The region was turbulent in the late 1940s and the early 1950s. Civil war in China was followed by a bloody war in Korea. In the 1960s, clashes on the Sino-Soviet border were common. Several objective conditions emerged by the mid- and late 1970s to create a peaceful, if tense, equilibrium. Put simply, they are

- the military weakness of Japan as a matter of official Japanese policy
- the military weakness of China as modern technologies made the Chinese industrial base increasingly obsolescent
- the growing modern military threat from the Soviet Union toward China as well as the United States and Japan
- the deadlock between the two Koreas
- the large U.S. military presence which not only countered Soviet military power but also insured the military balance in Korea and made good relations between Japan and South Korea possible.

Some of these conditions were created intentionally, and some grew out of circumstances. There are a variety of reasons, some political, some economic, why Japan chose not to rearm. The United States chose to defend South Korea as part of its growing concern with Soviet international intentions in the late 1940s. The Soviet Union chose to pursue its enormous military buildup in the Far East beginning in the mid-1960s, partly because of Chinese behavior but also because of a domestic political struggle—created and lost by Khrushchev—that affected military policy as well as other Soviet policies.[4] China chose not to subordinate its foreign policy to Moscow but rather to oppose the Soviet Union more and more openly, especially in international communist party circles and diplomatic circles. China's reasons derived both from domestic economic and political concerns and a deep emotional desire to escape a long period of foreign humiliation and influence.

Other conditions were not intended. China did not want to see its industrialization programs fall farther and farther behind until its military power was severely undermined. Allaying mutual fears between Japan and South Korea has been an unanticipated by-product of the U.S. military presence in both countries. The political and military deadlock on the Korean peninsula has constantly been opposed by both Koreas; neither wants it as a permanent condition, but neither has had the power to alter it. And the list could continue.

The neorealist theorists could hardly explain the present equilibrium convincingly without resorting to several of what Waltz calls the "second image," or domestic structural factors. The balance of power in Northeast

Asia is not only a product of mechanistic interactions among states. It is equally a function of domestic political and economic dynamics in the region and in the larger world. And it depends heavily on the competencies of leaders of states and their governmental staffs. In other words, as we search for variables that can upset the regional power balance unfavorably from a U.S. viewpoint, we must look at several classes of possible causes. At the same time, we must avoid the kind of reductionism that looks at everything, because the set would soon become infinite.

Our analytical starting point is state leaders' intentions. What do they apparently intend to do? What goals do they seek? What is Moscow trying to achieve in the region? What are Japan, China, and the two Koreas trying to achieve? What are their strategies for reaching those goals? These questions provide the primary structure for the analysis. Accordingly, we offer a case study of each state, seeking to understand its strategies toward all the other states. This leads to a duplication of treatment of a number issues, but looking at them from different capitals' perspectives provides different viewpoints.

State interests and goals do not stand alone as the arbitrary creation of leaders. Leaders certainly play a strong role in their definition, and they play a key role in the choice of strategies, but interests, goals, and resources for their pursuit derive from historical experience, domestic political constraints and dynamics, human capital, geography, economics, and perhaps several other factors. In each case, therefore, we devote attention to these factors without trying to be comprehensive. How do we select? No rigid criteria can be set, but in general we try to choose those that seem to bear most critically on state goals and strategies. This approach naturally risks omitting important factors. The critical reader may well see things that should have been included. That does not necessarily ruin the analysis, however. The analysis might help that same reader see more easily how a neglected factor would change the conclusions.

If that happens, the analysis has succeeded in stimulating further analysis within a clarifying structure. Why is that a success? First, American strategic thinking about the region is not nearly as extensive and textured as it is about Europe, the Middle East, and Central America. A few regional experts probably have a comprehensive grasp of Northeast Asia, but when reading much of the policy literature on the area, one is struck by the lack of such a perspective. Most of the literature is sharply focused on one country. China was the most popular in the 1970s and early 1980s, and interest in Japan overtook it as the U.S.-Japan trade balance became highly unfavorable to the United States and ill feelings toward Japan increased. The Soviet Union comes in third, and the Koreas have been woefully neglected in fourth place. Strategic treatments of the larger East Asian and Southeast Asian regions appear occasionally, but they are short on investigation of states' strategies in the region and long on advice for U.S. strategy.

Our analyses of each country and the region as a whole are far from exhaustive, and country experts may quarrel with some of them. The claim for originality, and more important, utility, for U.S. strategy, however, is based on the comprehensive approach and the search for key factors driving change that could upset or alter the balance of power in a manner adverse to U.S. interests. The test of their success is not whether they include every interesting development in the regional states and region at large, but rather whether they identify all of those that bear critically on the strategic equilibrium.

The heavy emphasis on national strategies and goals can reduce the treatment of some larger regional and global factors that are beyond the control or outside the interest of the various national leaders. Patterns of economic development, demographic trends, cultural currents, migrations, and extraregional forces are examples of such factors. Nor does this study include a comprehensive military assessment. Significant discontinuities are noted in several cases; for example, the considerable reduction of Soviet military forces in the region. Nor are shifts in capital investment and general changes in trade patterns given much attention. We might be missing something important here, but not because such things have not been considered. Instead, we may have misjudged their larger significance for the regional strategic balance.

Finally, we have mostly omitted an explicit treatment of one major power in the region: the United States. Its role is included by implication and sometimes explicitly, but our aim is to leave open U.S. strategy as something to be maintained or altered in light of other dynamics in the region. In other words, a discussion of the role of the United States is relegated to the conclusion, and even there the study is limited in its prescriptions. This seems appropriate because our aim is to try to stimulate fresh thought about U.S. power in the region, and that goal is better served by setting the issue aside until we have a comprehensive view of the major forces at play and the probable directions of change. What the United States should do about the region is more properly the subject of another study based on the findings and criticisms of this one.

The study begins with Soviet strategy because it has changed most dramatically in the last few years. Next come China and Japan, the big powers central to the region. Finally, we examine the Koreas—the small powers in the region, states long intent on change which might now find the opening they have sought. The final chapter is a fairly lengthy attempt to integrate the four main chapters into a regional perspective and to introduce an American strategic viewpoint.

Foreshadowing the findings, let us observe here that the end of the Cold War does indeed promise to upset the regional equilibrium. The process of change has only begun, trailing the dramatic events in Europe. It could lead to a serious destabilization, but it need not. The United States can prevent it, but it can also exacerbate it. Moreover, the American public's focus on Japanese-American trade relations to the exclusion of strategic military and political dynamics is a serious threat to our orderly management of the inchoate change described in this book.

NOTES

[1] See his "Back to the Future," *International Security*, 15, Summer, 1990, pp. 5-55.

[2] See Kenneth Waltz's *Man, the State, and War* (New York: Columbia University Press, 1959, p. 12) for his three "images" or theories about how to find the major causes of war: "with man, within the structure of the separate states, within the state system."

[3] See his unpublished paper, "Balance, Concert, Anarchy, or None of the Above," written for a Council on Foreign Relations study group chaired by Gregory Treverton in 1990-91, for a textured and compelling critique. See Hoffman in "Correspondence," *International Security*, 15, Fall, 1990, pp. 191-92, for an ill-tempered response to Mearsheimer. Robert Keohane, same issue of *International Security*, also criticizes Mearsheimer; Bruce M. Russett and Thomas Risse-Kappen, "Correspondence,"*International Security*, 15, Winter, 1990, pp. 216-19, offer yet two more dissenting views. This spirited debate over the validity and applicability of international relations theory focuses wholly on Europe in the post-Cold War era. Northeast Asia, strangely, draws no attention.

[4] See Stephen S. Kaplan, *Diplomacy of Power* (Washington, DC: The Brookings Institution, 1981), pp. 137-42, for the change in Soviet military policy toward China. On the domestic side, see George W. Breslauer, *Khrushchev and Brezhnev as Leaders* (London: George Allen and Unwin, 1982), pp. 89-98. Khrushchev fell into a serious quarrel with the Chinese leaders, which was carried on publicly as a issue of ideology and military doctrine in the nuclear era; yet he was trying to hold Soviet military spending down. Thus he was not eager to react to the Chinese challenge with a buildup of Soviet forces, which the military and some party leaders, e.g., Brezhnev, favored; at the same time, he had alienated most of his support for his domestic policies.

CHAPTER 2

Changing Soviet Strategy Toward Northeast Asia

Background

During World War II, East Asia was a secondary theater for the Soviet Union, one in which hostilities were intentionally avoided until Germany's defeat. By entering the war very late, however, Stalin was able to make some territorial gains. Taking several of the Kurile Islands from Japan and making border adjustments at the expense of China, Stalin set the structure for future tensions with both countries. He was able to install a "people's democracy" in North Korea, dividing the Korean peninsula and creating the conditions for future conflict and tensions there. With a very small military effort and skilled diplomatic efforts in Teheran, Yalta, and San Francisco, Stalin staked out a large strategic presence in East Asia. He failed, however, to obtain Soviet occupation of about half of Japan's Hokkaido, and he expected to see the Chinese Nationalists rule China for the indefinite future; he believed that there was little chance of the Chinese Communist Party winning the civil war.

The big problem for Moscow came with Mao's victory over the Chinese Nationalists in 1949. Stalin neither anticipated nor desired it. Mao's deep differences with the Soviet Communists dated back to the late 1920s when he rejected their tactical advice and based his movement among the peasantry instead of the urban workers. Now Stalin had to welcome this old communist adversary and his new People's Republic of China into the socialist bloc. To the West it looked like a major Soviet victory, but in time it would become a major Soviet burden.

U.S. strategy toward the region was far from clear even by 1950, but Stalin's instigation of the North Korean invasion of South Korea forced clarity in a matter of days. The war brought a solid U.S. military commitment to South Korea; a U.S. military buildup that continued after the war; a series of security treaties with Japan, Taiwan, and South Korea; and an economic recovery program analogous to the Marshall Plan for Europe.

Thus the lines were drawn between "two camps" in Northeast Asia. They remained clear for a decade, but began to cloud because of the inchoate Sino-Soviet split. The process of change was slow: three decades passed before U.S.-PRC normalization in 1979 caused a new alignment.

The Break with China

China was never wholly integrated into the Soviet bloc, and by 1957 hints of a split were evident. The PRC expected Moscow to deliver what it could and would not: the financing of Chinese industrialization. In the early 1960s, the split was an open secret, and after Brezhnev came to power, Moscow quit pretending that all was well and began a two-decade military buildup in the region, aimed primarily, although not wholly, at the PRC.

The number of Soviet ground forces rose from about 15 divisions in the mid-1960s to more than 60 divisions by the early 1980s. The Pacific Fleet became the largest in the Soviet Navy. SS-20 missiles were deployed not only to locations that threatened Europe, but also China, Japan, and Korea. A "high command," a new military headquarters between the General Staff and the frontal and fleet commands, was established in the late 1970s, reflecting both the large scale of the buildup and greater readiness for wartime operations. Four divisions and frontal aviation units were moved into Mongolia.[1] To add depth to the thin Soviet line of communications to the Far East, a second rail line, the Baikal-Amurskii Magistral, was built through extremely difficult terrain.

China could not meet the military competition on equal terms. The Chinese strategic nuclear forces did grow moderately, however, presenting a threat that greatly troubled the Soviet leadership. Chinese attempts to modernize tank and aircraft production achieved only modest results because isolation from the Western and Soviet economies severely retarded the country's industrial and technological base. The Chinese leadership, therefore, responded largely in political arenas—for example, by charging the Soviet Union with "hegemonism"—and mobilized as much of world opinion against Moscow as possible.

In party circles, the PRC competed with Moscow for leadership of the international communist movement. The origins of this struggle date back at least to 1957, and it caused much trouble for Moscow in maintaining its policy of support for "national liberation movements" in Southeast Asia, Africa, and Latin America. In Vietnam, China slowly lost influence to the Soviet Union, although it had never had much influence to lose. In a sense, the U.S. commitment to South Vietnam, viewed in Washington by Secretary of State Rusk as aimed at the containment of China, was objectively helping Moscow with the same goal, a goal of much greater importance to the Soviet Union than to the United States.

In the diplomatic arena, Brezhnev quite early advanced the concept of an "Asian Security System" intended to isolate China. It never caught on except in India and Vietnam, but it reinforced Chinese hostility toward Moscow.

In 1978, as U.S.-PRC normalization appeared more likely, Brezhnev abandoned all sense of caution toward China and began to consider it "enemy number one." The Soviet invasion of Afghanistan, the military buildup on the Sino-Soviet border, and the Soviet-sponsored Vietnamese invasion of Cambodia provided three points of bitter contention between these two giant states. These issues would remain the centerpieces of Soviet-Chinese confrontation until Gorbachev's new strategy in 1986.

Soviet Strategy Toward Japan

Japan, of course, was solidly in the U.S. sphere, and Moscow responded by treating the Japanese government as little more than a lackey of Washington. To the extent that Moscow had a strategy toward Japan, it was dictated by basic Marxist-Leninist analysis of class struggle within Japan. Small ruling circles were believed to be exploiting the large working class. In this view, working-class leadership could ally with other opposition groups and eventually win power. The schedule for success was never rigid, but the logic and final outcome were never doubted, at least officially.

Recent Soviet analysis during *glasnost* reveals just how rigid and mechanistic this strategy was, and still is to some degree. One critic, G. F. Kunadze, is particularly blunt, almost to the point of mocking it.[2] He argues that Moscow focused on "mass action" against the Japanese government, particularly by the political left, and considered all political opposition as "objectively" against the United States. This had to be so in the Soviet ideological view, because the Japanese government was attributed no domestic legitimacy. It was only an arm of U.S. control. Not only was the Japanese working class disenfranchised, but all other groups as well. Therefore, the proper policy focused on popular-front tactics intended to exploit anti-American feelings.

This strategy naturally excluded any concession to Japan on the Northern Territories. To grant them would concede legitimacy to the "puppet" government. For a long time, the broader Japanese public did not identify strongly with these territorial claims.[3] They were mostly the concern of the government. Eventually, however, the public became more aware of Soviet stubbornness on the issue; that awareness slowly made the public—including the political left—see the return of the Northern Territories as a matter of national pride. In Kunadze's view, the Soviet strategy actually worked against the government's goal of weakening the Japanese government by mass domestic opposition, particularly opposition led by the left. The Soviets' unwillingness to compromise on the Northern Territories instilled in the Japanese public a deep-rooted, broad-based hostility toward the U.S.S.R. over Japanese territory grabbed by Stalin at the end of the war.

A Soviet public opinion poll, reported in 1990, compared Japanese and Soviet attitudes toward each other. A majority of Soviet citizens—56%—were quite positive toward Japan, and only 1% clearly negative. Japanese respondents, by contrast, overwhelming held a negative view of the Soviet Union: 79%. Only one-fifth of the Soviet respondents saw Japan as a military threat to the U.S.S.R., while more than three-fifths of the Japanese saw the Soviet Union as a military threat to Japan. A series of other questions revealed a parallel set of asymmetrical perceptions.[4]

A second fundamental error in Soviet strategy, according to Kunadze, was its failure to recognize that the Japanese security tie to the United States was very much in Japan's self-interest. It not only freed Japan of defense burdens, but, more important, it facilitated its economic growth and foreign trade. The Soviet tactic of agitating against the U.S.-Japanese security relationship, rather than weakening the Japanese government in the eyes of the masses, simply fortified anti-Soviet feeling among the Japanese public, because disengagement from the U.S. could be seen as a threat to Japanese prosperity. At the same time, Soviet policy seemed to be aimed at countering the growing Japanese regional influence, influence surprisingly achieved without a Japanese military component. Indeed, why should the Japanese public find a reduction of Japanese influence an appealing goal? Thus Kunadze rhetorically reasoned to Soviet readers.[5] He also rebuked past Soviet leaders for letting their ideological blinders keep them from wondering how Japanese influence could increase despite the virtual absence of military power. They had insisted, despite the absence of evidence, that Japanese militarist circles were achieving rearmament.

Locked into this self-defeating strategy dictated by Marxist-Leninist assumptions about class struggle and international imperialism, Moscow was doomed to make no progress in expanding its influence in Japan. Instead, the strategy excluded the Soviet Union entirely from expanding relations with Japan, and denied it all the economic advantages of deepening cooperation.

At the same time, the U.S. opening to China allowed Japan to follow suit, and the subsequent improvement of Japanese-Chinese relations was yet another adverse strategic development for the Soviet Union. The Brezhnev period carried this paradoxical strategy to its dead end, and when Soviet policymakers began to indulge in "new thinking," they had to address the mess created by more than 40 years of ideological misperceptions of the dynamics of Japan's domestic and foreign policies.

Soviet Strategy Toward the Koreas

Since the Korean War, Soviet relations with the two Koreas have remained frozen in a well-known pattern. The DPRK began as almost entirely a Soviet client state, but Chinese participation in the war gave the nation a strong tie to China as well. To the degree that Soviet policy toward the DPRK shifted over the past four decades, it was the result of the DPRK playing off the PRC and the U.S.S.R. against one another. In the 1980s, for example, when the DPRK wanted to improve the quality of its military forces, Moscow gained the upper hand in Pyongyang by supplying advanced aircraft and other more modern weapons. Beijing simply could not offer what Pyongyang wanted, and Moscow could. Today, therefore, the DPRK finds itself more dependent on Moscow as the winds of change blow.

The ROK remained an implacable enemy, a lackey of U.S. policy, in the eyes of Moscow. Ties with the DPRK made that attitude imperative, but it also fit the ideological perceptions that defined Soviet strategy toward Japan. This approach has only recently begun to change, with the "new thinking" in Soviet foreign policy. If it continues, this process might eventually lead to dramatic changes on the Korean peninsula and in relations between Moscow and Seoul. As Russian foreign policy succeeds Soviet foreign policy, it appears all the more likely.

Under Stalin, Soviet strategy toward the United States hardened the boundaries between the Soviet Bloc, or "socialist camp," and the Western allies, the "imperialist camp." Stalin showed considerable interest in the territories contiguous to the U.S.S.R., and virtually none in the rest of the Pacific region. He seemed content to try to digest China and part of Korea into his camp after failing to win all of Korea.

Khrushchev, by contrast, reached back to Lenin's global strategy, and put Moscow in a larger arena of competition. "Peaceful coexistence"—that is, a "specific form for international class struggle"—was the label belatedly attached to Lenin's strategy after its promulgation in 1921. Its key elements were

- establishing correct state-to-state relations with imperialist countries
- expanding party-to-party relations worldwide while continuing to support class struggle and revolution
- establishing economic ties with the Western industrial states in order to further the industrialization of the Soviet economy
- helping bourgeois "national liberation movements" in the Third World break the grip of the European colonial powers on their Third World possessions. In other words, bourgeois nationalists in the colonies, although objectively class enemies, could play a "progressive" role in undercutting the imperialist system. Local communists, therefore, should strike tactical alliances with these movements.

The aim of this strategy was to gain time for strengthening Soviet economic and military power and thereby to change the "correlation of forces" between socialism and capitalism. Essential to the strategy, but not widely advertised, was the buildup of Soviet military power. Imperialism could not be expected to surrender peacefully; therefore, it was taken for granted that there would be a military showdown at some point.

This strategy, modified for the world of the 1950s, required a much more active Soviet policy in states such as Indonesia, the Philippines, and the Southeast Asian states. The strategy required far less change in regard to Northeast Asia. In principle, it could have led to improved ties with Japan and South Korea, but Moscow's unchanged stance on the Northern Territories and North Korea ruled that out.

Although the Third World component of Khrushchev's policy yielded scant results in most areas, it did put Moscow firmly on the side of Ho Chi Minh. Eventually, with the end of the war in Vietnam, it brought three new clients—a united Vietnam, Cambodia, and Laos—into the Soviet orbit.

Khrushchev's Third World policy also involved Moscow in supporting the Bandung Principles, concepts supported by Third World leaders in South and Southeast Asia. Convened at Bandung, Indonesia, the Bandung Conference attempted to promote unity among the new post-colonial states. Moscow backed the principles, desiring to support national-liberation movements against Western powers. It was an appropriate tactic for Khrushchev's new version of the "peaceful coexistence" strategy. In the "new thinking" in Soviet policy, those principles were reaffirmed.[6] They were not tied, however, to the "international class struggle" as they were in the past, but rather meant to signal a commitment to the international system of sovereign states.

Khrushchev did not push the military component of "peaceful coexistence" as strongly as his successor, Brezhnev. Dealing with the role of nuclear weapons was troublesome for Khrushchev because of Soviet assumptions about the inevitability of war and because Khrushchev apparently also saw them as a way to provide a cheaper defense posture. Priorities changed after Khrushchev's overthrow. As part of Brezhnev's "peaceful coexistence" policy in the 1960s and 1970s, the military component received almost all of the priority. This, of course, was when Soviet forces on the Chinese border grew from about 15 divisions to more than 60, and when the Soviet Pacific Fleet expanded considerably, projecting a significant naval presence not only into the Pacific but also into the Indian Ocean. In other words, the Soviet military was challenging both China and the U.S.-led alliance in Northeast Asia.

The central elements of Soviet strategy toward Northeast Asia appear to have been as follows:

- dramatically alter the military balance in the Soviets' favor

- support domestic political movements within Japan, South Korea, and the United States which opposed the U.S. military alliance system
- try periodically to expand economic access to Japan and the United States
- isolate China in Asia.

The Soviet strategy toward the United States was, of course, to split Japan from its close security ties to the United States. As Soviet critics point out today, that aim was wholly unrealistic without a Soviet willingness to make territorial concessions to Japan. Moreover, it greatly underestimated and misjudged Japan's interests, not only those of the government and the ruling circles but the population as a whole. As Soviet analysts belatedly realized, the U.S.-Japanese security tie brought Japan into the community of Western industrial democracies—precisely what the Japanese economy needed for recovery and growth. The result, of course, was general prosperity for the Japanese and growing Japanese prestige in world politics. Soviet ideological precepts seem to have blinded them to the effect of this factor on Japanese society.

The consequences of the Soviet strategy were hardly what Moscow desired. By the early 1980s, it was clear that a dead end had been reached. Rather than breaking the U.S. security position in the region, Soviet policy had strengthened it. In the overall Asian balance of power, Moscow had a strong position in Southeast Asia and in India. Against this position, the United States had not only maintained its hold on the rimland states—Japan, South Korea, and Taiwan—but had also struck up a strategic relationship with China and Pakistan. The Moscow-New Delhi-Hanoi triangle was intersected by an axis linking Washington, Tokyo, Seoul, Beijing, and Islamabad. Pyongyang tended to play off Moscow and Beijing against each other, eventually coming down more clearly on Moscow's side. Moreover, the economic and military power of the U.S.-led axis was formidable, compared to the relatively weak forces within the Soviet-led triangle of states. To be sure, Soviet military power held a large edge in ground forces—threatening China, and, to some degree, Japan and South Korea—but the overall balance was heavily against the Soviet Union. The result was an equilibrium which Soviet strategy did not have the power to upset short of openly resorting to war.

Notwithstanding its great military forces in the region, then, Moscow had maneuvered itself into a very weak strategic position. In doing so, it had brought about a remarkable strategic stability in Northeast Asia, one it did not like but which its old policies were unable to shake. G.F. Kunadze expressed his country's position: "The result was a paradox: in order to bring the new political thinking into play, we necessarily required a new crisis or total cul-de-sac in our previous policy. The peasant does not cross himself until it thunders."[7] In other words, the failure had become too great to ignore, making a new strategy imperative.

Gorbachev's New Strategy

The first step in "new thinking," as manifested in Soviet foreign policy, was Gorbachev's redefinition of "peaceful coexistence." He broke with the stereotypical ideological thinking about how to undermine the U.S. security structure in the region, virtually eliminated "international class struggle" from the concept, and introduced the new concept of "humankind interests."[8] That ideological revision opened the door in the U.S.S.R. for a fundamental rethinking of Soviet strategy toward Northeast Asia in particular and the "Asia-Pacific-Region" (APR, in the Soviet lexicon) in general.

That done, policy changes could follow. Accordingly, the bases for a new strategy were first articulated by Gorbachev in his July 1986 Vladivostok speech.[9] His September 1988 speech in Krasnoyarsk carried these concepts farther in some particulars.[10] Therefore, both documents merit attention. In Vladivostok Gorbachev set forth five thrusts for policy action.

First, and most expansive, the U.S.S.R. would seek bilateral relations with all states in the region. China and South Korea, of course, would be the critical new targets in this regard. Changes in bilateral relations with other states were also spelled out. With Japan, wider economic cooperation would be sought. The United States, Gorbachev said, had to be recognized as an Asian power, because the security problem could not be solved without it. He also spoke of Southeast Asia and other states, invoking the Bandung principles. But for Northeast Asia, the primary concern in this analysis, they are only tangentially relevant.

Second, Gorbachev voiced unequivocal support for nuclear nonproliferation in the Asia-Pacific Region. Taiwan, South Korea, and North Korea were the targets of this statement, and possibly Japan in the long run.

Third, he called for putting limits on naval forces in the APR as a whole. Entangling the U.S. Navy with limits clearly was the key target for this thrust, but Japan's growing fleet no doubt was also in mind, with possible application even to that of South Korea in the longer term.

Fourth, he spoke of a radical reduction in forces on the Sino-Soviet border. Here Gorbachev was conceding to one of the big three issues of dispute with China.

Fifth, he called for confidence-building measures among all states in the region, declaring that the APR needed a Helsinki-like forum for dealing with these measures and many other matters. In other words, he sought a multilateral diplomatic forum to overarch all bilateral relations. The advantages of such a forum for Moscow were several. It would allow for more Soviet initiatives in setting the agenda in the region. It would allow Soviet diplomats to try to build coalitions to constrain U.S. policies. And it would provide a vehicle for easing several reluctant parties, including the United States, into arms-control discussions which they have consistently resisted for this region.

The differences between Europe—where the Helsinki process first took root—and Northeast Asia are numerous, but perhaps the most critical one is the lack of an East Asian counterpart to the NATO-WTO confrontation in Europe. Except for the small neutral states, Europe in the Cold War was essentially divided into two opposing coalitions. In East Asia, there is no such tidy dualism. China plays an independent game to the extent possible. South Korea is more concerned with the North Korean threat than with a direct Russian/CIS confrontation. North Korea plays Moscow against Beijing. The complexities in Southeast Asia are even greater. Why Gorbachev expected serious progress on such a proposal is unclear. It was a non-starter from the beginning.

Sixth, and separately, Gorbachev talked about Afghanistan in his Vladivostok speech, expressing his intention to withdraw Soviet forces from that country. It was a major step, intended to stimulate a diplomatic revolution in the APR as well as in Europe and Southwest Asia.

Two years later, at Krasnoyarsk, Gorbachev reiterated most of these ideas, but he was more specific on several of the military-security issues, declaring that the Indian Ocean should be made a "zone of peace," and calling for a conference on naval forces and the creation of a multilateral negotiating mechanism. He also offered to pull Soviet naval forces out of Cam Ranh Bay in exchange for the U.S. withdrawal from its military bases in the Philippines. That is, he pressed home those thrusts which had received the weakest response after his Vladivostok speech.

In both speeches Gorbachev also emphasized economic cooperation, but he was short on detail and merely suggested better relations in a number of trade and scientific research areas.

He also restated his frequent commitment to the "deideologization" of Soviet foreign policy and invited the states of the APR to do likewise. Precisely what did this mean for those other states? U.S. policymakers normally do not think of their own foreign policy as ideologically based, and therefore the Soviet demand tended to be seen as nonsense or interpreted as concerning only the Soviet Union, China, North Korea, and the Marxist-Leninist regimes in Southeast Asia. To Soviet policymakers, however, U.S. policy *is* ideologically based, and U.S. security alliances are seen as designed to defend and expand Western liberal democracy and market economies. A Soviet scholar, Rafik Shagi-Akzamovich Aliyev, has made this point explicitly.[11] In his view, it would be a mistake for the U.S.S.R. to try to gain "more genuine equality" in the military area because the United States does not accept "deideologization" of foreign policy. Its military power underpins its ideological position, and the only "constructive" Soviet approach is economic penetration of the region. Aliyev's larger argument seems to be an attempt to edge the Soviet Union toward greater acceptance of U.S. ideology.

In some respects, the aims of this new strategy are fairly transparent. Although the U.S. security dominance could not be broken by "class struggle," it might be reduced by engaging the United States in multilateral negotiations, as in Europe, so that other states could be enticed to put pressure on the United States for military force reductions. In other words, the United States would be admitted to the region, but the price would be military reductions. This was a change from the old aim of ousting the United States entirely from Japan and South Korea, but in no sense did it abandon the goal of weakening the U.S. military presence and the concomitant decline in U.S. political influence. Packaged as a radically new policy, it retained some potentially destabilizing aims of the old strategy. From the Soviet viewpoint, however, this policy probably seemed likely to promote stability, because unilateral Soviet force reductions in the region were destined to occur soon anyway. In a purely U.S.-Soviet context this interpretation might make sense, but in the regional context it falls short: the Soviet reductions would be concentrated on China, whereas U.S. forces—as even some Soviet analysts admit—serve other important regional functions, such as preventing a major Japanese rearmament program.

Another major objective of the new thinking was to alter, if not eliminate, the Moscow-Washington-Beijing triangle as a strategic factor. It would, of course, remain a factor, but it could be made to lose much of its former strategic significance. To this end, Gorbachev proved willing to pay the price China had long asked—movement on three issues: troops on the Sino-Soviet border, Vietnamese withdrawal from Cambodia, and Soviet withdrawal from Afghanistan.

The final aim was to gain economic assistance from Japan, South Korea, and even the United States in developing the Soviet Far East. This was perhaps the principle aim of the "new thinking" in this area, although it was to follow improvements in the security area. Just as economic stagnation had been a major factor in prompting *perestroika*, getting the dynamic East Asian economies to help in the Soviet Far East was worth significant concessions. The political and military concessions he offered strongly support this inference, but Gorbachev was not very clear on how the Soviet "command" economy would be able to integrate with the "market" economies of East Asia.

This inference is an important one, because it offers a basic measure of the success of the new Soviet strategy. The strategy's ability to achieve economic growth for the U.S.S.R. would determine whether it was worth the concessions. If it worked in the security area and weakened the U.S. military position in the region, that would still not solve the fundamental domestic problems confronting *perestroika*—that is, the U.S.S.R.'s economic problems.

As many of the "new thinkers" in Soviet academic institutes emphasized, the economic prosperity of the East Asian states wholly bypassed the Soviet Union. The old Soviet policy had reached a political and military dead end because it denied the Soviet Union the fruits of the dynamic economic and scientific developments of the region. The new strategy, however, failed to spell out how to involve the Soviet economy and how to integrate it into the process. It was merely asserted as an aim. Yet it seems to have been the main objective: the military-security aims were subsumed within it, and the political aims were the preconditions for it.

The economic component of the strategy seems to have implicitly assumed that domestic economic reform would remove all the obstacles that had so long prevented Soviet economic integration into the world economy. As debate among Soviet political analysts would soon reveal, however, there were differing views on this assumption—not to mention the elementary misunderstandings regarding how the Soviet economy would have to change if the country were to enjoy the kind of growth seen in Japan and South Korea.

The new vision of the APR, therefore, was bold, dramatic in its reach, and enormous in its implications. In fact, it suffered from too much boldness: it was not very believable when it was announced, and improbable domestic economic reform was required for its key component to succeed. Several Soviet political and economic analysts and policymakers seemed to believe that such dramatic gestures alone would be enough to prompt enthusiasm among all parties and whip up a degree of excitement sufficient to shake the old regional structure and reshape it to Moscow's advantage. It seemed to offer something to everyone, while ignoring the incompatibility of many of its premises. And it contained some transparent hooks for members of the U.S.-led security system, especially the United States and Japan, which would allow Moscow to drag them into major military concessions, particularly in naval forces.

The Implementation of the New Soviet Strategy

Along with its difficulties, Soviet strategy had its successes. In China it had its greatest effect. In South Korea it transformed the relationship between the two countries. It met coolness in the United States and swung Japan from cautious optimism to angered disappointment about the return of the Northern Territories. Let us look at each case in some detail.

China

By yielding on all three of China's demands against the Soviet Union, Gorbachev achieved remarkable progress with Beijing. The Soviet withdrawal from Afghanistan clearly demonstrated that Gorbachev's Vladivostok speech was more than mere talk. Another concrete action in support of its rhetoric was the inclusion of SS-20s deployed in Siberia in the INF treaty. After the December 1988 announcement of a Soviet unilateral force reduction, the Soviet military began steps for withdrawal of its ground and air forces from Mongolia. Moreover, about 200,000 of the 500,000-troop cut was to be taken in the Far East. In the spring of 1989, Moscow put pressure on Vietnam to withdraw from Cambodia, and Hanoi ostensibly obliged in the fall of that year.

Not surprisingly, such sweeping and unambiguous actions impressed the Chinese, and they rewarded Gorbachev with an invitation to Beijing. Although the student demonstrations in Tiananmen Square during Gorbachev's May 1989 visit threw the Soviet and Chinese domestic policies into sharp contrast, Gorbachev did not let that distract him from his goal of normalization of relations. Not only did he achieve that goal, he also got a commitment to begin party-to-party contacts, which soon led to the reestablishment of full party ties. The Chinese party leader, Jiang Zemin, broke a 34-year hiatus and journeyed to Moscow in May 1991 to keep up the momentum in party relations.[12]

At the time of the Beijing summit, Alexander Yakovlev—then a Politburo member—judged the change achieved by Gorbachev by saying that if he were writing a book about it, he would entitle it *Thirty Years and Three Days*—that is, thirty years of unfortunate relations and three days of reconciliation.[13] Clearly, the Soviet side saw Soviet-Chinese reconciliation as a major achievement, the first in a series of changes the new strategy would achieve.

In the 18-point joint communiqué issued at the summit in Beijing, the PRC accepted most of Gorbachev's principles for changing the relationships in the APR.[14] There was little in them the Chinese opposed anyway. Both sides called for all powers to renounce "hegemony" in the APR and pressed for a greater role for the United Nations. They agreed to expand economic cooperation and declared their mutual respect for state sovereignty and "peaceful coexistence." Gorbachev agreed to support Beijing's position on Taiwan, but he was also able to insert in the communiqué a demand for Soviet "new thinking" in international affairs and to get Chinese support for the Bandung principles—something China had never really opposed.

The price of normalization was so high for the Soviet Union that one might wonder if China paid anything at all. If it did, it was in its willingness to take a conciliatory line toward India, Moscow's counterweight to China in the days of confrontation. And it probably included a cooperative attitude toward future Soviet initiatives on the Korean peninsula.

Perhaps more significant, however, was China's willingness to go along with Moscow's redefinition of the Moscow-Washington-Beijing triangle. Both sides insisted that they were able to move to normalization without any significant change in their relationship with Washington. As a Soviet analyst, N.G. Fedulova, described it in the fall of 1990, the "triangle" is an objective reality, but it has lost its former character of having an anti-American and an anti-Soviet leg.[15] A similar view was offered by V.I. Ivanov, who declared the situation ". . . new because there is no fear that any two will encroach on the third."[16] Gorbachev was quite careful, therefore, to try to neutralize the old game of playing the China "card" or the Soviet "card." Two years later, when Jiang Zemin came to Moscow as Chinese party leader, Gorbachev would once again emphasize that "Soviet-Chinese relations are not some kind of card in a geopolitical game."[17] In the new climate Moscow had created with Washington, the old card game had lost much of its former significance. Or so it seemed. The Tiananmen Square incident put great strain on U.S.-Chinese relations, which President Bush moderated by refusing to go along with sanctions called for by Congressional and media leaders. PRC-U.S.S.R. normalization gave the Chinese leaders a stronger foreign policy position from which to resist American pressure.

Nonetheless, normalization was no small achievement. The Soviet occupation of Afghanistan had healed the breach in U.S.-Pakistani relations and drawn the PRC and the U.S. into closer cooperation against the U.S.S.R. The axis that U.S. policy had built from Tokyo through Beijing to Islamabad would not necessarily collapse, but Gorbachev had removed some of its key reinforcing factors. Although the U.S. position in Asia remained strong, it was somewhat weakened on the mainland. More important for Gorbachev, he had reduced some of the remarkably strong anti-Soviet feeling in the region, which China and the United States had exploited throughout the 1980s.

On the economic front, the Soviet side heralded the opening of a railroad from Sinkiang to Kazakstan, cooperation in science and technology, and increased border trade. While all this may have sounded like a major new departure, it promised very little help for the deeper economic crisis in the U.S.S.R. That would depend on other states in the APR: Japan, the United States, and South Korea.

Overall, the normalization of relations with the PRC has to be put down as a success for the new Soviet strategy. It was a prerequisite for any further thawing of the Soviet Union's frozen position in Asia and the Pacific. At the same time, it may also prove small compensation if the thaw fails to occur uniformly throughout the APR. Marshal Yazov's visit to Beijing and Jiang Zemin's visit to Moscow give the relationship a hint of its earlier character:

military arms transfers and party factions predominated. For example, the Soviet Union would sell China a squadron of its modern fighter, the SU-27, at a "friendship price."[18]

Japan

Unlike China, Japan was much less responsive to the new Soviet policy. Shevardnadze courted the Japanese and was able to visit Tokyo. Japanese delegations were brought to Moscow as part of a comprehensive campaign to prepare for the unprecedented Japanese-Soviet summit meeting in Tokyo in April 1991. For all the effort, however, little serious progress was achieved.

In the official Soviet view, the fault was with Japan. While the Soviet Union withdrew from Afghanistan, signed the INF treaty, and offered to pull out of Cam Ranh Bay, the Japanese complained all the more about the Soviet military danger, refused to engage in arms-control talks, ruled out compromise on the Northern Territories, and cast doubt on Soviet sincerity. In comparing Japan to the United States and Western Europe, Soviet Deputy Foreign Minister Ivan Rogachev called Japan "more Catholic than the Pope."[19] As noted earlier, the climate of *glasnost* and "new thinking" prompted some serious internal Soviet rethinking of the country's policy toward Japan. Although these efforts have had some impact on official thinking, they have hardly carried the internal debate. Moreover, the growing split between the Union regime and the republics complicated things for Gorbachev. Indeed, in January 1990 Russian President Boris Yeltsin visited Japan and advanced a four-stage plan for returning the Northern Territories. Because the process would require 15-20 years, however, the Japanese were not particularly impressed.[20]

The best insight into the internal Soviet debate is provided by the Far East expert G.F. Kunadze. He insists that Soviet policy proceeded on the mistaken assumption that ". . . the laws of development are automatically on the side of socialism.[21] He admits that Soviet leaders tried to correct this mistake, but he believes that the Soviet Union could not succeed because it was not willing to pay the "political price" for what everyone agreed was in the Soviet economic interest—a sharing of Soviet resources in the Far East with Japan in exchange for a share in Japanese economic know-how and technology. He sees the main task of Soviet policy as preventing the decline of Soviet influence in the APR and asserts that unlimited economic relations with Japan are essential to that end. The new Soviet strategy failed to address even the basic obstacles to progress in this direction.

The Soviet Union, Kunadze notes, was unwilling to pay the price of those improved relations: meeting Japanese conditions for a peace treaty. Kunadze blames Stalin for seizing the Northern territories and failing to sign a peace treaty in 1946 in San Francisco. Since then, Moscow has refused to yield on the Japanese territorial claims. Until it does, no real progress will be possible. That Soviet officials could make a strong legal case for Soviet possession of the Northern Territories does not impress Kunadze.

Why was Soviet strategy still so unyielding even in the climate of "new thinking"? Kunadze's answer is that the role of ideology not only consistently guided Soviet policy toward Japan in the past but retains a strong grip even in today's changed political climate. New ideas at the top of the policy hierarchy, he explains, must be filtered down through the bureaucracy for implementation, and at the lower levels the old ideological concepts still hold sway. And each narrow specialist adds his own distortions. "The result," Kunadze adds, "is a vicious circle in which information is prepared and filtered in such a way as to conform to the leadership's existing views," reinforcing the old ones and squeezing out the new ones.

Thus the ideologically biased lenses of the apparatus kept military factors in the center of the picture so that they continued to dominate Soviet policy thinking. Kunadze's judgment in this regard is confirmed by the high priority given Soviet military concerns even in Gorbachev's new principles enunciated at Vladivostok and Krasnoyarsk. Similarly, the Soviet Union's failed efforts to create a Helsinki-like multilateral forum were primarily concerned with reducing military forces in the region. At almost every meeting sponsored by the Soviet Union on the region, the agenda was dominated by military security matters with economic and political factors a secondary component.

The logic of the Soviet strategy seems to have been that dealing first with military issues would open the door to progress on other matters. Although he concedes a certain amount of truth to that logic, Kunadze insists that in regard to Japan it missed the main point. There will be no movement with Japan until Moscow is willing to make concessions on the Northern Territories. Gorbachev's visit to Tokyo six months after Kunadze published this assessment certainly vindicated his analysis.

A second price the Soviet Union's successor states must pay, in Kunadze's opinion, is recognition that the Japanese-American security relationship is very much in the interest of all the people of Japan, not just the government. This relationship includes Japan in a family of states in which it can profit enormously from trade, gives it a growing political role, and costs it very little in military expenditures. Several Soviet analysts share with Kunadze this recognition that military power has proved unimportant in Japan's emergence as a major power—something Soviet ideological precepts rule out by definition. According to the old "stereotypical" Soviet view, the fact that Japan's influence has increased means that Japan must be building up military power. This, he suggests, explains the persistent but groundless Soviet charge of reemerging Japanese militarism. Kunadze and other Soviet critics believe that the Soviet leadership made a gross error here, both in policy and in analysis of the real situation in Japan. Ideological assumptions drive the analysis so strongly, in fact, that evidence of militarism is manufactured out of thin air. In reality, the Japanese-American security tie has prevented Japanese military resurgence and permitted spectacular economic growth. No post-Soviet strategy can make sense unless it rests on a clear recognition of these facts.

The best explanation of the lack of progress on the economic front has been offered by Rafik Shagi-Akzamovich Aliyev, one of Kunadze's colleagues at IMEMO (Institute for Economics and International Affairs.[22] He restates the case for the Japanese-American military tie, and argues that Japan's economic access to Western markets might well be jeopardized if the tie were broken. Moreover, such a break could create a Japanese "Gaullism" focused on the Northern Territories. Even the Japanese Communist Party wants them returned! Aliyev finds the Soviet goal of reducing the Japanese security tie to the United States "absurd."

His most important argument, however, concerns the obstacles to Soviet-Japanese economic cooperation. Progress was blocked by the Soviet command economic system, which would not allow sufficient economic autonomy in the Far East to permit an effective Japanese economic engagement there. In his view, ideas afoot in Moscow for a set of special economic zones in the Far East would not work. The economic ministries would interfere, and the special zones would fail. His proposed remedy, therefore, emphasized blocking all such interference. He suggested three elements for a new approach. First, the Far Eastern region of the U.S.S.R. had to have complete economic autonomy. Second, it had to develop a multistructured economy based on the market. Third, economic autonomy for the Soviet Far East must not contradict the sovereignty of the Moscow center.

This concept did recognize the critical role of permitting market economic relations on Soviet soil if there were to be any real prospect of interdependency with the Japanese economy. Running a multistructured system—that is, a market sector parallel with a planned sector—might, however, have been easier said than done. Finding a halfway house between a command economy and a market system proved impossible during three decades of search in East Europe. Why should an answer suddenly turn up in the Soviet Far East? Still, Aliyev does get to the root of the economic cooperation problem. Without a genuinely free market in the Soviet Union—at least in the Far East—Japan could not be expected to take a serious interest in widening economic cooperation. On this point, Aliyev got very close to the core of the problem without fully acknowledging what a genuine solution requires.

Aliyev also sharply challenged the emphasis on the Vladivostok-Krasnoyarsk principles: they were dominated by military concerns. He considered it a great mistake for Moscow to seek greater military equality in the APR. Soviet military power was wholly adequate for defensive purposes without any U.S. reductions. If they were to increase their influence in the APR, what the Soviet Union really needed was economic penetration.

The APR concept also troubles Aliyev. For him it makes no sense. What defines it? To define it economically, its borders would have to include the entire Western economic world, because its states are economically linked to Europe, North America, and other areas. As a purely geographical definition, including all the Pacific Ocean and Indian Ocean littoral states, it is equally incoherent for policymaking. Aliyev has a valid point, and it may explain some of the contradictions in Gorbachev's new strategy. Because it embraces too much, the new strategy is not a useful generalized label under which to articulate well-coordinated policies. That also makes it easy for most states within the region to ignore or disregard its initiatives.

As mentioned earlier, Aliyev also doubts the wisdom of the Soviet demand that all countries accept "deideologization" of their foreign policies. The American ideological approach is essential to that nation's military and economic policies, and it has brought prosperity to the East Asian rim. Soviet policy would be more wisely directed at trying to share the prosperity rather than reducing the American military presence. To coin a metaphor, Aliyev is essentially arguing that in the Far East the Soviet Union got on the military train and missed the economic train. It could not catch the economic train by trying to reorganize the military train. It had to transfer trains outright.

Actually, Japan, rather than the United States, was the big stumbling block for Soviet strategy. Soviet difficulties with Japan reflected basic problems with the Soviet approach to the region as a whole. Economic differences created a "Great Wall" that kept the Soviet Union out of the region, and the wall could not be breached by military and political means alone. "New thinking," as reflected in Gorbachev's new strategy, has failed to confront this reality clearly and directly.

Against this background, Gorbachev's visit to Japan was destined to achieve very little, although the billing raised expectations quite high. In the aftermath, the Japanese press accused the Soviet Union of turning its "ugly" side toward Japan while showing the better side to Europe. The availability of perceptive analyses by several Soviet thinkers such as those mentioned earlier, however, makes it unlikely that Gorbachev and his foreign ministry officials were unable to anticipate the disillusionment that would follow a summit with no progress on the Northern Territories. How, then, is the whole affair to be explained?

Even if Gorbachev actually wanted to yield on the Northern Territories, it is improbable that he could have overcome the sharp domestic resistance to such a concession. Shevardnadze resigned because of sharp internal criticisms that he had given away the Soviet strategic position in Central Europe, especially in Germany. Refusing to defend Shevardnadze, Gorbachev had drifted to the political right throughout 1990. The party and military "conservatives" were hardly in the mood for another sacrifice of Soviet influence and control.

On the other side of the political spectrum, Yeltsin and "Democratic Russia" (a liberal political party in the Russian Republic) were challenging Gorbachev. Since early 1990, Yeltsin had kept Gorbachev on notice that the Northern Territories are Russian and cannot be given back to Japan without Russia's agreement. And as we noted, Yeltsin's scheme for their return—requiring a 15-20 year process—does not appeal to Japan.

In a word, Gorbachev did not have the domestic political power to pay the political price required for a major breakthrough with Japan. Perhaps he believed that he could buy a breakthrough on the "installment plan." As he joked in Tokyo, the lengthy talks were setting "a Guinness record" for such meetings, but in the end the Japanese refused to sell on easy long-term credit.[23]

The Koreas

Soviet strategy toward South Korea enjoyed more success than that toward Japan, but where it may lead and the dynamics it may create in Northeast Asia are both unclear and somewhat disturbing. Nor is it clear that Soviet policymakers grasp the implications of their initiatives.

For several years, North Korea and South Korea have sparred with one another in the diplomatic arena, the North insisting on a unified Korea, the South arguing for a two-Korea approach as a near-term political solution. As Soviet analysts point out, no real movement is possible without agreement among the other powers in the region, especially the United States and the Soviet Union, but also including China and Japan.

South Korea took an indirect approach to Moscow, first improving ties in East Europe—notably with Hungary, Poland, and Czechoslovakia after their attendance at the 1988 Olympic Games in Seoul. Hungary accepted diplomatic ties with Seoul in February 1989, setting an example the others quickly followed. The ROK was thus able to prove that socialist countries (as these were at the time) could have profitable ties with both Koreas. The Soviet leadership was impressed sufficiently to explore South Korea's opening, and progress came swiftly.

Again, the newfound freedom of academic expression in the Soviet Union gives us some insight into the changing Soviet view of the two Koreas, just as it did for Japan. In the fall of 1989, Vasili Mikheyev noted that signs of flexibility were appearing in the positions of both the ROK and the DPRK.[24] Although he recognized that the two sides were still far apart, he insisted that the improved international climate permitted Moscow and Washington to give the process new impetus. Normalization between Moscow and Beijing, in his view, added dramatic possibilities for progress toward a Korean political solution. Changing Japanese attitudes—

reflected in a willingness to establish diplomatic relations with the DPRK—and unofficial U.S.-DPRK contacts were also noted as encouraging signs. Such an optimistic judgment, so contrary to the old official line, foreshadowed the reversal of Soviet diplomacy toward Seoul that would soon occur.

Gorbachev's San Francisco meeting with President Roh Tae Woo in June of 1990 marked, of course, a major step in the new Soviet policy toward Korea. Less than four months later, normal diplomatic ties were established. Positive results for Gorbachev were evident in January 1991, when Seoul offered $3 billion in loans to the Soviet Union over the next three years, and Deputy Prime Minister Maslyukov said after the deal was signed that the Soviet Union would be willing to sell arms to the ROK "for defensive purposes."[25] Moscow, therefore, is clearly thawing its once-frozen position on the Korean peninsula. Seoul is making it economically profitable and thereby increasing the fluidity of the situation. The forces of change are inchoate, but they are likely to grow in strength and in number. That is, more parties are likely to become concerned and seek to influence the outcome. Japan and China hardly look benignly on the prospects of a reunified Korea, but that is precisely what Seoul would like the new fluidity to facilitate. Whereas at present Japan and China are disturbed about the North Korean nuclear weapons program, with a unified Korea that concern would be all the greater. The South Koreans, of course, realize that North Korea has strong cards to play in this game, including the military-offensive card, which makes it risky for South Korea to press ahead without caution.

It is difficult, however, to see how this process, unless Moscow decides to abandon it, can fail to undermine the DPRK's very existence. Once entangled with the ROK and its powerful economy, the DPRK will be no more a match for the ROK politically than East Germany was for the Federal Republic. The situation is significantly different in the details—particularly in the greater legitimacy enjoyed by the Pyongyang government because it does not depend on Soviet forces to prop it up—but the potential for a rapid collapse of the DPRK is not to be wholly discounted, just as aggressive military behavior to preempt a collapse is not to be ruled out. What, then, did Moscow promise the DPRK to get it to go along?

Perhaps nothing, but if there was something, the answer must lie in Japan's policy toward the Koreas and the possibility of bringing the United States along in the search for a Korean political solution. The ROK's policy of two Koreas is not likely to remain its policy once the process of change gains momentum. Why should it not try to displace the DPRK government? A Korea united under the ROK could become both a strong economic power and a military factor of great weight, perhaps eventually acquiring nuclear weapons. Likewise, the DPRK's policy for a unified Korea can hardly remain its goal. The DPRK's survival would seem to require a two-Korea outcome, the ROK's old formula. To get the cooperation of the North

Koreans—assuming that the Soviet Union is not simply ignoring them—the Soviets must promise some formula that perpetuates the DPRK as a viable state.

Here Moscow's strategy seems to depend on the involvement of the United States, China, and Japan. If all three can be persuaded to support some form of DPRK, then Seoul's power in the political endgame might be checked.

Once South Korea became aware that this was Moscow's policy, of course, Seoul could be expected to withhold economic assistance to Moscow, canceling the very thing that started the new ROK-U.S.S.R. relationship. One is left only with paradoxes, not clear answers to this puzzling question.

China, for its part, can hardly desire a united Korea under Seoul, with all the attendant economic, military, and political consequences. Therefore, Beijing can probably be counted on to support the DPRK's continued autonomy in some form. Yet China has apparently decided to improve its relations with South Korea, perhaps moving to full recognition in 1992.[26]

Although Japan has kept good relations with Seoul by supporting its policy toward Pyongyang, it may be no more enthusiastic than China about a unified Korea with a market economy. The logical way for Japan to slow that outcome, if not prevent it altogether, would be to recognize the DPRK and quietly support its continued autonomy, even in some kind of Korean confederation. As a future prospect, an economically and militarily strong, united Korea would be bound to prompt a Japanese review of its own rearmament plans. Perhaps Korea's deeply rooted hostility toward Japan has withered so completely that it is no longer a significant political factor. It would not be prudent, however, to assume that such feelings are dead. Japan is most unlikely to do so. More than any other state in the region, Japan is unlikely to take a benign stance toward the prospect of a unified Korea.

How the United States would approach this process is not so clear. It would be hard pressed to oppose it if Moscow favored it, and it would be even harder pressed if Japan and China opposed it. Yet a South Korea frustrated in its effort to win the whole peninsula would be a difficult ally for Washington if the United States were seen as part of a coalition supporting the independent existence of the DPRK. Moreover, the U.S. policy of sponsoring good relations between the ROK and Japan, getting both sides to repress a history of terrible colonial relations, would be enormously complicated. U.S. forces could hardly remain in Korea; yet they are the mainstay not only in the military balance on the peninsula but also in the securing of congenial ROK-Japanese relations. The major U.S. lever for balancing its uneasy allies would disappear, and what would replace it is difficult to conceive. Therefore, Korean reunification could easily undermine the strategic position of the U.S. in Northeast Asia, probably causing a complete military withdrawal.

Perhaps Moscow will eventually prove willing to abandon the DPRK outright. Speculating about this possibility, Mikheyev argues that although it might be a "subtraction" from the socialist camp, a democratic, independent, and unified Korea could play a "constructive" role as a "balancing factor" in big-power relations in the APR. Both China and Japan, however, would be seriously displeased. And U.S. forces would have to withdraw, weakening U.S. influence as a stabilizing element.

Many factors might come into play on the Korean peninsula, and we have probably overlooked several of them here. The main point is that once the process of change acquires momentum, it will be difficult to anticipate where it will end. As we look for factors that could upset the strategic equilibrium in Northeast Asia, Korea certainly must be included as a major one. Soviet leaders may have launched a policy the ultimate consequences of which they do not understand. Alternatively, perhaps Moscow understands it well and is gambling on becoming the guarantor of the security of a unified Korea.

Soviet Strategy Toward the United States

The main Soviet objective toward the United States in Asia was revealed by its Soviet critics. It was to improve the Soviet military position, not by increasing its own forces but by reducing U.S. forces there, particularly naval forces. Gorbachev's Vladivostok principles make that quite apparent, and the Soviet effort to create a multilateral negotiating mechanism in the pattern of the Helsinki process suggests the same inference.

Once entangled in such a process, the United States could be confronted by pressures from a number of states, including some of its allies, to reduce its military forces in the region. None of the U.S. allies seems so disposed—quite the contrary—but things could change. As the Soviet analysts point out, the concept of "deideologization" of foreign policy—that is, of equal security for all APR states—would undercut the U.S. position. The bait in this trap, of course, was Soviet acknowledgment that the United States is an APR power and that it must participate centrally in the process of change.

As the Soviet critics point out, however, this process would not only damage U.S. interests; the Soviet Union itself might not like the results. A "Gaullist" Japan determined to retrieve its Northern Territories is hardly in the Soviet (or Russian) interest. Nor is a unified Korea which is both an economic and military regional Leviathan.

A number of Soviet commentaries over the past couple of years have expressed frustration at the lack of response to Gorbachev's new strategy, particularly from Washington.[27] More frequently voiced have been accusations that the U.S. harbors Cold War attitudes and wants to gain a military advantage in the region. In fact, much of the Soviet commentary betrays a sense of puzzlement and frustration toward the United States over its unresponsiveness.[28] On the whole, then, in Moscow's view the anticipated response to the Soviet initiatives did not materialize on schedule.

Conclusions

The old Soviet strategy toward Northeast Asia contributed to the region's stability. The Soviet military threat provided strong incentives for the maintenance of the American security system there, and even allowed Washington to develop a strategic relationship with China. This was by no means the outcome intended by the Soviet leaders, but rather the result of misperceptions on their part and paradoxes in the logic of their strategy.

The new strategy was intended to destabilize the region, not in a military sense but in a political and economic one. By breaking up the old stability, the Soviet Union believed it could create a new stability in which it would play a fundamentally different role. Rather than an outside actor, it would be the central inside actor. As an insider it would profit both economically and politically. In reducing (although not eliminating) U.S. military power in the region, the Soviet Union would also gain militarily.

Even a cursory examination of the new Soviet strategy, however, reveals that it, like the old one, suffered from a number of contradictions. The military goals it sought could undermine the military stability of the region. The economic goals were wholly unrealistic unless a transformation of the Soviet economy to a market basis was achieved. This change cannot be ruled out, and it is more likely to happen in an independent Russia, but it would take a long time. And only then could the Russian economy profitably interact with the thriving economies of Japan and Korea.

The new strategy has had positive results only regarding China and, to some extent, South Korea. On all other fronts, it appears to have been stymied. Moreover, in the one place where it was not blocked—Korea—it promises to generate a number of troubling outcomes if it succeeds.

The tumultuous events in Moscow in the summer and fall of 1991, of course, appear to have brought the demise of the Soviet Union. In its place a number of successor states are struggling to establish their independence within a "commonwealth," leaving highly uncertain whether a single foreign policy toward East Asia will be continued for them all. For all intents and purposes, Russia has taken into receivership Soviet foreign policy in that region, and with or without a commonwealth, Russia is bound to have the dominant, if not the only, voice in that policy.

Will this change greatly affect our analysis of the impact of Gorbachev's strategy toward the region? Not significantly. Gorbachev had gone about as far as he could without major domestic economic change, and that change was bound to undercut the existence of a central Soviet state. The foreign policy line coming from Boris Yeltsin and his foreign minister, Andrei Kozyrev, does not suggest efforts to reverse what Gorbachev did in East Asia except in ending party-to-party relations with China. It is also likely to put added economic pressures on North Korea because supplies of oil and military spare parts from Russia will probably require hard currency for payment. Moreover, much of the "new thinking" by Russian scholars is more likely to find a receptive audience in Foreign Minister Kozyrev, who has wholly abandoned Marxism-Leninism.

Another consequence of the passing of Soviet power is already becoming manifest in Russian Far East economic relations with other regional states. Initiatives by factory managers and local government officials are opening up more direct economic interaction with Japan and Korea. Moscow does not appear to be fully in control of the local entrepreneurs and officials in Vladivostok, Khabarovsk, and other cities in the Russian Far East. They are forced—or left—to look after their own interests during the dramatic transformation in Moscow.

The truly significant consequences of Gorbachev's strategy toward Northeast Asia have been to remove Soviet military power from its stabilizing role and to leave Russia in the throes of dramatic social, economic, and political transition. For the next few years, therefore, Moscow is unlikely to play a strong role in the region except when and where the other regional powers invite it to do so. Recipient of foreign assistance is more likely to be its central role.

Such a rapid decline of Soviet and Russian power in the region, of course, only sharpens our original question. What does it mean for the strategic equilibrium of the region? The tentative answer has to be that it has upset it, and that it has prompted the beginnings of basic changes in Korea that affect the interests of Japan, China, and the United States. Although he can hardly have intended this outcome, Gorbachev inadvertently stimulated the beginnings of major changes in the regional balance of power, changes that could become highly destabilizing unless the other powers in the region anticipate them and work out adequate arrangements for a new equilibrium.

NOTES

[1] JPRS-TAC-91-010, Apr. 29, 1991, p. 34, "Soviet Ambassador on Withdrawal From Mongolia," puts the Soviet troop strength in Mongolia at 67,000.

[2] JPRS-UWE-90-012, Oct. 29, 1990, pp. 2-12, "The New Thinking and Soviet

Policy Regarding Japan," an article by G. F. Kunadze, analyzes the history of the policy and the requirements for change.

[3] *Ibid.*

[4] JPRS-UWE-90-007, July 23, 1990, pp. 52-58, "Soviet Union-Japan: How We See Each Other."

[5] JPRS-UWE-90-012, Oct. 29, 1990, pp. 2-12, Kunadze, *op. cit.*

[6] See Gorbachev's Vladivostok speech of July 28, 1986, TASS.

[7] Kunadze, *op. cit.*, p. 3.

[8] Gorbachev offered some rough ideas on his new directions in a Central Committee Plenum speech in December 1984. In 1986 he got the 27th Party Congress to accept a new definition of "peaceful coexistence," but the rationale was not all that clear until his book, *Perestroika*, was published later that year.

[9] See TASS, July 28, 1986, for the full text.

[10] See TASS, Sept. 16, 1988, for the full text.

[11] JPRS-UWE-91-001, Jan. 8, 1991, pp. 19-27, "Soviet Policy in the Asia-Pacific Region Viewed," Aliyev's article in *Mezhdunarodnaya politika i mezhdunarodnye otnoshenia*, 9, September, 1990, pp. 88-96.

[12] See Francis X. Clines, "Chinese Party Chief Mending Relations in Moscow," *The New York Times*, May 16, 1991.

[13] FBIS-SOV-89-097, May 22, 1989, p. 17, "Yakovlev Interviewed on the Summit," Moscow TV, May 21, 1989.

[14] FBIS-SOV-89-095, May 18, 1989, pp. 16-18, "USSR-PRC Joint Communique on Soviet Issued," Moscow TASS, May 18, 1989.

[15] JPRS-UWE-90-010, Sept. 13, 1990, "USSR-US-PRC Relations and Some Tendencies in International Development," pp. 17-25.

[16] JPRS-UWE-91-001, Jan. 8, 1991, "USSR's Role in Asia Viewed," pp. 97-107.

[17] Francis X. Clines, *op. cit.*

[18] *Ibid.*

[19] See Rajan Menon, "Gorbachev's Japan Policy," *Survival*, 33, Mar./Apr., 1991, pp. 158-72, for this quote and a good summary of the Soviet irritations with Japan.

[20] *Ibid.*

[21] *Op. cit.*

[22] Aliyev, *op. cit.*, JPRS-UWE-91-001, Jan. 8, 1991.

[23] See Gorbachev's remark in FBIS-SOV-91-077, Apr. 22, 1991, p. 11.

[24] Vasili Mikheyev, "The Korea Problem in the Future," *International Affairs*, 9, 1989, 138-47.

[25] RFE/RL Daily Report 16, January 23, 1991.

[26] See FBIS-CHI-91-233, Dec. 4, 1991. The Chinese CPC General Secretary Jiang Zemin has reportedly told Kim Il-sung that there are no major obstacles barring diplomatic relations between Beijing and Seoul.

[27] See, for example, Yu. Lugovskoi, "The Krasnoyarsk Initiatives and Security of the APR," *Azii i afriki*, 2, Feb. 1989, pp. 5-8, translated in JPRS-UIA-89-014, Sept. 11, 1989, pp. 7-11.

[28] See Aleksei A. Kirichenko, "Vladivostok 88: Hopes and Prospects," *Mezhdunarodaya ekonomika i mezhdunarodnye otnosheniia*, 2, Feb. 1989, pp. 138-41, and V. Voronstov and A Muradyan, "APR Security: Concepts and Reality," *Far Eastern Affairs*, 1, Jan. 1990, pp. 19-36. The former article reports on negative U.S. attitudes at a conference of academics in Vladivostok in October 1988 including scholars from 36 countries.

CHAPTER 3

China's Strategic Role in Northeast Asia in the Post-Cold War Era

By Andrew Y. Yan

Background

Since the early 1980s, China has been increasingly active in international economic and diplomatic relations. The primary focus of Chinese foreign policy, however, has been on Northeast Asia—defined here as including China, Japan, North and South Korea, the Soviet Union, Taiwan, and Hong Kong. This region has vital strategic importance to China. Its security concerns focus on this area: the principal threats to Chinese national security come from the long and disputed Sino-Soviet border as well as from the volatile situation on the Korean peninsula. China's military power does not extend beyond this region, even though its strategic nuclear weapons can reach any corner of the world. Northeast Asia is home to China's largest trading partners—Hong Kong, Japan, Taiwan, and South Korea. This region is also where Chinese political and cultural influences have been strongest.

The collapse of the socialist bloc and the end of the Cold War make it imperative to reassess the probable role China will play in the new strategic environment of Northeast Asia. Since World War II, Northeast Asia has been dominated by the rivalry of the United States, the Soviet Union, and China. Three major dimensions underlie the postwar strategic equilibrium in Northeast Asia: first, the expansion of Soviet military power on the Asian mainland and in the Pacific; second, the application of America's extended deterrence commitments, most prominently in the United States-Japan alliance but extending to other regional actors; third, weak Chinese military and economic power and its pursuit of an autonomous political and military capacity. The strategic balance in this region has been primarily between the U.S.-Japanese alliance and the Soviet Union. China has played a secondary role, and its position in this strategic equilibrium has been derivative.

Taking a broad historical view, we can see that Chinese foreign policy is a function of its historical legacy and its domestic political and economic dynamics. Our analysis will treat Chinese foreign policy and strategy as a dependent variable, taking as the independent variables China's domestic political and economic institutional configuration, state and societal interactions, economic imperatives, policymakers' worldviews, and official ideology. Of course, these independent variables are themselves products of history. Viewed from this perspective, Chinese foreign policy in the past 40 years has been strongly influenced by a set of factors including deep-rooted *traditional attitudes*, modern *nationalist impulses*, a genuine *revolutionary aspiration*, and an official Marxist-Leninist *ideology*.

Tradition leads Beijing's leaders to assume China's greatness, cultural superiority, and historic integrity, and it convinces them that China deserves a leading role in the world. Like past Chinese rulers, they have faith in China's capacity to achieve its basic goals without becoming dependent on others. China's modern history of humiliation at the hands of the Western states also leads Beijing to be extremely concerned about external influence and involvement, and leaves it vacillating between dependence and autonomy.

This historical legacy, cloaked in modern nationalism, motivates Beijing's leaders to build a strong nation-state, strive for total independence within certain time limits, and oppose any compromise of China's sovereignty. It also impels Chinese leaders to try to minimize Western influence within China and to struggle against all forms of what it perceives as imperialism and colonialism in international affairs.

Ideology and revolutionary aspirations also affect China's foreign policy in very significant ways. Marxism-Leninism has provided an effective rationale for venting Chinese feelings of having been deeply wronged by the 19th century colonial powers. For more than a quarter-century, China has been ruled by first-generation revolutionary leaders strongly committed to certain universalistic, messianic goals. These leaders have called for revolutionary change not only in China but worldwide. Viewing the world in distinctive Marxist-Leninist-Maoist terms, they have seen international problems through lenses quite different from those of other Communist as well as non-Communist leaders. Although the revolutionary component in Chinese foreign policy has declined since the late 1970s, there is no doubt that ideology will continue to influence China's approach to the world in important ways.

In this chapter we will analyze China's likely impact on the strategic equilibrium in Northeast Asia. First, we will briefly review China's historical legacy; then we will turn to China's current domestic political and economic dynamics. Part three of this chapter is based on these analyses, and it treats Chinese foreign policy and strategy toward the Soviet Union, Japan, the two Koreas, Taiwan, and the United States. Our prime concern is Chinese foreign policy after the Tiananmen crackdown in June 1989. For better or for worse, the Tiananmen crackdown stands out as a watershed not only in China's domestic political development but also for a fundamental transformation of the whole socialist bloc. We will conclude with an assessment of the role China is likely to play in Northeast Asia in the years to come and its possible implications for U.S. policy toward this region.

The Historical Legacy

China's relations with Northeast Asia are almost as old as Chinese civilization itself. China's contacts with Korea date to the first century B.C., and direct contacts with Japan were established in the following century. This 2,000-year linkage between China and its Northeast Asian neighbors can be divided into four periods: the *Sino-centric* period (3rd century B.C.- 19th century A.D.); the period of *victimization* (1840-1950); the period of *challenge* to the international order (1950-1976); and the period of *participation* in the world system (1976 to the present).

During the first and longest period, from the Qin and Han dynasties in the third century B.C. to the late Qing dynasty in the nineteenth century A.D., China regarded itself as the "middle kingdom"—the center of the world. No outside power was able to shake the foundations of this self-centered sense of the world. This was the golden age of *Sino-centrism*. The main pattern in China's foreign relations in this period was the interaction of a relatively advanced Chinese agrarian culture with less sophisticated nomadic peoples on the periphery. During this period Chinese material and cultural influence extended greatly into Korea and Japan as well as other Asian countries.

Throughout the second period, which extended roughly from the first Opium War in 1840 to 1950, China was the *victim* of an expanding imperial order. First the Russians, then the British, the French, the Germans, and finally the Japanese and the Americans entered China for profit, influence, and territory. Weakened by economic decline, political decay, and technological backwardness, China suffered great humiliation and material and territorial losses during this period. Through the Aihui Treaty and the Tianjin Treaty in 1858, the Peking Treaty in 1860, and the Yili Treaty in 1881, Russia absorbed about 1.8 million square kilometers of Chinese land. Through the Aihui Treaty alone, "Russia seized a piece of land from China which is as large as France and Germany combined."[1]

The humiliation at the hands of the West, Russia, and Japan, coupled with China's strong sense of cultural superiority and historical integrity, created a powerful urge toward *nationalism* and a *revolutionary aspiration*. This complex has gripped the imagination of three generations of Chinese and pushed them into an increasingly critical analysis of the international order and Chinese society. The Chinese Communist Party (CCP) seized power in 1949, ending 150 years of rebellion and revolution in China; thus began the third period in China's foreign relations. During the quarter-century of Maoist rule, a revolutionary China regarded itself as the *challenger* of the postwar international economic and political order that centered on the United States. Chinese leaders were committed to restoring national unity, protecting territorial integrity, modernizing the economy, and regaining a degree of international influence and prestige. Nationalist impulses have prompted the new Chinese leaders to move national security and territorial integrity to the top of the political agenda. They have also created a dilemma for Chinese leaders: a choice between autonomy and dependence on the socialist bloc. Inspired by the revolutionary impulse, Chinese leaders despised the existing international system and portrayed China as one of the principal challengers of the prevailing international order.

Sino-Soviet relations played a fundamental role in Chinese foreign relations in the early part of this period. China's new revolutionary leadership believed that a close relationship with the Soviet Union would be the best strategy for pursuing its goals, particularly given the common ideological commitments of the two countries. In the early 1950s, therefore, China adopted a foreign policy of "leaning to one side," that is, toward the Soviet Union. Gradually, however, the Soviet leadership's arrogance and the Chinese leadership's mistrust eroded the Sino-Soviet alliance. Beijing became convinced that Moscow was attempting to exercise over China political and economic control that would sacrifice Chinese interests in Moscow's dealings with the United States. Moreover, lingering territorial disputes, especially in Manchuria and Xinjiang, contributed to a deterioration in the relationship. By 1956, the Sino-Soviet alliance had begun to fray; in 1968-69, it led to a military confrontation on their common border, along the Amur river.

Although Beijing continued to regard the United States as an imperialist power during this period, its relations with Washington gradually evolved after the Korean War. By the late 1960s, increasing Sino-Soviet tensions had convinced Beijing that its principal adversary was not the United States but the Soviet Union. At the same time, Washington, bogged down in a protracted conflict in Vietnam, was eager for a bold diplomatic initiative that might increase its leverage over both Hanoi and Moscow. As a result, Beijing and Washington moved rapidly toward a mutual rapprochement in the early 1970s, arranged during Henry Kissinger's secret visit to Beijing in 1971 and sealed with Richard Nixon's subsequent trip the following spring. At this point, the principal factor driving the two countries toward a more normal relationship was their common concern for Soviet expansion in East Asia. Indeed, by the end of the 1970s, Chinese leaders had begun to talk about a "united front" with the United States against the Soviet Union, and American officials described China as a partner in a quasi-alliance. Soon, the improvement of Sino-American relations was further reinforced by economic considerations, as China began to look abroad for the advanced technology it needed to accelerate its economic development. The changing Chinese-American relationship was formally marked by diplomatic recognition in 1978.

During this same period of time, China's policy toward Japan and South Korea was strongly influenced by Beijing's relations with the United States. During the 1950s and 1960s, with Sino-American tensions at their height, China maintained no relations whatsoever with South Korea, which it regarded as little more than a puppet of the United States. During the same period, China criticized the Japanese government for its military alliance with the United States and for its continuing diplomatic relations with Taiwan. Meanwhile, it cultivated political and economic ties with sympathetic groups and individuals inside Japan, in the hope of luring Japan away from the anti-Chinese economic embargo and military alliance created by the United States. When Sino-American relations started to improve in the 1970s, however, Chinese attitudes toward South Korea and Japan also began to change. Within seven months of Nixon's visit to China in 1972, Beijing and Tokyo had normalized their diplomatic relations, and China began expressing support for the Japanese-American alliance.

China's relations with North Korea were shaped during the Korean War. When Beijing's alliance with Moscow was strong, its relations with Pyongyang were also relatively stable. When the Sino-Soviet relationship deteriorated, North Korea preserved cordial relations with both Moscow and Beijing. Sometimes it played the honest broker's role between its two giant neighbors. The turmoil of the Cultural Revolution briefly disrupted Beijing's friendly ties to Pyongyang, but the damage done by the Red Guard movement was quickly repaired.

This third stage in China's foreign relations also witnessed periodic efforts to promote the reunification of Taiwan with the mainland, sometimes through the use of force and sometimes through political overtures to Taipei or the United States. Both strategies created strains in the relationship between the United States and Taiwan, whether by sowing doubts in Washington over the wisdom of its alliance with the Nationalists, or by raising questions in Taipei about the long-term durability of the American commitment. Beijing's *rapprochement* with the United States in the 1970s represented a major breakthrough in this strategy, although it did not lead to any immediate signs that Taipei was prepared to consider reunification with the mainland.

With the death of Mao in 1976 and the rise of Deng Xiaoping, China entered a new era in its foreign relations. Domestic development and reform, reinforced by the perception of international detente, had a far-reaching impact on Chinese foreign relations. Having established normal diplomatic relations with the United States and Japan, China felt much more relaxed about the Soviet threat. Realizing the bitter fruits of self-reliance and the attendant economic backwardness, and particularly stunned by the rapid economic development of its smaller "four little dragon" neighbors, China began to *participate* actively in the international system. China's domestic policy moved in dramatically new directions. After 10 years of turmoil caused by the Cultural Revolution, the Chinese economy was on the verge of collapse. Economic modernization was given the highest priority on the national agenda. Development was pursued through policies that marked a drastic departure from the Maoist and Stalinist models of the past. Society was granted more autonomy from the state, the economy more autonomy from the plan, the government more autonomy from the party, and intellectual and cultural life more autonomy from ideology.

Several significant changes are evident in China's foreign policy and strategy in this period. First, Chinese leaders increasingly acknowledged the durability and legitimacy of the existing international system, becoming more and more actively involved in it. Beijing has joined virtually every major international organization and has taken an active and constructive role in their work. Second, China has shown an interest in ensuring a peaceful international environment, particularly in East Asia, so that its society can devote its energies to the tasks of modernization and reform. China has adopted what might be called a policy of "omnidirectional peaceful coexistence," featuring a reduction of tensions with virtually all of its former adversaries. Although military modernization is one goal of China's modernization, the military budget actually declined steadily from 1980 to 1989.[2] Third, Beijing has engaged in unprecedented foreign economic interactions, in the belief that opening China to the outside world will greatly accelerate modernization and economic reform. From 1976 to 1989, China's foreign trade increased from US$13.4 billion to US$82.6 billion.[3] Fourth, China has adopted a foreign policy of pragmatism and flexibility. Ideology and revolutionary aspirations have quietly faded away. Instead, Chinese leaders increasingly deal with issues on a pragmatic, case-by-case basis, with explicit reference to national interests.

Current Domestic Dynamics

The Tiananmen Square incident stands out as a watershed in China's domestic political and economic development. Its impact on Chinese foreign policy, however, has been limited. More than a decade of reform in China has left the current Chinese leadership little choice but to follow the imperatives of the reform process. By 1988, China's reform effort ran into a series of economic and political difficulties. Whereas earlier success in rural areas was remarkable, the reform process encountered serious trouble as it moved to the urban industrial areas and began to shake the very framework of the ownership structure. The economy began to overheat: over many years, consumer demand was stimulated by bonuses and pay well above productivity-level; investment by enterprises and local governments was promoted without adequate financial discipline, producing inflation; and central-government budget deficits were increased by earlier moves to let provinces retain a larger share of total revenues. These economic problems, coupled with the price reform of 1988, led in turn to massive corruption, especially within the party and government bureaucracies. A dual price system offered irresistible opportunities for personal enrichment. Goods bought at low state prices could be sold for much more on the private or even black market. Official corruption was more than just widespread; it was conspicuous. Rampant corruption led to deep discontent and demoralization throughout Chinese society. As various conflicts and tensions accumulated, the antagonism between state and society sharpened. These problems had all the makings of a social explosion.

Against this background the events of May-July 1989 in Beijing can be seen as a panic-reaction by the elderly leadership against the logic of China's own reform program. The leadership failed to understand, or at least to accept, the fact that economic and technical development is inextricably linked to political liberalization.

In a basic sense, the problems China has encountered reflect the "halfway nature" of socialist reform and the paradoxical choice between efficiency and equity, stability and growth, full employment and improved economic outcome, and supply and demand. Lack of clearly defined property rights undermined the incentive for long-run development and led to various forms of predatory business practices, chronic excess aggregate demand, and inflation.

The Tiananmen Square incident exacerbated these problems. Although Beijing has made an effort to present to the outside world a favorable picture of the Chinese economy, a close look reveals its deeply institutionalized problems.

After the Tiananmen crackdown, the Chinese government responded to the economic problems by tightening central administrative control over the economy. It pulled back part of the decentralized power, implemented an austerity program, tightened credit, and launched a campaign against the private sector in both rural and urban areas. Because the private sector now accounts for about 35% of commerce and 40% of industrial output—compared to 80% of agricultural production—these policies significantly retarded economic growth in general and industrial production in particular. In both 1989 and 1990, growth rates of GNP and industrial production fell to around 3.5-4.0% and 6.0-7.5% from their respective 1988 counterparts of 11% and 17%.[4] Production efficiency deteriorated further. According to the Minister of Finance, Wang Bingqiang, state enterprises, one of the government's main sources of revenue, have even become a cash drain. In the last two years, losses at state enterprises exceeded profits by a ratio of nearly 8 to 1.[5] Because of the risk of provoking unrest among workers, the government is afraid to close factories that lose money. Subsidies to such factories thus absorbed nearly a third of government revenues in 1990 and more than half in the first half of 1991.[6] Because of sluggish demand, a great number of factories sat idle. The disguised unemployment rate is very high. In the Beijing area more than one-third of the state-enterprise workers receive only their basic salary without any bonus—which ordinarily accounts for 50% to 80% of their income. In some factories more than half the workers are in this situation.[7] Their condition is further worsened by the fact that about one-third of a worker's wage is paid in government bonds. The conflicts between local governments and the central government have intensified since the center sought to recapture fuller control without stifling local initiative. This antagonism surfaced in the debates between leaders from the coastal provinces of Guangdong, Liaoning, Fujian, and others over the Eighth Five-Year Plan for Chinese economic development. The debates were so intense that the government had to postpone the National Congress from June to October, and then to December 1990, to provide time to arrange compromises on the proposed plan.[8]

The June crackdown jeopardized China's position in the international market. The political risk of investing in China has increased. Although corporations (with the exception of Taiwanese firms) have maintained their existing business operations in China, they have been very reluctant to increase their investment. In 1989 and 1990, China's tourism industry, the source of more than $2 billion in hard currency annually, declined about 20%.[9] The West's suspension of military sales and high-level contacts led to a sharp decline in China's imports of technology and equipment. Although in early 1990 the World Bank and the Japanese government resumed loans committed before the Tiananmen incident, few governments or business corporations want to take the political risk of making new loans to China.

Moreover, the loss of foreign earnings occurred at a time when major foreign debt servicing payments were due. In late 1988, China admitted foreign debts of some $40 billion, including $7.3 billion in short-term loans. The authorities claimed to have stabilized the foreign debt at this $40 billion figure which, they said, carried a debt-service ratio of 15%.[10] The situation has been further aggravated by a 20% devaluation of the yuan at the end of 1989. China's debt-service obligations are about to peak, and some Western estimates suggest that in 1990 debts due for repayment may total $9 billion. In addition, the Minister of Finance has acknowledged a domestic bond debt of 80 billion yuan, of which 30 billion was due to be repaid in 1990.[11]

The economic problem worsened further as China's political situation deteriorated. In China, all major and many minor economic issues are essentially political. The Tiananmen incident was a vivid indication that the current government had lost its popular legitimacy. The government's capacity to govern has declined sharply. It can no longer rely on the corrupt party organization to control society; nor can it use the bankrupt official ideology. It has instead leaned on military and security forces as its sole means of retaining power. There are, however, clear signs of instability within the military and security apparatus, which has been unable to prevent more than 100 dissident leaders from escaping abroad. Despite the conservatives' quiet purges within the military and security forces, it is an open question whether the armed forces will continue its support for a highly unpopular and ineffective leadership or whether the military itself will split during the forthcoming succession crisis. Even with the replacement of reformist party General Secretary Zhao Ziyang by Jiang Zemin, the ex-mayor of Shanghai, the leadership crisis is far from over. The younger leaders of the current government lack the popularity, vision, and strength of personality necessary to lead the country out of its crisis. These younger leaders are greatly dependent on Deng Xiaoping and other senior leaders, who are in their eighties and whose health, like their credibility, is in decline.

The on-going repression has intensified dramatically the antagonism between the society and the state. Chinese society has used sustained noncooperation and passive resistance to challenge the repression. Most people, particularly urban residents, have distanced themselves completely from the government, refusing to follow political campaigns. Others have lost all interest in politics. Peasants refuse to pay high taxes, and workers do not work efficiently. Continued political instability and a deepening power struggle within the top leadership have discouraged local authorities, especially at the provincial level, whose power has been increased significantly by the decentralization process during the past decade. Furthermore, information flow can no longer be regulated. The development of advanced electronic and other information technologies has brought Chinese individuals and groups much closer to the outside world. That seems likely to strengthen both nongovernmental and transnational groups—in any case, those groups and interests that are not under direct government control.

China now faces an intractable paradox. On the one hand, reform seems deadlocked: without political reform, economic reform cannot go further, but the aged leaders and incumbent bureaucrats with vested interests will not allow political reform. As long as Deng Xiaoping is alive, there is little hope for change. On the other hand, however, with one-third of its national product now effectively connected with the international market,[12] it is almost impossible for China to return to its original self-reliance and isolation. Participation in the international system imposes new constraints on the government. As suggested by Chen Yizi, former senior adviser to party leader Zhao Ziyang and director of the National Institute for Economic System Reform, "Under current Chinese leadership, it is impossible to solve the fundamental problems with the Chinese economy no matter who is in power. However, it is also impossible, no matter who is in power, to return to a self-isolated state because ten years of reform has fundamentally transformed the Chinese economic structure."[13]

China's Strategy Toward Northeast Asian Countries

Thus far, the main trend in Chinese foreign policy in the post-Mao era has been toward stabilization rather than disruption. China's overwhelming concern with its economic development leads Beijing to seek a peaceful international environment and to forge economic links with virtually every conceivable trading partner. It has also produced greater flexibility and pragmatism in its foreign policy and a reduction of tensions with many countries that were once China's adversaries. The domestic political and economic difficulties after Tiananmen gave China's foreign policy a generally "inward-looking" tendency. The country's strategy was principally aimed at protecting its domestic authority. China's policy in Northeast Asia, therefore, seems Janus-faced. On the official level, its policy seems quite rigid and unyielding to any outside pressure. Chinese leaders have condemned a "bourgeois liberalization" and "spiritual pollution" caused by the openness of its economy. On the practical level, however, China has employed ambiguity and pragmatism in its dealings within the region. As evidence of this pragmatism, note that China's foreign trade increased 10.46% of its GNP in 1989 and 18.24% in 1990.[14]

In general, China wants to use what seems to be a period of relative stability in great-power relations to develop its own economic base and also, therefore, its longer-term defense potential. At least four characteristics can be identified in Beijing's strategy toward Northeast Asia since 1989. First, China has sought better relations with the other regional powers in Northeast Asia and greater influence in this region, both to offset Western pressure and to have more access to the international markets which would help ease its economic problems.

Second, although Beijing has sought businesslike relations with both the Soviet Union and the United States, the triangular relationship has deteriorated and left China with less room to maneuver between the two. Nevertheless, some leeway remains. A warmer relationship with Moscow, for example, would offset pressure from the United States. With the collapse of the Soviet Union, however, even this leeway may have vanished.

Third, the world situation looks to be less threatening in the foreseeable future. Security issues seem to be losing importance relative to international economic considerations. As one senior Chinese observer put it: "The East-West Cold War is approaching an end, the world economy is continuously going toward integration, the interdependence among various nations becomes more obvious, and there emerges a positive trend towards relaxation."[15]

Fourth, with the diminishing of the Soviet threat, the Chinese believe that friction between the U.S. and its allies in Northeast Asia will increase. This would leave China new opportunities and leverage against the United States.

The Implementation of China's Strategy

China's strategy toward Northeast Asia varies greatly from state to state. Let us, therefore, review each in some detail.

The Soviet Union

The normalization of Sino-Soviet relations achieved by the May 1989 Gorbachev summit visit to Beijing eased China's biggest security concern. Soviet forces withdrew from Afghanistan and Mongolia, and the cessation of Soviet support for Vietnam and Cambodia greatly reduced tensions in East Asia. In April 1990, Prime Minister Li Peng paid a state visit to Moscow and signed a formal document that outlined guidelines for the mutual reduction of armed forces along the 7,000-km Sino-Soviet border. As a follow-up to this agreement, high-level teams of Soviet and Chinese experts met in Moscow in September to discuss concrete details of its implementation. During General Secretary Jiang Zemin's most recent visit to Moscow, China and the Soviet Union signed a formal agreement regarding their border in northeastern China, the result of a compromise by both sides but largely by the Soviets.[16] Undoubtedly, the signing of this agreement was an outstanding event in bilateral Sino-Soviet relations because it signified improvement in one of the most sensitive areas of that relationship. It was also the first international document that envisaged actual arms reduction in the Northeast Asian region.

The economic cooperation between the two countries has improved rapidly. In 1989 and 1990, two-way trade between the two increased 12.7% and 15%, respectively. Total trade has grown from $363 million in 1982 to $3.7 billion in 1989, a tenfold increase.[17] In 1990, Sino-Soviet trade totalled US$4.38 billion, up almost 20% over 1989, making the Soviet Union China's fifth-largest trading partner.[18] Moreover, these figures do not include trade between border regions in the two countries. In 1989 and 1990, for example, Xinjiang and Heilongjiang provinces signed separate treaties with their Soviet neighbors, on regional economic cooperation and trade-on-barter terms.[19] During Li Peng's April 1990 visit, a major long-term agreement on bilateral economic and scientific cooperation was concluded. That included large Chinese exports of consumer goods to the Soviet Union on credit terms by which the Soviets agreed to provide financial and technical assistance to China for the construction of nuclear power plants. On March 28, 1991, China announced a 1.5 billion Swiss franc business loan to the Soviet Union. Moscow will repay the loan in mechanical goods.[20] During Jiang's May 1991 visit, China made another $750 million business loan to the Soviet Union.[21]

Exchanges between the two military establishments picked up immediately after the Summit in 1989. During Soviet Deputy Prime Minister Belousov's October visit to Beijing, the two countries reached an agreement by which the Soviet Union would sell China 24 SU-27 ground-attack aircraft at a "friendly price," that is, considerably below international arms trade prices. In March 1991, a Soviet aircraft-performance squadron visited China, and MIG-29s and SU-27s took part in the show as high-ranking Chinese military officials looked on. This seems to imply that there are ongoing deals between the two nations which could lead to the sale of the most advanced Soviet aircraft to China.[22] In May 1991, then-Defense Minister Dmitri Yazov headed a large military delegation to China. Chinese sources reported that this was the first major military visit from the Soviet Union in more than 40 years.[23]

In short, the deep freeze in Sino-Soviet relations was ended, and a new stage was begun. Both sides have powerful motives for continuing this process of cooperation. Each believes that its most urgent priority for the next decade or more is to modernize its economy; this will require a peaceful international climate, reduced defense spending, and a calm border. Both countries hoped to take advantage of the dynamic economic development in Northeast Asia and increase their flexibility and maneuverability in the Moscow-Beijing-Washington triangle. Besides, barter trade between the two saves scarce foreign exchange for both countries; for the Soviet Union this was and remains important.

The demise of the Soviet Union, of course, raises fundamental questions about the future. Russia quite clearly is the successor to the Sino-Soviet rapprochement, and the nature of a new Russian strategy is far from clear. Although the Sino-Soviet relationship since normalization was taking a positive direction, it faced serious limits on how far it could go. Soviet military presence in the region was still large, and Soviet ties to Vietnam and India hardly pleased Beijing. Finally, the issue of the historically disputed territories was not settled. To what extent do these limits apply to Russia?

The end of the Soviet power and the Soviet Communist Party creates a disjuncture in the Moscow-Beijing relationship. The newly established party-to-party relations have vanished. Although the Chinese communists in recent decades had no intimate relations with other ruling parties, they now have no foreign communist parties of significance for support, something that must disturb the aging Chinese communist leaders while it must please the younger Chinese proponents of political reform. The Soviet military is disintegrating, creating great uncertainty about what Russian military forces will be left on the border and in the Pacific fleet. Moscow is most unlikely to retain its close and supportive relations with Vietnam and India. In other words, the changes work both for and against improved relations.

In the short run, both states are likely to be cautious about each other. Gorbachev's liberalizing domestic policies had already introduced a serious constraint in the relationship after the Tiananmen massacre. Yeltsin's abolition of the Soviet Communist Party and commitment to democracy and a market economy can only make that constraint stronger. Given the unsettled territorial disputes and the emergence of independent states in Central Asia, the basis for renewed points of rivalry is strong. China could well be tempted to meddle in the politics of some of the Central Asian states, supporting the residual groups of communists there. At the same time, Beijing will hardly want to jeopardize its relations with other states in the region. It needs cooperation with Japan, South Korea, and the United States in order to cope with its own economic problems. One thing is sure. The old U.S.-Soviet-Chinese triangle has lost its strategic significance, and it is not likely to become a U.S.-Russian-Chinese triangle in the next several years.

In sum, China got much of what it sought in its rivalry with Moscow through normalization, but the course of Soviet domestic politics has created a wholly new basis for Sino-Russian and Sino-Central Asian relations. Given the domestic weaknesses of both Russia and China, the structure of a new strategic relationship is likely to emerge slowly.

Japan

The Sino-Japanese relationship is a central factor in Northeast Asian international politics, but it has been a derivative rather than a primary strategic dimension. China and Japan have enjoyed a relatively undisturbed pattern of accommodation for the past two decades within the regional strategic context. China's vulnerability to Soviet power and America's desire to counterbalance Soviet capabilities provided a political logic for Chinese security strategy. The seemingly inexorable quality of Soviet military modernization contributed to Sino-U.S. accommodation. Beijing tacitly endorsed the American military presence in East Asia, including the U.S.-Japan alliance and the increase of Japanese military capability. Although Beijing remains ambivalent about the long-term implications of Japan's power and national goals, near-term exigencies have dictated greater Japanese involvement in China's strategic plan in the late 1970s and early 1980s. The United States encouraged such collaboration, but expectations of American-Japanese-Chinese security coordination were more notional than real. Only in the late 1970s—when China advocated an anti-Soviet "united front" strategy to escape its own isolation and deny Moscow a potential political bridgehead along the Pacific rim—was there ever a putative strategic pattern, and it did not last long.

The normalization of Sino-Soviet relations, however, helped transform the security framework of East Asia. In essence, the Soviet Union was no longer prepared to sustain an open-ended military confrontation with the PRC, and the Chinese responded to this opportunity. Although Sino-Soviet relations retained elements of conflict, the two sides were prepared to pare back their past military deployment on a step-by-step basis. The demise of the Soviet Union, of course, will probably cause a rapid decline of Russian military power in the region.

At the same time, there are major uncertainties in the minds of Chinese leaders about the sustainability of the American regional security role. The United States is now far less prepared to assume a disproportionate responsibility for its Asian allies, a tendency reinforced by mounting budget constraints. Nationalistic grievances within the region are further calling into question the capacity of the United States to maintain access to bases and facilities upon which the forward deployment of American naval and air forces depend. Although the United States remains the ultimate guarantor of Japanese and Korean security, American policymakers could be losing their ability to provide for comprehensive regional security.[24] At the same time, the United States has placed increased pressure on its more-prosperous regional allies for "burden sharing" and contribution to global security requirements, most recently in the Persian Gulf. The future role of Japan, and the extent to which it assumes added responsibility for security in Northeast Asia or in other locales, has therefore become a pivotal issue in Sino-Japanese relations.

The changing strategic equilibrium had led Beijing to rethink its previous endorsement of a larger Japanese defense effort. Japan's January 1987 announcement that its defense expenditures would surpass one per cent of its GNP constituted a symbolic threshold for the Chinese. This triggered strong responses from Beijing, including an attribution to Japan of larger political ambitions.[25] To China, this defense increase indicates the emergence of a more powerful and potentially more assertive Japanese state. In January 1989, *Guoji wenti yanjiu*, the quarterly publication of the Institute of International Studies of the Ministry of Foreign Affairs, published an extraordinarily detailed assessment of Japanese defense policy and military capacities.[26] According to the author, Japanese defense concepts have evolved steadily from "'defense in place,' strictly limiting defense to Japan's soil ... and passively meeting an enemy attack, to serious attention to pre-combat preparations and achieving victory early in a war;

from the idea of annihilating the enemy on the beaches to annihilating the enemy at sea; and from combat in coastal waters to combat on the high seas." At the same time, the author asserted, the Japanese were also laying the foundation for far-more-elaborate, high-technology programs of national defense, including space-based defense.

These trends, along with a steady enhancement of American-Japanese defense collaboration to a distance of 1,000 nautical miles beyond Japan's home islands, have demonstrated that past Japanese constitutional restraints on military activity "have gradually become dead letters, and their binding force weakened long ago." Moreover, such trends bespeak "the consequences of the nationalist ideological trend running wild." All these trends, the author further observed, were taking place at a time of diminished East-West tensions, and with growing pressures for reduction of military expenditures on a worldwide basis. Subsequent Chinese commentaries asserted that the United States has simply goaded an already willing Japan, with Soviet military activities in Asia serving "as a major pretext for (Japanese) arms expansion."[27]

Japan has also been ambivalent toward China. It is concerned about the long-term implications of China's power and goals. The Japanese well understood that an isolated and poor China, as it was in the 1960s, was a destabilizing factor in Asia. And China's modernization and reform have opened up new avenues of long-term cooperation for Japan. After the Tiananmen massacre, the Japanese government was visibly reluctant to join the West in economic sanctions against China. As a regional power, the Japanese argued that for the United States, China is only an "element" in its global strategy, but for Japan, China is not a mere "diplomatic card" whose value changes with the exigencies of international relations. China has strategic significance for Japan, especially in light of the increasing friction between Japan and the U.S. The Sino-Japanese relationship could offer the Japanese leverage in their relations with Washington.

Above all, the economic factor stands out as the most influential element in Sino-Japanese relations. Japan is China's second-largest trading partner—if one considers Hong Kong as a separate country. Bilateral trade amounted to $19.3 billion in 1988.[28] Japan's investments in China are exceeded only by those of Hong Kong and the United States. China is one of Japan's largest manufacturing bases outside Japan itself. China's immense potential market seems irresistible to Japanese businessmen. Japanese trade with and investment in Hong Kong have boomed: Japanese banks are said to account for some 56% of the country's bank deposits and Japanese department stores have some 30% of Hong Kong's retail sales.[29] In fact, after December 1989 Japan became the largest investor in Hong Kong.[30]

Nevertheless, difficulties remain in Sino-Japanese relations. There have been ups and downs since 1978. The difficulties have been exemplified by a series of incidents between the two nations: the high-school textbook incident in 1982; the 1983 Kyoto Court decision concerning a student dormitory; the Yasukuni Shrine Visit incident and subsequent anti-Japanese movement among Beijing students in 1985; and early in 1991 a Chinese demonstration prompted by the territorial dispute over the small Diaoyu island in the South China Sea. The memory of the brutal Japanese invasion of China still exists in the minds of many Chinese people. As Chinese leaders have often commented on Sino-Japanese relations: "Past experiences, if not forgotten, offer good lessons for new ones" (*qianche buwang, houshi zhishi*). These very emotional and sensitive issues will cast a shadow over Sino-Japanese relations for some time to come.

The Two Koreas

The relationship between China and the Republic of Korea (ROK) has developed very rapidly. In 1990, two-way trade between the two countries reached $3.8 billion, about five times the value of Chinese trade with its long-standing ally North Korea. The ROK is very enthusiastic about regularizing its relationship with Beijing, just as it has tried to do with Moscow. At the Asian Games in Beijing in September 1990, the ROK not only sent a large delegation but also donated 400 cars and spent about $15 million for billboard space. In October, China and the ROK exchanged trade-liaison offices in Beijing and Seoul, under the fiction that neither of the two governments is directly involved. Even so, one of Deng Xiaoping's sons, Deng Zifang, recently visited Seoul to discuss economic ties. While neither the father nor the son holds any official Chinese position, the message was lost on no one.

For Beijing, there are several rationales behind the move. Strategically, the normalization of Sino-Soviet relations greatly reduced Beijing's anxiety on its northern border. The Korean peninsula thus occupies a much more prominent position in China's security agenda. China has a large stake in the Korean peninsula. A unified Korea with strong economic and military power, possibly with a nuclear capability, would be a threat to China's security. Beijing would clearly be unhappy to see this happen. The Korean peninsula is the only place in the world where a military confrontation directly involved the four great powers—the United States, the Soviet Union, China, and Japan. China is also undoubtedly worried about North Korea's evolving nuclear capability. The establishment of relations with the ROK will give Beijing leverage in the strategic equilibrium, not only to balance the power of the U.S. and Japan, but also against the potential threat coming from the northern part of the peninsula.

Economically, China has benefited greatly from its ties with the ROK. The Asian Games are a vivid example. China has encouraged foreign investment, particularly high-tech investment from the United States and

Japan. The results, however, have been disappointing so far. For one thing, foreign firms, particularly Japanese companies, are reluctant to invest in China; for another, more fundamentally, high-tech investment from the developed countries is not profitable in a labor-intensive country such as China. Investment in low and medium technology from the newly industrialized countries (NICs) is much more attractive. This reality is reflected in the fact that the largest foreign investor in China is Hong Kong, a country whose manufacturers have profited greatly by moving labor-intensive plants to neighboring Guangdong province. South Korean investment in low- and medium-tech industries is thus best suited to China's economic development. For China, investment from the ROK will also lure Japanese business, and especially serve to attract investment from Taiwan. Therefore, by luring investment from Taiwan, the Sino-ROK relationship offers China not only economic benefits, but also strategic gains.

For Seoul, China holds a special position in the Korean peninsula's power equilibrium. Both Koreas view China as friendly. Beijing therefore could serve as a go-between in the Korean reunification process. As the Soviet threat diminished and the U.S.-Soviet rivalry eased in Northeast Asia, and as the U.S. showed signs that its policy after the Cold War might be more "inward-looking," Seoul began to worry that it might be abandoned by the United States.[31] America's pressure on military "burden sharing" and U.S.-ROK trade disputes have stimulated an anti-U.S. feeling and nationalism in South Korea. Stronger ties to China would give the ROK firm leverage in its bargaining with the United States.

South Korea's economy is now shifting from labor intensive to capital intensive. Social unrest and workers' demonstrations have brought a rise in wages. In 1987 and 1988, ROK wage increases averaged 17% and 14%, respectively.[32] This situation was worsened by an 8% appreciation of the won against the U.S. dollar in 1987, and a further 13.7% increase in 1988. The ROK is losing its comparative advantage in exactly the industries in which China has the most potential in the short to medium term. Economic relations with China will greatly accelerate the ROK's economic development by shifting textiles, shoemaking, simple electronics, and other labor-intensive industries to China.

By any standard, North Korea is clearly a loser in the changing strategic equilibrium in post-Cold War Northeast Asia. The establishment of Moscow-Seoul diplomatic relations in October 1990 signified the loss of one of North Korea's most important socialist friends. Except by demonstrating its anger in words, Pyongyang knows it has nothing with which to offset what its old friends have done. For North Korea, the only alternative is to rely on its only significant remaining ally—China.

Beijing has maintained a good relationship with North Korea since the Korean War. The Chinese call their relationship with North Korea "the friendship cemented with blood in the war." This sentimental rhetoric reflects the crude fact that 250,000 Chinese, including the oldest son of Mao, died during the Korean War. This emotional bond has had great impact on Sino-North Korean relations and has shaped the basic pattern of this relationship. Since the late 1970s, China has pursued pragmatic economic reforms. In the meantime, North Korea followed China's Cultural Revolution, launching a movement called *chollima*—named after a legendary horse which could gallop 1,000 ri (about 250 miles) in one day. The ideological divergences between the two separated them somewhat in the mid-1980s. In the latter part of that decade, however, when conservative forces again dominated Chinese politics, Beijing and Pyongyang resumed a warmer relationship.

After the Tiananmen incident, the West pressed an economic embargo and temporarily suspended governmental contact with Beijing. In the meantime, the Socialist bloc has experienced a fundamental transformation. Only Cuba, North Korea, and China have retained an orthodox Marxist-Leninist ideology. Isolation and ideological similarity have pushed China and North Korea into a closer relationship. On March 14-16, 1991, the new General Secretary Jiang Zemin made an official goodwill visit to Pyongyang at the invitation of President Kim Il Sung, who met him at the Sunan airport. A half-million people welcomed Jiang, lining the road from the airport to downtown Pyongyang.

In addition to the historical and ideological factors, North Korea occupies a critical position in China's security agenda. This little northeast neighbor of China maintains the world's fifth-largest army, including a potential nuclear capability. As the U.S.-Soviet rivalry eases, North Korea may pose the region's most important and prickly problem.

North Korea's economy has fallen into sharp decline. Its GNP for 1989 was estimated at $21.6 billion, and per capita GNP at $987,[33] roughly one-tenth and one-fifth, respectively, of South Korea's ($210.1 billion and $4,968). During 1987-89, North Korea's rate of economic growth averaged less than 3% per annum; in 1989 it was 2.4%. North Korea appears to be increasingly left behind by the economic advances of the capitalist South and the demise of Communism elsewhere. It is once again a "hermit kingdom" left in unhealthy isolation—unhealthy for it and for everyone else. And as one of China's leading experts on North Korea warns: "cornered dogs bite."

The leaders in Pyongyang are well aware of the country's weakened position in Northeast Asia. In fact, its foreign policy has become rather more realistic. Kim Il Sung, in his 1990 New Year address, openly admitted the necessity of a readjustment in North Korean foreign policy, stating that "the way of building socialism should also be steadily improved and perfected in keeping with changes in the situation."[34] North Korean leaders judged that it would be unrealistic to try to stop old friends among the socialist countries from establishing diplomatic ties with the Seoul government. Instead, North Korea opted to counterbalance the loss by developing ties with Japan and the United States. Beijing, in Korea's view, can help Pyongyang on these important strategic issues by playing the role of go-between. Starting in 1989, North Korea held councillor-level meetings with the U.S. in Beijing; by November 1990 eight such meetings had taken place. In September 1990, two Japanese delegations visited Pyongyang—one, from the ruling Liberal Democratic Party (LDP), was led by former Deputy Premier Kanemaru Shin, and the other, from the Japan Socialist Party (JSP), was led by Vice-Chairman Tanabe Makoto. On September 4, 1990, Premier Yon Hyong-muk arrived in Seoul and met his South Korean counterpart, Kan Young-Hoon, and held the first intergovernmental talks since the national division of 45 years ago.

China remains the closest ally of North Korea, its only dependable one. There are, however, difficulties in their relationship. North Korea has a very bad image among the Chinese. Its endless political campaigns, ideological indoctrination, and enchanted loyalty to the "loving father" are reminiscent of the painful Chinese Cultural Revolution. In addition to their dislike of North Korea's patrimonial politics, leaders in Beijing are also uncertain about the young Kim's political intentions and goals. Nevertheless, as long as Deng Xiaoping and his old colleagues live, the relationship between Beijing and Pyongyang will continue on the current path.

The United States

The Sino-U.S. relationship is probably at its lowest point since Nixon visited China two decades ago. China remains angry over the Western economic sanctions led by the United States after Tiananmen Square. China has yet to yield officially to any Western pressure since the brutal crackdown of June 1989. It accused America of intervening in its domestic affairs and attempting to subvert its government. It pretended to be a victim of Western sanctions and continues to insist that any bilateral difficulty is entirely Washington's fault. On the practical level, however, Beijing is well aware that its weight in U.S. strategic considerations is decreasing. The end of the Cold War and the détente in the Soviet-U.S. relationship, together with China's own immense economic and political problems, leave little room for China to maneuver between the two superpowers. Its old strategic-counterweight position in the Moscow-Washington-Beijing triangle has been fundamentally altered—if the triangle retains any strategic significance at all.

Chinese leaders also understand that U.S. relations with its allies in Europe and Asia will be more difficult to manage in a period when the "Soviet threat" has disappeared. The secret missions of National Security Advisor Brent Scowcroft and Deputy Secretary of State Lawrence Eagleburger to Beijing in July and again in December of 1989 made it clear to Beijing that Washington needs its cooperation on a number of crucial international-strategic issues. First, in Beijing's view, Washington needs China's cooperation on a broad range of global and regional issues in Bush's U.N.-centered "new world order" policy, from missile sales and nuclear nonproliferation to cooperation in regional conflicts. The Gulf War vividly showed Beijing that its veto power in the U.N. Security Council could offer strong leverage in its relationship with the U.S. That point was underlined in November 1990, one day before a critical Security Council vote on Iraq. The U.S. State Department announced that the Foreign Minister of China, Qian Qichen, was coming to Washington for talks with Secretary Baker and President Bush—while insisting that this was not a departure from its policy against official exchanges.

The second area in which China perceives that the U.S. needs its cooperation is in the Pacific region. Sino-American relations are a critical element in the successful management of the security issues in the Korean Peninsula, Indochina, and the Taiwan Straits. Because of Beijing's special relationship with Pyongyang and the Khmer Rouge, Washington cannot attain peaceful settlements in the two regions and in the Taiwan straits without China's cooperation.

China's post-Cold War strategy toward the United States, therefore, again appears to be Janus-faced. On the official level, China has tried to stand firmly and pretend to be a victim of Western sanctions. On the practical level, China has taken steps to ameliorate America's anger, although very much at its own pace. Under pressure from the American Congress, it lifted martial law in Beijing and released a large number of students who were involved in the June 1989 demonstrations. It allowed the return of Voice of America correspondents, Peace Corps volunteers, and Fulbright scholars. It also announced that it was no longer selling medium-range missiles to Syria. In June of 1990, it allowed the prominent dissident and astronomer Fang Lizhi to leave China, giving him safe passage to Great Britain from his refuge in the American Embassy. In July 1990, China sent to the United States a delegation of major cities' mayors headed by one of its smoothest and most moderate politicians, Zhu Rongji, who was the mayor of Shanghai and is now the vice premier. More recently, to placate the U.S. Congress's anger over its huge $10.8 billion trade deficit last year and preserve its Most Favored Nation (MFN) status, China sent a large delegation of more than 100 people to the United States in May 1991, to purchase more than $700 million in American goods.[35]

As for China's own interests, it wants to use what seems to be relative stability in great-power relations to develop its own economic base and also, therefore, its longer-term defense potential. Good relations with the United States are crucial to its overarching goals of developing the economy and reunifying with Taiwan. For economic development in China, the United States remains the most important source of technology, capital, and markets. In 1990, China exported to the United States about $15.2 billion in merchandise, which accounted for about one-fourth of its total exports. With a $10.5 billion trade surplus, it has surpassed Taiwan to have the second-largest trade surplus with the United States.[36] In its economic-modernization effort, China regarded the United States and Japan as the two most important countries for technology transfer. While Japan remains China's largest trade partner, the United States is the largest foreign investor in China. With its ambivalent feeling toward China's strengthening of economic and military power, Japan has been very reluctant to invest in long-term projects. Chinese officials widely hold that the Japanese are only interested in selling goods to China, not in helping China modernize.

The United States also plays an important role in China's aim for reunification with Taiwan. The old Chinese leaders have put national reunification at the top of their political agenda. Deng Xiaoping has designated national reunification as one of the three overarching tasks for China in the rest of the twentieth century. He has stated that he wants to see China reunited before he dies, lest he be unable to close his eyes when he "meets Marx." Current political liberalization in Taiwan makes Beijing much more worried about Taiwan's independence movement. The United States still remains Taiwan's closest friend and largest military supplier. Beijing well understands that without the United States' support, the independence movement may become a permanent obstacle to unification. Beijing realizes that the current international situation and huge discrepancy in economic development between the two Chinas make the cost of using military force to unite Taiwan too high. The best way, in Beijing's view, is to persuade the Nationalist government of Taiwan to negotiate. So far the Nationalist government of Taiwan still refuses to have any direct contact with its mainland counterpart, although trade and investment from Taiwan to mainland China have increased dramatically in the last two years.[37] The only country influential enough to play the role of go-between is the United States.

The Sino-U.S. relationship should also offer Beijing leverage in its relationship with Japan. As noted earlier, the shadow of the Sino-Japanese War has long darkened bilateral relations between Beijing and Tokyo. Chinese leaders have worried about Japan's military expansion. The Japanese mine-sweepers' visit to the Persian Gulf after the Gulf War made Beijing very apprehensive. Beijing believes that a strong relationship with the United States could counterbalance its relationship with Japan, and perhaps force Japan to behave more favorably toward China.

China also needs United States help with its military modernization. Since the late 1970s, the U.S. has played an important role in the modernization of China's defense system, including selling advanced radar systems and logistics and electronic equipment. Since 1985, China has acquired from the United States the following: avionics to upgrade its most advanced J-8 interceptor, large-caliber ammunition, artillery-locating radars, anti-submarine torpedoes, and commercially available items such as helicopters, naval gas-turbine engines, coast-defense radars, and a variety of communications equipment. The United States and China have jointly established tracking stations in Xinjiang and Shanxi. Altogether, the United States has been significantly involved in China's military modernization.

Overall, Chinese leaders believe that China's relationship with the United States is critical to its national reunification and strategic interests, as well as to its economic and military development. The past two years have shown that Beijing is willing to compromise with the United States to gain long-term interests, even though it uses tough official rhetoric so that its leaders can save "face."

Nevertheless, in the post-Cold War era there remain three areas of potential conflict between these two powers. The first is over values. Current Chinese leaders are still officially committed to orthodox Marxism-Leninism; the so-called four cardinal principles (the leadership of the Communist Party; the proletarian dictatorship; the Marxist-Leninist and Maoist ideology; and persistence along the Socialist path) are still enshrined in the first article of China's constitution. With the old revolutionary leadership in power, conflicts resulting from value differences are bound to influence Sino-U.S. relations. The second potential conflict is China's arms sales and regional issues. Last year, China surpassed France to become the third-largest arms seller in the world. China's sales to the Middle East and other parts of the world have caused a strain in Sino-U.S. relations. China remains the largest military supplier of Cambodia's Khmer Rouge. During the Iran-Iraq war, China is believed to have sold to Iran alone some $30 billion worth of arms, including some Silkworm missiles.[38] Although China has promised not to sell the mid-range missile to Syria in the near future, potential conflicts still remain in the long run.

The third area of possible tension between China and the U.S. is Taiwan. Along with the Korean Peninsula, the Taiwan Strait is the most potentially explosive area in Northeast Asia. Although the United States no longer has formal diplomatic relations with Taiwan, many on Capitol Hill and in the White House remain sympathetic to their old friend Taipei. The continuing American interest in a peaceful future for Taiwan—an interest that Washington has consistently reiterated since the Shanghai Communique of 1972—contradicts China's insistence that the Taiwan question is a domestic matter in which no foreign power has the right to interfere.

Conclusions

Overall, our analysis suggests that post-Cold War Chinese foreign policies and strategies toward Northeast Asia are a function of China's historical legacy and current domestic political conflicts and need for economic development. In sum, four conclusions can be drawn regarding the characteristics of China's strategy toward Northeast Asia in the post-Cold War era.

First, China's immense domestic political and economic problems and its overwhelming concern for economic development have given its post-Cold War foreign policy an "inward-looking' tendency. Its strategies are conducted principally with a view to safeguarding domestic authority and solving domestic problems. Consequently, China wants a peaceful environment in Northeast Asia for the foreseeable future. Its policies and strategies toward this region, therefore, seem Janus-faced: they are rhetorically unyielding on the official level but open to compromise on the practical level.

The economic and political problems China has encountered are closely associated with the "halfway-nature" of its socialist reforms. Without drastic political reform, these problems are not likely to be resolved while the existing, centrally planned political and economic system remains. In the near future, therefore, China will concentrate on its immense political and economic problems and will be unlikely to devote much money to military expenditures. Although China has increased its military budget in the last two years, the increase merely covers inflation. China spends only about $10 per capita on its military, and this amount is among the lowest in the world.

Second, China's post-Cold War strategies have inherited a paradoxical historical legacy: on the one hand, centuries-long Chinese history and tradition convinces Beijing's leaders that China deserves a leading role in the world. Like past Chinese rulers, they have faith in China's capacity to achieve its basic goals without becoming dependent on others. On the other hand, China's more recent history of humiliation at the hands of the West also makes Beijing extremely protective of its national integrity and cautious about external influence and involvement. This paradox has led and will continue to cause Beijing to vacillate between dependence and autonomy. Issues of national sovereignty and national integrity, therefore, will be extremely sensitive for Chinese leaders, and they will find little room for compromise. This also suggests that in the years to come, China is unlikely to form any kind of formal alliance with other great powers in the world. It is more likely that China will continue to pursue an independent foreign policy.

The third characteristic of the post-Cold War foreign policy of China is the rise of nationalism in China. As the grip of ideology over Chinese society gradually weakens, and China's economic and military power gradually strengthen, nationalism has emerged as a potentially threatening force for the long run in Northeast Asia. Nationalism is reflected in the continuing mistrust of foreign economic and cultural presences in China, in the desire for economic and strategic independence from stronger powers, in the insistence on reunifying China on Beijing's terms, and even in some assertions of China's rights to a leadership role in Asia. At present, China is still a great defensive power. Coupled with the projected growth of China's military and economic strength, emergent Chinese nationalism is understandably of considerable concern to her neighbors. Clearly, the region faces the need to accommodate Chinese aspirations—a process which will not be easy and could produce a disaster.

Fourth, the determinants of China's post-Cold War foreign policies contain great uncertainties. China's foreign policy is a function of domestic political struggle and economic development. We pointed out earlier that China's future political development is far from certain. The Tiananmen incident and subsequent repression have intensified the antagonism between the state and society and exacerbated the succession crisis. The current leadership in Beijing is greatly dependent on Deng Xiaoping and other senior leaders who are in their late eighties and whose health, like their credibility, is in decline. It is almost certain that when Deng passes away, there will be a great change in China's domestic politics. It is unclear just what impact this will have on China's foreign policies, but its foreign policy will change. It may be, as John Fairbank once said, that the "one thing certain about China is uncertainty."

In general, China will play a critical role in the economic development and strategic equilibrium in Northeast Asia. In the foreseeable future, China will remain a great defensive power and a backward country. In the long run, however, China is most likely to become the most important challenge to American interests in Northeast Asia.

NOTES

[1] F. Engles, "The Russian's Success in Far East," *Collection of Marx and Engles Works*, vol. 12, p. 662, Beijing, 1975 (in Chinese).

[2] *Annual Statistics of China*, National Statistic Bureau, Beijing, 1990.

[3] *Almanac of China's Foreign Economic Relations and Trade*, Ministry of Foreign Economic Relations and Trade, Beijing, 1990.

[4] *Annual Statistics of China*, 1990, National Statistics Bureau, Beijing, 1990; and *People's Daily* (foreign edition), Feb. 23, 1991.

[5] *People's Daily* (foreign edition), Mar. 29, 1991.

[6] *Ibid*.

[7] See the *Delegation Report* from Chinese Young Economist Society, 1990.

[8] About the debates, see *New York Times*, June 20, 1990; and *People's Daily* (foreign edition), Dec. 25, 1990.

[9] *Annual Statistics of China*, National Statistic Bureau, Beijing, 1990.

[10] Financial Budget Report to the National Congressional Assembly by Minister of Finance, Wang Bingqiang, Beijing, Mar. 1990.

[11] *Ibid.*

[12] *Annual Statistics of China*, National Statistic Bureau, Beijing, 1990.

[13] Chen, Yizi, *China: Ten Years Reform and the Democratic Movement in 1989*, LianJin Press, Taipei, Taiwan, 1990.

[14] *Far East Economic Review*, Feb. 1991.

[15] Xu Kui: "The Prospects of Sino-Soviet Relations," *Foreign Affairs Journal*, Beijing, June 1989, p. 30.

[16] *People's Daily* (foreign edition), May 17, 1991.

[17] *Almanac of China's Foreign Economic Relations and Trade*, Ministry of Foreign Economic Relations and Trade, Beijing, 1990.

[18] "Improved Sino-Soviet ties based on self-interest: market forces," *Far Eastern Economic Review*, May 30, 1991.

[19] *People's Daily* (foreign edition), Dec. 20, 1989 and Mar. 1990.

[20] *People's Daily* (foreign edition), Mar. 28, 1991.

[21] *People's Daily* (foreign edition), May 17, 1991.

[22] *People's Daily* (foreign edition), Mar. 25, 1991.

[23] *People's Daily* (foreign edition), May 11, 1991.

[24] Please see the Japanese and Korean chapters for Japanese and Korean views on the decline of America's strategic role in this region.

[25] On Chinese responses to the one percent decision, see Whiting, *China Eyes Japan*, especially pp. 134-141.

[26] Ge Gengfu, "Changes in the development of Japan's defence policy and defence capacities," *Guoji wenti yanjiu*, no. 1, January 13, 1989.

[27] Xi Zhihao, "Japan is stepping up arms expansion," *Jiefangjun bao* ("Liberation Army Daily"), Aug. 28, 1989.

[28] *Ni-Chu Keizai Kyokai*, Tokyo.

[29] Between 1985 and 1988-89, Japanese investment in Hong Kong rose from US$131 million to $1,662 million. During the same time, U.S. investment there rose from $44 to $729 million. *Financial Times*, Jan. 30, 1990, p. 22.

[30] *New York Times*, Dec. 25, 1989.

[31] Discussions with officers in the ROK Ministry of Foreign Affairs.

[32] *Principal Economic Indicators*, Seoul, Bank of Korea, Apr. 1989.

[33] National Unification Board, "Overall assessment of the North Korea economic situation for 1989," Oct. 1989.

[34] *Pyongyang Times*, Jan. 1, 1990.

[35] *People's Daily* (foreign edition), May 5, 1991.

[36] See *Far East Economic Review*, Asia 1991 Year Book, Feb. 1991; *People's Daily* (foreign edition), May 11, 1991; and *New York Times*, A1, May 16, 1991.

[37] Taiwan has so far invested some $660 million in more than 3,300 projects in mainland China. Taiwan has surpassed the U.S. and become the largest investor in terms of number of investments. See *People's Daily*, Apr. 20, 1991.

[38] Huang Xiang, "Sino-U.S. Relations over the Past Year," *Beijing Review*, Feb. 15-28, 1988, pp. 25-27.

CHAPTER 4

Japan's Strategic Role in Northeast Asia in the Post-Cold War Era

By Andrew Y. Yan

Background

Japan's strategic and economic interests in Northeast Asia are difficult to overstate. For the last 40 years, Japan's main security concerns have been a militarily assertive Soviet Union and the volatile situation on the Korean peninsula. Japan draws about 43.3% of its raw materials from the Asian-Pacific area, and 68% of its exports go to this region.[1] In 1990, its exports to the U.S. alone accounted for 37% of its total exports.[2] Japan mainly invests in the United States, Hong Kong, South Korea, Taiwan, and China. In 1991, these countries accounted for about three-fourths of Japan's total $400 billion in foreign investment. The United States, China, Taiwan, and South Korea are also the major foreign manufacturing bases for Japan.

In the more than four decades since World War II, the main source of stable security relations in Northeast Asia has been the U.S.-Japan alliance, as a weak and independent China balanced a militarily assertive Soviet Union. The U.S.-Japan Treaty of Mutual Cooperation and Security has been the cornerstone of Japanese security strategy. The end of the Cold War, however, has fundamentally changed the structural equilibrium in this region. The U.S.-Japan alliance was based on the traditional Cold War system of international relations. The disintegration of this system means that the threat posed by the Soviet Union in particular, or by international communism in general, has largely withered away.

Several factors contributed to this fundamental transformation. The first and probably most important factor was the absolute decline of the Soviet Union's economic and military power, along with the fundamental transformation initiated by Mikhail Gorbachev. Central planning suffocated the Soviet economy, and the rigid ideology stifled people's freedom and creativity. The Soviet economy became unable to sustain massive military expenditures. Gorbachev's *perestroika* was intended to strengthen the bankrupt Soviet economy. Its foreign policy toward Northeast Asia, as part of its overall policy of détente, changed from military confrontation to security cooperation, and even attempted to secure economic collaboration.

The second factor contributing to the transformation of the region was the relative decline of American influence and Japan's emergence as an economic superpower. Since 1985, Japan has replaced the U.S. as the largest creditor in the world; at the same time the U.S. has become the largest debtor. In 1988, Japan, with its new Official Development Assistance (ODA) program, surpassed the United States to become the world's largest official contributor to Third World development. Third, the rapid economic development of newly industrialized countries in this region altered regional politics. Since the 1960s, Taiwan, South Korea, and Hong Kong have led the world in rates of economic progress. Their economic development, combined with Japan's, has made Northeast Asia the most rapidly growing region in the world in this century. Finally, there was a reforming China. The implementation of China's open-door economic policy in the last decade allowed the Chinese economy to grow at double-digit rates. China's coastal regions—notably Guangdong and Fujian provinces—have been actively integrated into the Northeast Asian economic ring. Trade between China and Japan, Hong Kong, Taiwan, South Korea, and the Soviet Union has increased dramatically in the last decade.

As the region has entered a transitional period, so has Japanese foreign policy. Today, in a world where geopolitical and geostrategic interests are increasingly determined by economic factors, Japanese foreign policy has changed significantly.[3] For more than 40 years Japan has been the junior partner in U.S.-Japan relations. Today, however, Japan's enormous economic power and growing economic friction with the United States are turning Japan's foreign policy from passive to active, from dependent to autonomous.

This chapter will analyze Japan's strategy toward Northeast Asia in the post-Cold War era. First, it briefly reviews postwar Japanese foreign policy. It then turns to an analysis of the reactive nature of Japanese foreign policy. The third part focuses on the post-Cold War Japanese strategy toward the Soviet Union, China, the two Koreas, and the United States. Since the basic configuration of the strategic relations in this region remains unchanged, the increased activeness of Japan's foreign policy will have crucial consequences on regional strategic relations. This chapter concludes, therefore, with an assessment of the role Japan is likely to play in the region in the years to come.

A Transitional Stage in Japan's Foreign Policy: A Historic View

Japan's postwar foreign policy evolved through five phases. In the first phase, Japan moved from total disarmament to a self-imposed, internally directed security role during the U.S. occupation from 1945 to 1952. In the second, through the end of the 1970s, Japan became a compliant follower of the United States, focusing its attention on domestic economic development. In phase three it was a gradually awakening junior partner in bilateral security affairs. The United States came to acknowledge, in the mid-1970s, that the U.S.-Japan relationship was an "alliance." During the tenure of prime Minister Yasuhiro Nakasone, in the early to mid-1980s, Japan entered its fourth phase, as a member of the Western alliance with a growing impact on regional politics. Recently, Japan has entered a new, transitional phase. Since the mid-1980s Japan has become a global economic superpower, with an undeniable role in the international political and economic arenas. With the end of the Cold War, the decline of U.S. economic power, and intensified friction with the U.S. on trade and investment issues, Japan has pursued a more independent and multidirectional foreign policy. U.S.-Japan relations have become a "global partnership," although a frequently troubled one.

The relationship between a victorious United States and a defeated Japan in the immediate postwar period was determined by the overwhelming economic and military power and strategic interests of Washington. Initially, the U.S.-led occupation forces undertook sweeping reforms to construct a demilitarized and democratic society and a capitalist economy. Under U.S. protection, Tokyo pursued what has come to be known as the "Yoshida strategy." Shigeru Yoshida, the first postwar Japanese prime minister, argued that Japan should align itself with the United States for defense. While supporting the development of a Self-Defense Force (SDF) to supplement American efforts, he vehemently opposed Dulles's request for major Japanese rearmament. Yoshida gave the following reasons: Japan was a weak economic power, Article 9 of the Constitution prohibited rearmament, the Japanese had a psychological aversion to the military after the tragic Pacific war, and a rearmed Japan would frighten its neighbors.[4] In exchange for America's obligation to defend Japan, Yoshida offered to permit the stationing of United States troops in his country.

The Cold War and U.S. strategic interests in Asia halted the demilitarization process in occupied Japan. Two weeks after the outbreak of the Korean War in June 1950, the National Police Reserve was established. In July 1954, the internal security force was enlarged and reorganized into the Ground, Maritime, and Air SDF. At the same time, the United States provided $2.1 billion in aid to the faltering Japanese economy. The U.S. also slowed down the breakup of the nation's powerful business groups (*zaibatsu*)[5]. Furthermore, Washington provided support to the conservative, pro-American political forces in Japan, which were united in 1955 under the banner of the Liberal Democratic Party (LDP).

Japan's reentry into the international political system during this period was also largely prompted by U.S. strategic interests in Asia. Japan's sovereignty was restored fully by the 1952 San Francisco Peace Treaty. The Soviet Union and its allies did not sign the treaty, however—thus preventing Japan from settling the status of the Soviet-occupied territories to the northeast of Japan (the "Northern Territories"). The United States continued to administer the Bomim Islands until 1965, and the remainder of the Ryukyu Islands—including Okinawa—until 1972. When Okinawa was returned, it housed one of the largest American forward bases in the world.

The 1952 Security Treaty between Washington and Tokyo placed Japan even more firmly into the U.S. strategic orbit. The treaty provided for the stationing of U.S. military bases, facilities, and personnel in Japan. Reflecting the overwhelming U.S. dominance in military power, the treaty obligated the United States to defend Japan against aggression, but did not require a reciprocal commitment. In 1960—over the vehement and sometimes violent objection of opposition forces in Japan—the Treaty of Mutual Cooperation and Security was signed. This treaty obligated both parties to assist each other in case of armed attack on territories under Japanese administration, although it was understood that Japan would not come to the defense of the United States, because the Japanese Constitution prohibited the dispatch of armed forces abroad. Notes accompanying the treaty required prior consultation between the parties before Washington undertook major changes in its troop deployments or equipment stockpiling in Japan. The treaty required a one-year notice of revocation after 1970. These changes reflected the gradual increase in Tokyo's assertion of sovereignty and Washington's accommodation to it.

Japan's relations with its Asian neighbors were also largely determined by the U.S. policy of keeping Japan in its strategic orbit and steering it into the capitalist economic system. One example of this policy was the delay, until 1972, in normalizing relations between Japan and China. Likewise, the signing of a peace and friendship treaty between Tokyo and Beijing was delayed until 1978.

In the 1950s and 1960s, Japan was gradually allowed to become a full-fledged member of the U.S.-led international capitalist system. Japan joined the United Nations, the IMF, the World Bank, the Economic Commission for Asia and the Far East, GATT, and other international organizations. In the 1960s, Japan achieved the highest level of domestic economic growth in the postwar world. Economic growth enabled the ruling LDP to consolidate its political support. This helped protect the Japan-U.S. security relationship. By the end of the 1960s, Japan had become the dominant regional economic power. At the same time, a majority of the Japanese had come to accept the bilateral security link with the U.S. and the Self-Defense Forces as part of the status quo.

Japan's "economic miracle" in the 1960s shielded the country against major external disturbances. Japan survived several external shocks: the

Nixon Doctrine (announced at Guam in 1969), the 1971 U.S.-Chinese rapprochement, the 1971 "New Economic Policy" of the U.S., the 1973-74 oil crisis, and the U.S. withdrawal from Vietnam. Following these major disturbances, Japan emerged as a confident junior partner in the U.S.-Japan relationship.

At the same time, Japan began to question Washington's political leadership. On the one hand, improved U.S.-Chinese relations since the 1970s have been welcomed in Japan as an important contribution to the reduction of tension in East Asia in general and on the Korean Peninsula in particular. On the other hand, the manner in which Washington pursued its policy of reconciliation with Beijing in the early 1970s generated much resentment in Japan. As is well known, the Nixon Administration's decision to effect a rapprochement with the PRC came as a surprise—even a shock—to Tokyo. Despite the pro-Beijing sentiments that had grown in Japan over the years, and despite significant trade and other commercial relations that had developed between Japan and the PRC in the 1960s, Japan's official policy had been to follow the U.S. lead in blocking Beijing's bid to replace Taipei in the United Nations and refusing to recognize Beijing. Many in Japan simply felt betrayed by Washington's 1972 decision.

A few years later, in 1978, President Carter reversed his decision to withdraw U.S. ground troops from Korea. This act likewise weakened the credibility of U.S. security commitments in the region. The following year, Washington's inability to extricate itself from the Iranian hostage crisis further reduced U.S. credibility as a global political leader. After the Soviet invasion of Afghanistan in 1979, Tokyo clearly realized that Washington needed its allies to help contain the growth of the Soviet military under Brezhnev.

Although President Reagan's major defense buildup through the mid-1980s temporarily halted the erosion of U.S. military capabilities, Japanese leaders remained uncertain about the future of nuclear deterrence and the U.S.-Soviet military balance. Moreover, continuing pressure on Tokyo to share more of the defense burden cast doubt on the will and ability of the U.S. to underwrite its security commitment to Japan. Such were the conditions when Nakasone took office in 1982. Nakasone was a new type of Japanese leader, willing to speak in unequivocal terms about Japan's importance as a member of the "Western alliance" and about Japan and the United States sharing a "common destiny." During his premiership, which lasted until the Autumn of 1987, Nakasone undertook major efforts to increase Japan's defense capabilities and intensify its security cooperation with the United States. Since 1980, Japan's defense budget has increased by over 5% per year. Tokyo also pays more than 40% (or $2.8 billion) of the cost of the American military presence in Japan. In absolute terms, Japan spent $30 billion on military spending in 1990—the third-largest such outlay in the world.

All this transpired against a background of steeply rising U.S. federal budget deficits brought on by President Reagan's combined policies of tax cuts and military buildup. By 1986 the budget deficit reached $221.2 billion, and the federal debt was $2.1 trillion.[6] As a result, the United States became heavily dependent on Japanese capital to finance its trade and current-account deficits—and remains so, although the deficits have declined somewhat. The deterioration of U.S. industrial competitiveness—reflected in its huge current-account deficits—seemed an inverted image of Japan's growing strength in trade and finance.

The visible signs of U.S. decline in financial power and trade have caused an increasing number of Japanese to question the U.S. leadership in the Western system of alliances. The most articulate expression of Japanese apprehensions emerged in Japan's debate on comprehensive security. The 1980 report by a task force appointed by the late Premier Masayoshi Ohira declared as follows:

> In considering Japan's security, the most fundamental change that took place in the international situation in the 1970s is that the clear U.S. superiority, in both military and economic dimensions, came to an end.[7]

Militarily, said the report, since the mid-1960s the United States had refrained from an arms buildup while the Soviet Union continued its military expansion, changing the military balance globally and regionally. As a consequence, the report asserted, "U.S. military power can no longer provide the nearly sufficient security it once did to its friends and allies," and "it had become necessary for U.S. friends and allies to strengthen their self-help efforts particularly in the area of conventional forces, and credibility of the U.S. 'nuclear umbrella' can no longer be maintained without their cooperation with the United States." The report concluded that the "Pax Americana [was] over," and the age of "peace through burden-sharing" had begun.[8] Another report, prepared in 1985 by a private advisory group to Prime Minister Nakasone, presented a virtually identical view of the change in U.S. power and its consequences for international peace and security.[9]

By the time Noboru Takeshita succeeded Nakasone, the Japanese had accepted a global, activist role. No longer was Japan satisfied with the traditional bilateral, U.S.-Japanese framework which had defined their international role. Nor was it content to follow U.S. leadership passively. Takeshita's foreign policy was based on four basic principles: ensuring continuity in Japan's diplomacy, developing Japan's foreign policy on its own will and initiative, placing the highest priority on developing the Japanese-U.S. relationship, and making Japan a "nation contributing more to the world."[10]

The pursuit of a more active, independent, and multilateral foreign policy was echoed vividly in a speech delivered late last year in Tokyo by

Takakazu Kuriyama, the Vice-Minister of Foreign Affairs. His speech declared that

> For minor powers, the international order is essentially a given factor, and the goal of diplomacy for such countries is to maintain its own security and to ensure its economic interests by best adapting themselves to the existing international order. . . . The foreign policy of postwar Japan maintained such a passivity, and enjoyed peace and prosperity, taking maximum advantage of the international order maintained by the United States.
>
> However, . . . Japan, as an important member of the industrial democracies, can no longer conduct a passive foreign policy, regarding the international order as given. Today, Japan must actively participate in the international efforts to create a new international order, in order to ensure its own security and prosperity. It is in this context that Japan's foreign policy must outgrow, as soon as possible, that of a minor power to the foreign policy of a major power.[11]

The pursuit of a more independent and multilateral foreign policy has been propelled even further by an upsurge of nationalism in Japan in recent years. In 1989 a member of the Diet, Shintaro Ishihara, co-authored with Sony Chairman Akio Morita a highly provocative book, *The Japan That Can Say No*. It quickly became a best-seller in Japan. Also in 1989, the Liberal Democratic Party (LDP) lost their majority in the Upper House of the Japanese Diet for the first time in their 40 years of domination over Japanese politics. The more nationalistic and anti-U.S. Japanese Socialist Party (JSP) gained a large share of votes at the expense of the LDP. The intensified friction of economic relations between the U.S. and Japan and the U.S.'s stress on "burden sharing" have strengthened Japanese nationalism. In September 1990, a threat from the U.S. Congress to begin withdrawing American forces until Japan paid "all" the military costs involved in their presence brought forth the following outburst from the chief of Japan's Defense Agency: "The U.S. Congress lacks common sense. Japan did not ask for the stationing of the U.S. forces. We will have to say 'Please take the forces home.'"

The Reactive Nature of Postwar Japan's Foreign Policy

One striking characteristic of postwar foreign policy in Japan has been its reactive nature: the state failed to undertake major independent foreign-policy initiatives even though it had the power and incentive to do so. It mainly responded—erratically, unsystematically, and often incompletely—to outside pressures for change, whether concerning security or economic issues.[12] As a result, it is difficult to find a systematic Japanese foreign policy in the postwar era—except for Tokyo's uneven efforts to adapt to the international order of the superpowers.

This reactive nature of postwar Japanese foreign policy is rooted in Japan's historical legacy, the character of the postwar international system, and Japan's domestic social and political structure. Japan was defeated in the Second World War, of course, and has been occupied by American troops since the end of that conflict. Japan's aggression during World War II left its neighbors extremely sensitive to Japanese foreign policy. A low-key and passive foreign policy promised to reduce this sensitivity and thereby facilitate Japan's concentration on economic reconstruction. Postwar Japan also depended on the United States for security and economic reconstruction. In the early stages of the U.S.-Japan relationship, U.S. financial aid and industrial contracts during the Korean War played a critical role in reviving Japan's economy. Today the U.S. has become the largest market for Japanese goods. In 1990, more than one-third of Japan's exports went to the United States. Also, Japan lacks natural resources. In the same year, it imported more than half of its food and 99.8% of its energy. For the sake of its very survival, therefore, Japan must be alert to the slightest international pressures.

Despite the importance of the international environment and its own historical legacy, particularly during the early postwar period, Japan's reactive behavior in the late 1980s cannot be explained without examining its domestic social and political structure. In contrast to the situation of the 1950s and 1960s, the international economic order of the 1980s clearly allowed for and encouraged Japanese activism, especially in view of the declining capabilities of the United States, economic stagnation in Western Europe, and Japan's own broad-based economic, technological, and, increasingly, geostrategic leverage on the global scene.

Japan's domestic political structure, however, undercuts an active foreign policy in several respects. Perhaps most important among them is the fragmented character of state authority in Japan which makes decisive action more difficult than in countries with strong chief executives, such as the United States or France. The problem of domestic coordination is compounded by the lack of a functionally oriented administrative corps and clearly defined ministerial responsibilities that can clarify bureaucratic disputes over jurisdiction. Japan has, as Karel van Wolferen puts it, "a hierarchy, or complex of overlapping hierarchies, without a top."[13]

To be sure, Japan has powerful national ministries such as the Ministry of International Trade and Industry (MITI) and the Ministry of Finance, which can act decisively on narrow issues within their individual areas of technical expertise (e.g., technical standards for consumer electronics or the establishment of research cartels for integrated circuits). But on broad, complex questions of global economic and strategic issues, the Japanese government cannot help but be reactive.

Domestic interest-group pressures and the government's unusual sensitivity to them further intensify this reactive character. In contrast to the United States, Japan has a relatively weak defense lobby, few émigrés with irredentist concerns, and relatively few powerful indigenous multinational enterprises with global geostrategic interests. The most powerful interest groups (aside from large umbrella-like business federations such as Keidanren, which has 600 corporate members and is too unwieldy to direct an activist foreign policy) are agricultural federations and regional chambers of commerce dominated by small business. These parochial groups have virtually no international interests other than to resist foreign encroachments into Japanese domestic markets.

The influence of interest groups on policymaking has been enhanced by the increasing policy role of the LDP and its powerful Policy Affairs Research Council.[14] Improved expertise, information, and staff support, together with the growing ability to control bureaucratic promotions (the result of over 30 years of continuous power) have enhanced the LDP's policymaking influence. Japan's system of medium-sized electoral districts forces as many as five members of the largest political parties (especially the ruling LDP) to run against one another in the same electoral district; therefore, extremely small shifts in the total vote can be crucial to a candidate's election prospects. As a result, LDP legislators tend to be highly sensitive to constituency pressure, especially from relatively well-organized grassroots pressure groups such as agriculture and small business organizations. Most of these groups have no clear ideology for conducting international relations other than their own parochial responses to foreign pressure.

Finally, the changing government-business relationship has helped make Japan's foreign policy reactive. Although the Japanese bureaucracy remains powerful, the private sector has acquired a self-confidence and assertiveness that are reinforced by its accelerating internationalization. Prime Minister Toshiki Kaifu's cabinet has been widely regarded as a weak government because it has weak intraparty backing and lacks an LDP majority in the Upper House. Indeed, in 1989, the Japanese government changed prime ministers three times in less than one year—an event unprecedented in postwar Japanese politics. During the Persian Gulf Crisis, the Kaifu government proposed to send SDF officers overseas. The government finally withdrew the proposal, however, fearing that the Diet would dismiss it. This was the first time in Japanese postwar history that the government withdrew a proposal before a Diet debate. Most recently, the main figure in post-Cold War foreign policymaking—the powerful LDP Secretary-General Ichiro Ozawa—resigned because of the failure of the LDP in the Tokyo mayoral election. The weakness of the current government seems likely to restrict its capacity to conceive and implement an active foreign policy in the post-Cold War era.

Japan's Strategy Toward Northeast Asian Countries

Every sovereign country is concerned with its national security. National security, however, is an ambiguous term. In a narrow sense, it means defense against outside invasion. In a broader sense, it means building international and domestic conditions that will preserve and promote national interests and protect them from all sorts of threats, actual or potential. Today, Japan is without doubt an economic superpower. In the current transitional world order, however, the question of whether Japan can use its enormous economic strength to balance its military and political weakness is the central problem for Japanese leaders. Moreover, Japan's economy is still fragile because of its dependence on importing energy, food, and industrial resources, and its need for export access to international markets. Therefore, for Japan, security means securing stable supplies and protecting trade and investment in the international market. This is especially true in the post-Cold War period, when the military threat from the Soviet Union has diminished. It would be no exaggeration to say that security for Japan is really economic security. Under current circumstances, a stabilized Northeast Asia with an open economy would be best suited to Japan's interests in the region. Japan's strategy toward this region, therefore, should seek to safeguard these interests.

In the early 1980s, a task group appointed by Prime Minister Masayoshi Ohira proposed a so-called Comprehensive Security (*sogo anzen hosho*) as the general direction for Japan's foreign policy. Although "comprehensive security" remains an ambiguous concept, in essence the policy postulated three levels of national-security measures for Japan: first, with the decline of U.S. power, Japan needed to strengthen its capacity for self-help and self-defense; second, Japan should try to render the international system conducive to Japan's security, including increasing its Official Development Assistance (ODA) and cultural diplomacy; third, Japan should undertake intermediate-level efforts to build a favorable security environment in the region.[15]

From this general perspective, Japan's strategy toward Northeast Asia in the post-Cold War era can be expected to have three elements. First, while remaining dependent on the U.S. relationship for its security, Japan will continue to increase its military spending in absolute terms. It will pursue a "global partnership" with the United States: it will not just share burdens; it will also share the decision-making on global issues. Second, Japan will continue to increase its economic penetration—through trade and investment—in Northeast Asia. The economy in much of this region will become more interdependent. Third, although the U.S. will remain Japan's main economic and security partner, its relative importance to Japan will decline. Japan will pursue relationships with other countries in the region in an effort to limit its dependence on the U.S., and in so doing Japan will gain leverage in its dealings with the U.S.

The Soviet Union

Japan's relationship with the U.S.S.R. (and now Russia) seems locked in a stalemate. Gorbachev's unprecedented visit to Tokyo in April 1991 yielded nothing more than a symbolic promise to continue to talk. Even the failed *coup d'etat* engendered little progress on the bilateral relationship. The stumbling-block preventing improved relations remains the territorial dispute over the four northern islands—Habomais, Shikotan, Kunashiri, and Etorofu.

Before Gorbachev's visit, the Japanese side had held high hopes. The Japanese hoped that Gorbachev would match his historic opening to Europe by returning at least Habomais and Shikotan. Several possible deals were suggested. Japan was reportedly ready to offer $26 billion in badly needed grants and credits to the Soviets in return for its concession on these islands.[16] The failure of the Tokyo summit, however, left the Japanese disappointed and angry and made the bilateral relationship even worse.

It is clear that the Soviet Union wanted to establish closer relations with Japan. Moscow is anxious to gain access to Japanese investment, trade, and technology and establish long-term economic and industrial agreements. It now recognizes that if the Soviet Union, or Russia, its successor, is to become a Pacific power and benefit from East Asia's economic dynamism, some form of *rapprochement* with Japan will be necessary. In the long term, it is also in Japan's interest to improve relations with Moscow—especially when friction with the U.S. is rising and China is getting stronger both economically and militarily. Tokyo also has long-term economic interests in gaining access to the huge natural gas, oil, and pulpwood resources in eastern Siberia and Sakhalin, and in regaining access to its traditional fishing resources in the northern seas.

Why, then, has progress towards a solution been so scant? Political constraints hamper progress on the territorial issue. Moscow was concerned that the return of all or some of the Northern Territories might set a precedent for the return of other territories occupied by the Soviet Union. In December 1988, a Soviet diplomat stated that "Moscow almost certainly could not move on the islands issues while international minority problems are unresolved."[17] Georgi Arbartov, the influential director of the Institute for the Study of the U.S.A and Canada, admitted in Tokyo in September 1989 that Moscow could not make any territorial concession because even the return of "one half of a small island" would "open up the whole Pandora's box of territorial questions."[18] The Soviet Union was also concerned that any concession to Japan could affect the U.S.S.R's still-unresolved territorial disputes with China, just as the Soviet concession along the eastern Sino-Soviet border before the Tokyo summit had raised Japanese expectations that similar progress might also be achievable on the Northern Territories.

The sweeping political changes in the Soviet Union also hampered resolution of the problem. The failure of the Tokyo summit reflected Gorbachev's inability to make any compromise. The end of the Soviet central government and the rise of nationalism in the successor republics after the attempted *coup* make territorial concessions even more difficult—if not impossible.[19] Moreover, as Andrei Piontkovsky of the Soviet Academy of Science's Research Institute for System Analysis argued in 1989:

> The broad issues are the competence of the Congress of People's Deputies, so a final decision will be taken by that body. And this circumstance must now be taken into account by all the sides involved in the talks (on the disputed islands), including the Japanese side. The creation of a new, full-time Soviet parliament, the Supreme Soviet, will bring profound changes in the internal political situation in the U.S.S.R. and also the process of decision-making in Soviet foreign policy, though the last fact has not been fully realized.[20]

The Soviet, now Russian, leaders may even fear that the return of the Northern Territories would encourage the Japanese to make further demands—perhaps for the northern Kuriles or even Sakhalin. Japan's escalation of its claims against the U.S.S.R. in the 1956 negotiations provides a precedent that confers credibility on such concerns.

The difficulties on the Japanese side are, if anything, more serious. Japanese policy has hardened into an "all or nothing" position. Any prime minister who accepted anything less would be in trouble on two fronts. This is especially the case for the current weak Kaifu government. Rivals in his party as well as the opposition would seek to exploit the "sellout" for their own political advantage. All parties accept the justice of the territorial demand, although there are considerable variations about just whether to demand four territories only, or all of Kuriles and a step-by-step approach, or a comprehensive settlement. In addition, those who—out of ideological or other motives—want to revive patriotic and nationalist feelings have an interest in blocking any accommodation and in emphasizing the "threat" from the north. The death early this year of Shintaro Abe, the powerful leader of the pro-Soviet faction in the LDP, made any territorial compromise by the Japanese government even more difficult.

The strategic dimension of the Northern Territorial issue also puts considerable constraints on its resolution. The Northern Territories can be used to guard the southern gateways to the Sea of Okhotsk from the Pacific. For Soviet/Russian naval forces, the Central and Southern Kuriles provide the most secure, ice-free passage into and out of the Pacific Ocean. The Sea of Okhotsk was a major deployment area for Soviet missile-firing submarines (SSBNs) operating out of Petropavlovsk on the eastern coast of the Kamchatka Peninsula. A new generation of long-range missiles enabled the Soviets to deploy their SSBNs in this type of highly defended bastion while keeping them in striking range of targets in the western United States. In other words, in the 1990s the Northern Territories have far greater strategic significance than they had in 1956, when the Soviets had been prepared to make concessions to Japan that would have resulted in at least two of the islands being returned.

The continued Soviet refusal to give up territories also served to keep alive the Soviet threat for Japanese public opinion, and hence justify the increase in Japanese military spending. This in turn has helped soften U.S. criticism that Japan is a security "free-rider" and assuage U.S. demands for "burden sharing." The increased defense expenditures, involving the purchase of a large amount of U.S. military hardware, have helped reduce the huge U.S. trade deficit with Japan. The unresolved Northern Territories issue thus has a positive function for the Japanese government in terms of both security and economic relations with the United States.

Aside from the political obstacles, there are economic obstacles to improving the relationship. Japan's trade with the Soviet Union never amounted to much more than 2% of its total foreign trade. Even at the height of the "Siberian boom" in the 1960s and early 1970s, it never exceeded 3%. In 1990, two-way trade between Japan and the Soviet Union was $2.8 billion, about one-quarter of the volume of the trade between China and Japan. Although Siberia's vast natural deposits remain a long-term attraction to Japanese business, their potential is heavily outweighed by adverse considerations. The enormous geographical and technical difficulties of extracting the resources of Siberia and of developing a solid industrial infrastructure will require massive investment with long time horizons. Moreover, the uncertainty of *perestroika* has made long-term investment even riskier. Moscow has also been short of hard currency, as a result of the decline in the price of oil and natural gas, which account for 80% of its foreign earnings. It could not afford, therefore, to buy the necessary equipment and technology. During the Tokyo summit, Gaishi Hiraiwa, chairman of the powerful Federation of Economic Organizations, told the Soviet visitors "[y]our country must lay the groundwork for the transition to an orderly market economy" because "the Japanese are simply not ready to pour money down a black hole."[21]

It seems unlikely that the stalemate will be broken soon. The two weak governments and the generally negative attitude of the Japanese toward the Soviet Union suggested that any substantial improvement was a long way off.[22] Whether the passing of the Soviet Union will lead to a conciliatory Russian foreign policy is not yet clear. Nevertheless, Moscow's intense desire to be a Pacific player and its need for Japanese investment and technological assistance in opening up the Russian Far East may be strong inducements for making the concessions necessary to achieve a *rapprochement* with Japan. The Northern Territories issue has been more forcefully stressed at times of general tension, but it seems to have been the excuse for, rather than the cause of, tension.

If a total Russian surrender on the issue is unlikely in the foreseeable future, it is also difficult to see the status quo remaining in place indefinitely. It might be impossible to abandon it altogether, but it could be set aside as a formal rather than a substantial issue, just like Chinese claims to large tracts of Soviet East Asia and the Japanese controlled Diaoyu (Senkaku) Islands. An influential Japanese analyst suggested that the islands be demilitarized and the question of sovereignty left unresolved. Senior Soviet officials echoed the idea.[23] A second possibility, hinted at by a senior official of Moscow's Institute of World Economy and International Relations in December 1988, would be to turn the islands into an "international buffer zone."[24] What this would mean in practice is not at all clear, however. A third option, and the one most frequently suggested, would be to return to Japan the Habomais and Shikotan (to which the Soviet claims are weakest) and to demilitarize the other two islands, leaving the question of their eventual status subject to ongoing or future negotiations. Gorbachev apparently raised the possibility of returning the two islands with Nakasone during the former Japanese prime minister's visit to the U.S.S.R. in July 1988. Although such a compromise is officially still unacceptable to the Japanese government, polls suggest that most Japanese would find such an accord "acceptable."[25] In any event, the problem has now passed to President Yeltsin of Russia.

China

Japan's relationship with China is both more intimate and more complex than its relationship with the Soviet Union. Sino-Japanese relations appear to have a dual structure which is built into their long history of interaction. The duality emerges in the conflicting sentiments among the Japanese of inferiority and superiority toward China. The inferiority complex comes from their sense of cultural debt to China and guilt for their record of aggression against China. The superiority complex derives from their assistance in China's modernization and contempt for China's backwardness. Similarly, Japan's political strategy toward China appears to be ambivalent. On the one hand, Japan recognizes China's strategic importance and its huge potential economic benefit to Japan; on the other hand, Japan worries about China's strengthening economic and military power.

Japan fully recognizes China's strategic importance. To Japan, China is not a mere "diplomatic card" whose value changes with the exigencies of international relations. As a permanent member of the Security Council of the United Nations and the only nuclear country in Asia, China carries broad strategic significance for Japan on all international matters. With Japanese foreign policy in transition, China takes on an added significance. The 1985 report on Japan's comprehensive security policy, prepared by a private advisory group to Prime Minister Nakasone, identified four major developments which forced Japan to change its foreign strategy: first, the rough parity between the U.S. and Soviet strategic capabilities; second, the decline in U.S. economic power and the combined problems of budget deficits in advanced countries and debt accumulation in the developing world; third, the emergence of a multilateral international system with the rise of China as an independent force on the international scene and an increasingly assertive Third World; and fourth, the dawning of a "Pacific Age," brought on by the new vigor of the region's newly industrialized powers.[26]

During the late Cold-War era, China was a de facto ally in the U.S.-Japan alliance to contain the Soviet military threat in Northeast Asia. With the Soviet military threat diminishing, however, many Japanese now realize that developments in China raise the possibility of several new security problems, ranging from Chinese refugees to an expansionist foreign policy in Beijing. A militarily assertive China could be the biggest threat for Japan in the long run. Tokyo also recognizes that the Japanese invasion during the 1930s and the memory of the Sino-Japanese War remain in Chinese minds. It takes little effort to revive anti-Japanese sentiments among the Chinese, as indicated by a series of incidents in Sino-Japanese relations since 1978 and the student demonstrations against the Japanese "economic invasion" at Beijing University in 1985.

In response to this sense of guilt and recognition of the strategic importance of not irritating China, Japan has played a low-key role, emphasizing the symbolic rhetoric of "friendship and cooperation." Japanese officials often use phrases such as *ichii taisui* ("neighbors across the strip of water") and *dobun doshu* ("same Chinese characters, same race") to emphasize their country's special relationship with China. Accordingly, Sino-Japanese relations have grown asymmetrically: China often takes a high-handed approach, bitterly criticizing "the revival of Japanese militarism"; Japan responds in a low-key manner, emphasizing its "special" relationship with China. This accommodation has helped maintain a relatively stable relationship between the two countries and in Northeast Asia. It is likely to continue in the post-Cold War era.

Economically, Japan's strategy has been to take advantage of economic opportunities as much as possible without providing significant technological assistance. Japan is China's largest trading partner (about $20 billion in 1990). It is also China's largest lender. In commemorating the 10th anniversary of the 1978 Sino-Japanese Peace and Friendship Treaty, Prime Minister Noboru Takeshita visited China in August 1988 with a huge package of government loans. The 810 billion yen he brought—the third in a series of loans—far exceeded the previous two packages, which had totaled 330 billion yen for 1979-1983 and 470 billion yen for 1984-1990. Japanese investment, however, has lagged behind that of the U.S. and Hong Kong. Japan has been reluctant to commit itself to large investments, and especially hesitant to transfer advanced technology. Japan's business behavior has thus been widely suspect in China. As we noted in the previous chapter, one high-ranking official in China's Ministry of Foreign Economics and Trade observed: "The Japanese are only interested in selling goods to China, but not at all interested in helping us with modernization."[27]

These economic issues have grown even more important with the end of the Cold War. With the intensification of its economic conflict with Washington, Japan is trying to reduce its market dependence on the U.S. China is the largest potential alternative. Unlike the situation in the Soviet Union, ten years of reform has fostered a huge market economy in the southern part of China, particularly in Guangdong, Fujian, and the other coastal provinces. China's capacity to absorb foreign investment is much greater than that of the former Soviet Union. Japan's long-term economic interest in China is reflected in its obvious hesitance to join the Western economic sanctions against China after the Tiananmen crackdown. This interest was also revealed by Japan's business relations with Hong Kong. Japan has taken Hong Kong as a bridgehead for its long-term economic investment in China. In this regard, it is useful to recall some data from the previous chapter. In December 1989, not long after Tiananmen, Japan became the largest investor in Hong Kong; Japanese bank deposits accounted for 56% of the deposits in Hong Kong banks, and Japanese department stores have about 30% of Hong Kong's retail sales.[28]

Japan has enjoyed a relatively stable and undisturbed relationship with China for nearly four decades. Tokyo's low-key posture has helped Japan maintain its relatively stable relationship with China, which in turn has been critical for the stability of relationships in Northeast Asia. A central question for Japan's long-term strategy is whether China can contain its domestic turmoil. After the Tiananmen crackdown, many in Japan began to worry about the possibility of China playing a spoiler's role in the region. They recognized that an economically desperate China could become disruptive and combative. China's gross national product (GNP) was nearly equal to that of Japan in 1960, but fell to one-quarter of Japan's in the 1980s and one-fifth by the end of 1990. China's per capita GNP in 1990 was roughly $300, while that of Japan was well over $20,000. It is commonly recognized that the gap in economic power between Japan and China will continue to grow rapidly. Today, China's trade with Japan accounts for one-third of Chinese foreign trade. This will continue to grow. Also, whereas China's foreign debt was estimated at $49 billion in 1989, Chinese foreign-exchange reserves were estimated at $17.5 billion. China will, therefore, have a serious repayment crisis in the 1990s, and 70% of this foreign debt is owed to Japan. This will give Japan a lot of leverage for changing its asymmetrical relations with Beijing.

Nevertheless, despite the long history of competition and the legacy of a bitter war, Sino-Japanese relations in the 1990s will remain on solid ground. Although disputes about the sovereignty of the small Diaoyu islands in the south China sea might be a disturbing factor in future Sino-Japanese relations, the more likely factor to disrupt the steady relationship between the two is a rapid reunification of the Koreas. A unified Korea with nuclear weapons is likely to lead to Japan's rearmament or even to Japan's acquisition of a nuclear arsenal. This could lead to a quick deterioration of Sino-Japanese relations.

The Koreas

Japan's relationship with South Korea has always been very delicate because of the legacy of Japan's occupation of the peninsula from 1910 to 1945 and the extraordinarily strong nationalist sentiment among Koreans. The era of Japanese colonial domination left most Koreans with a deep-seated bitterness towards their colonial oppressor. Public-opinion polls in both nations consistently indicate their people's mutual dislike. Koreans rank Japan as one of the countries they like least (second only to North Korea), and the Japanese rank South Korea third on their list of most-disliked nations (behind only the Soviet Union and North Korea). Even the normalization treaty and arrangements for long-term Japanese economic assistance, achieved by President Park Chung Hee and Prime Minister Eisaku Sato in 1965, were most unpopular in both countries. Accordingly, the textbook crises, the statements by cabinet ministers on Japan's imperialistic past, and the official visits to the Yasukuni shrine caused a comparable if not a greater uproar in Korea than in China. Today, Japan and South Korea are linked by geography, economics, and their mutual ties to the United States. But the Japan-South Korea relationship remains an uneasy association.

Japan has always regarded Korea as critical to its own security, and it fought two wars with China and Russia early this century to secure control over the peninsula. Historically, Japan has never had an easy time with Korea. The postwar partition of the Korean peninsula created both a point of military tension and a source of regional stability. The common threat Japan and South Korea perceived from the communist bloc to the north created a strong inducement to stress stable relations over historic hostility. Still, mutual suspicions have remained on both sides. Many Japanese, for example, perceive South Korea as more nationalistic and militaristic than Japan.[29] They express concern that an increasingly powerful Korea could eventually become not only an economic competitor to Japan but also a significant military power in Northeast Asia. Korean nationalism and the possibility of reunification only heighten these concerns. On the Korean side, there are worries about their country's economy growing too dependent on Japan and fears that a Japanese defense buildup will acquire its own momentum.[30] Note, for example, that Japanese Prime Minister Kaifu's decision to placate the United States by sending minesweepers to the Persian Gulf provoked a firestorm of alarmism in the South Korean press, even though the government adopted a measured, uncritical response.[31]

The uneasy relationship between Japan and South Korea not only stems from deep-rooted historic feelings, but more importantly from their divergent security interests. Japan's central concern has been a militarily assertive Soviet Union, and its first priority has been to regain the Northern Territories. North Korea has not been seen as a realistic independent threat to Japan. In the post-Cold War era, however, the Korean Peninsula will probably become Japan's paramount strategic concern. Two issues will particularly bother Japan: North Korea's nuclear capability and the possible reunification of the Koreas. South Korea's main threat comes from the North. South Korea has viewed the U.S.S.R. only as a secondary adversary, as an ally of their enemy. In fact, in the absence of a threat from the North, it is more likely that Korean security concerns would focus on Japan, rather than the Soviet Union, even less so Russia as long as it stays on a democratic course at home. In the post-Cold War era—with the disappearance of the Soviet military threat and the success of President Roh Tae Woo's *Nordpolitik* foreign policy—Japan will gain increasing importance in South Korea's strategic agenda.

In the short run, North Korea's possible nuclear capability is Japan's biggest security concern. Although some are still skeptical about Pyongyang's capacity to produce nuclear weapons,[32] Tokyo has never doubted North Korea's intentions or ability to do so. Many Japanese analysts have argued that North Korea's reasons for not going nuclear have been outweighed by Pyongyang's perception of a growing strategic need for nuclear weapons. Strategically, North Korea's nuclear weapons targeted against the South could deter U.S. nuclear strikes on the North in any North-South conflict. This is particularly important because, by the end of 1990, relations between Pyongyang and Moscow had sunk to an all-time low, primarily as a consequence of the U.S.S.R.'s decision to recognize South Korea. A North Korea that sees itself as abandoned by its major nuclear ally might perceive an even greater need for such a deterrent. And post-Soviet Russia is more likely to be seen as an enemy than an ally. The conventional military balance on the Korean Peninsula is also shifting in favor of the South. In 1989, North Korea's GNP was estimated at $21.1 billion—roughly one-tenth that of the South ($210.1 billion). To match the South's 5% of GNP in military spending, the North has been allocating 20-25% of GNP to the military. Even so, the military balance is moving inexorably in Seoul's favor—the

South's current military budget is already approximately double that of the North. By the end of the decade the South may well achieve conventional military superiority, much earlier if Russia fails to provide spare parts and new weapons to the North Korean military.

The outcome of the Gulf war—in which American equipment bested Soviet arms similar to those used by Kim Il Sung's forces—can only have underscored the North's feelings of insecurity. The North faces a no-win situation: attempting to match the South militarily will be ruinously expensive for an economy already burdened with huge external debt and in deep economic crisis. The North cannot maintain, let alone increase, its current crippling rate of defense expenditure. As Kim Chang Soon, a top South Korean expert on the North, pointed out, "After the Gulf, I don't think any North Korean leader believes they can win a war with their present weapons systems. They are developing nuclear weapons not to win a war but to deter war or avoid losing one."[33]

Pyongyang's economic problems are exacerbated by Soviet, now Russian, reductions in aid and, since early 1991, Moscow's policy of forcing the North to pay for Soviet goods—including the oil on which North Korea depends heavily—at world market prices and in hard currency. The nation's external debt is currently estimated at $5 billion, economic growth is slowing, trade with fraternal socialist countries is declining, agriculture is in deep trouble, and about 50% of the North's industry may be idle because of an energy shortage.

All of these problems, from the Japanese point of view, will force North Korea to acquire a nuclear arsenal. Katsumi Sato, a leading Japanese expert on Korean affairs, says that when Soviet Foreign Minister Eduard Shevardnadze visited Pyongyang in September 1990, North Korean Foreign Minister Kim Yong Nam told him that the new Soviet ties with Seoul had relieved Pyongyang of its obligation not to make nuclear weapons.[34] There is an emerging view in Japan that favors "rescuing" Kim economically in the interests of preserving stability in the peninsula, and thereby removing Japan's security concern. This argument rests on the assumption that continued economic decline and international isolation could lead Kim Il Sung to lash out at his old enemies while he still can. Wataru Kubo, a Japanese Socialist Party parliament member involved in preparing former Deputy Prime Minister Kanemaru's visit to Pyongyang in September 1990, argues, "Unless Japan normalizes relations, North Korea will feel threatened by a strong chain linking South Korea with Japan and the U.S."[35]

In the long run, the perceived nuclear danger will be compounded by Korean reunification. The demise of the anachronistic communist dictatorship in Pyongyang will surely bring about the unification of the Korea peninsula, which might well continue, although in a slow and perhaps ambiguous manner, the nuclear weapons program it would inherit from the North. A unified Korea with nuclear weapons, coupled with strong anti-Japanese sentiment among Koreans, will definitely constitute a security threat to Japan. Of course, this outcome would be highly dependent upon how the unification occurred and where the unified Korea anchored itself strategically. Under current circumstances, it is more than likely that a unified Korea would be under Seoul's leadership. Whether it would still ally itself with the U.S., however, is an open question. Given the rapidly diminishing Soviet military threat and the strengthening anti-U.S. sentiment among Koreans, especially within the younger generation, the continued U.S. military presence would also be in doubt. This could induce Japan to rearm, and possibly to acquire nuclear weapons. China, too, can be expected to react vigorously. Northeast Asia would then be facing a very dangerous situation.

Japan's strategy toward Korea, therefore, has aimed at preserving the status quo on the peninsula and at curbing North Korea's efforts to acquire a nuclear arsenal. This strategy was revealed vividly during last September's unprecedented visit to Pyongyang by two Japanese delegations, one from the ruling party LDP led by former Deputy Prime Minister Kanemaru Shin, and the other from the Japan Socialist Party (JSP), led by Vice-Chairman Tanabe Makoto. The Japanese seemed determined to move rather quickly toward diplomatic recognition of Pyongyang, dangling the prospect of billions of dollars in aid and the cost of a deteriorating relationship with the South. Japan backtracked only after Washington sent an intelligence team to Tokyo with satellite photos of a suspicious nuclear-reactor complex; Japan then told Pyongyang that there would be no normalization without full International Atomic Energy Agency (IAEA) inspection of North Korea's nuclear facilities.

Korean reunification will involve all the powers in the region. Although both North and South Korea seek to change the status quo, neither state has sufficient influence to force change without the participation of other major powers. Japan's potential role in Korean reunification is limited, however. The only leverage Tokyo has is economic. South Korea's economy has been heavily dependent upon that of Japan. In 1990, 30% of South Korea's total imports and 20% of its total exports were with Japan. Japanese direct investment accounted for about one-half of South Korea's total foreign investment.[36] To North Korea Japan can offer desperately needed foreign capital and technology, but how well Japan can use this leverage and maneuver between the two remains to be seen.

The United States

U.S.-Japanese relations will remain the primary axis of Japan's foreign policy, although the content of that policy has changed significantly over the years, reflecting changes in the relative economic strength of Japan and the United States. On the security side, although Japan has continuously expanded its military power during the past decade—and will probably continue to do so—the United States will remain Japan's ultimate protector for the foreseeable future. Motoo Shiina, a member of the Japanese Diet and one of the nation's top defense strategists, recently described the limits of Japanese military expansion this way:

> We have only 180,000 ground troops virtually without any reserves. We have a very limited air force and navy. We have no marines. It is clear that we cannot expand our major influence beyond our shores. It is impossible. Where would they go? To China? The Chinese have nuclear weapons and 3.5 million in their armed forces. You need a huge military force and a good sized defense industry to have a credible aggressive capability. For Japan, that would take at least ten years lead time. If we suddenly showed a desire, say, to purchase a thousand F15s, just placing an order would be recognized by anyone in the world as a potentially aggressive move and the other nations could react. Some countries could cut off our supplies. Even if we built our own defense industry, we would not have all the necessary inputs to maintain such an industry and build a full range of modern weapon systems. If potential inputs from other countries are suspended, we would be finished. Our capabilities do not reflect even the potential for an aggressive defense policy if you really look at the facts. Here our revived militarism is sheer nonsense. What we want to be sure of is that Hokkaido will not be occupied like our four northern islands. We want to ensure this by the policy of establishing a minimum defensive capability so that we can live in peace and prosper. That is all.[37]

Such a candid assessment of Japan's strategic weakness suggests that the U.S.-Japan Security Treaty will remain the foundation for Japanese security strategy. With the shifting of East-West relations from confrontation to dialogue, there is a new and contemporary significance for this security relationship. First, deterrence will remain the primary function of the treaty. However much the Soviet Union may have changed, its successor remains a military superpower with huge nuclear and conventional forces. Around Japan, the security environment remains unclear as the disposition of Soviet (presumably now Russian) naval and air power remains uncertain, China improves its military industrial base, and North-South tensions on the Korean peninsula continue. Under these circumstances, Japanese leaders are likely to see the U.S.-Japan security tie as essential for peace and security in Northeast Asia.

Second, the existence of a solid alliance between Japan and the United States has been a prerequisite for a serious dialogue between Japan and the Soviet Union. Only with this relationship would the old Soviet Union regard Japan as a nation it must treat seriously. It is also likely to remain indispensable to any effort to invite the new Russia into a new international order for the Northeast Asian region as a peaceful and constructive participant.

Third, the Security Treaty is the most important framework for stability and development in Northeast Asia and the Pacific. On the one hand, it is the crucial pillar for the continuation of an active U.S. presence in the region. Without this pact, the U.S. presence in Asia and the Pacific would be greatly curtailed, not only militarily but also politically and economically. On the other hand, the treaty lends international credibility to Japan's insistence that it will not become a major military power. This makes it easier for Japan's neighbors to accept a larger political role for Tokyo.[38]

The Japan-U.S. relationship is increasingly dominated by economic factors. Growing economic interdependence between the U.S. and Japan has transformed the old relationship from that of patron-client into an uneasy partnership. Economic frictions have spread from the field of trade into wider areas of investment, finance, and technology. Since the mid-1980s, the annual U.S. trade deficit with Japan has been around $50 billion—it peaked at $57 billion in 1987 and fell to approximately $38 billion in 1990. By the end of 1990, Japan had roughly $200 billion invested in the U.S., including about $50 billion in direct investment. This investment—ranging from Sony's $5 billion purchase of Columbia Pictures and Matsushita's $6.1 billion acquisition of MCA, to the Japanese holding of Rockefeller Center and the $800 million purchase of the world-class Pebble Beach golf course in California—has evoked a growing perception that Japan's economic and technological power represents the new threat to the United States' leading role in the world. In reality, it has provided a much-needed source of capital to the U.S. economy in light of the declining propensity of Americans to save.

Because it is highly subjective, the perception is all the more difficult to remove. It has stimulated a strong sense of mistrust towards Japan, and stirred a widespread suspicion among Americans that Japan does not behave fairly, whether in trade, technology transfer, or sharing of the defense burden. This perception, however, stems from two misperceptions: an overestimation of Japan's economic power and an underestimation of the overall strength of the United States. In fact, Japanese trade with the U.S. is much more favorable to American than is commonly perceived. Japan is America's best foreign customer by far, second only to Canada. Its imports from the U.S. totaled $44.5 billion in 1989, and are rising very sharply: up 18% from 1988-89 and 34% from 1987-88. Those figures are much higher than the growth of Japan's exports to the United States. Moreover, 60% of those U.S. sales were manufactured goods, and one-half of those were "high-tech" products. This means that in 1989 U.S. exports of manufactured goods to Japan totaled $27 billion—higher than U.S. exports to Germany and France combined.[39] On the investment side, over the past fifteen years the return on investment of U.S. manufacturing firms in Japan has been, on average, roughly twice the return realized by U.S. affiliates in Canada, the United Kingdom, and France.[40]

Critics invariably point to Japan's trade surplus—it sells more to Americans than it buys from them. But America's population—its market—is more than twice as large, and a per capita comparison reveals that each buys about the same amount from the other: in 1989, for example, $374 in U.S. imports from Japan per capita, and $360 in Japanese imports from the United States.[41]

Even with these difficulties and problems, the two economies have become increasingly interdependent since the beginning of the 1980s. In 1990, for example, 36% of Japan's total exports went to the U.S.. The U.S. also absorbed one-half of Japan's overseas investment. Japan is the largest purchaser of U.S. government bonds and securities. Thanks to this huge capital inflow, which began just as the Reagan administration began its major defense buildup, the U.S. was able to sustain both its huge defense buildup of early 1980s and one of the most rapid rates of overall growth and employment-creation among the major industrialized nations, without suffering a debilitating credit crunch. Japan is also a very attractive market for U.S. companies, because of the higher return on investment and high quality of labor. By the end of 1990, direct U.S. investment in Japan was approximately $18 billion, much of it in the high-tech sectors. The stakes are especially high in the electronics, banking, energy, and automotive sectors. Texas Instruments, for example, produced all the 64K RAM computer chips for its global operations in Japan, and IBM sources more than half of its IBM PC components there. General Motors, Ford, and Chrysler have all made heavy exports to the United States from Japan of both components and finished automobiles. Even in the semiconductor industry, Silicon Valley's relatively hard attitude toward Japan is moderated by a broad market segmentation: California producers specialize in microprocessors and customized chips, while Japanese producers specialize in commodity RAM chips. In fact, over a quarter of Japan's current exports to the United States are structurally linked to the production and marketing activities of U.S. firms on their home territory.[42]

This economic interdependence has made it increasingly difficult for Americans to devise ways to retaliate against Japan without hurting U.S. interests. This became quite apparent when the United States imposed tariffs on certain Japanese imports in reaction to Japan's dumping of semiconductors in the U.S. market in 1987-88. With the United States' huge foreign debt and intractable current-account deficit, the economic interdependence developed very much on Japan's terms, and it is likely to continue that way in the 1990s and into the next century. Although labor shortages and an aging population may slow Japanese economic growth somewhat, the asymmetric pattern of economic interdependence seems likely to continue, in light of Japan's high levels of savings and investment (about twice those of the U.S.), rigorous educational system (up to the college level), far-sighted corporate strategies, and low level of defense spending. Japan is quite aware of its leverage in its relationship with the U.S. In January 1991, Makato Utsumi, the Japanese vice minister of finance, bluntly commented—in public—that Japan would reduce its capital investments in America if Washington applied sanctions for not giving U.S. financial institutions opportunities in Japan similar to those enjoyed by their Japanese counterparts in America.

The economic interdependence has also driven both countries more deeply into each other's affairs. The Japanese see the current negotiations over the Structural Impediment Initiative (SII) as American intervention in their domestic affairs. The Japanese view such activities as "Japan-bashing," and have reacted with new assertions of nationalism. Nevertheless, Japan recognizes its heavy dependence on the U.S. market and U.S. defense forces, and it will probably continue to yield slowly and reluctantly to some U.S. economic pressures, confident that the Japanese economy can adapt without much difficulty. Given the tremendous upheavals in the communist world, it is likely to be years before anything resembling a new and coherent international system takes shape. It is more than likely that Tokyo will be careful not to move too far or too fast from the United States on key foreign-policy issues.

As the U.S. and Japan look to the future of a relationship that has fundamental global importance, the underlying structure of their bilateral ties has remained remarkably unchanged since the end of the Allied occupation nearly 40 years ago. The U.S. provides military security and also defends the open global markets for trade and finance that strongly benefit Japan and other U.S. allies. Nevertheless, the rapid accumulation of American foreign debt—and the increasing reluctance of foreign investors to fund it—suggest, with increasing urgency, that the status quo will not last indefinitely. The pressing challenge to both the U.S. and Japan is to find a means of smoothly sharing the economic burdens of global leadership and thereby to preserve an economic and security regime that has brought unprecedented prosperity to both countries and the world as a whole since its inception four decades ago.

Conclusions

As the Cold War winds down, Japan's strategy in Northeast Asia is entering a transitional stage. Its foreign policy has turned from passive to active, from dependence to autonomy, and from bilateral dependency to multilateral cooperation. In all, the following five conclusions emerge.

First, its security and economic dependence on the United States, and the reactive nature of Japanese policymaking, make it unlikely that Tokyo will abruptly break its foreign-policy path in any significant way. This suggests that the U.S.-Japan strategic alliance will remain the primary axis of Japan's foreign policy in the post-Cold War era.

Second, while remaining dependent on the U.S. for its security and economic expansion, Japan will continue the trend, which started in early 1980s, to increase its military expenditures in absolute terms. The relative importance of the U.S. to Japan will thus decline. Japan will also deliberately pursue relationships with other countries in this region, to limit its dependence on the United States. This, in turn, will increase its leverage in its dealings with the U.S.

Third, due to uncertainties in the domestic transformations in China and Russia, it is unlikely that Japan will change its relations with them significantly. With weak governments in Tokyo and Moscow, the Northern Territories dispute between Japan and Russia is unlikely to be resolved quickly. In the long run, with the continued strengthening of China's economic and military power, Sino-Japanese relations could become crucial to regional stability. Given the historical distrust between China and Japan and China's rapid economic development, it is possible that the PRC could replace Russia as Japan's primary rival in this region.

Fourth, the Korean Peninsula will remain Japan's biggest security concern for the foreseeable future—especially the possible nuclear capability of North Korea. The reunification of the Koreas would definitely present a great challenge to Japan, both economically and strategically. It is clearly not in Japan's interest to see the two Koreas reunited, but Japan's influence over this matter is limited. It is conceivable that Japan's strategy toward the Korean Peninsula will be to try to maintain the status quo there.

Fifth, U.S. military presence is pivotal to the long-term stability of the region. Diminishing Soviet power in this region might increase tensions between China and Japan or Korea and Japan. The United States is the only power acceptable to all countries in the region, because of its geographical remoteness and its history of regional involvement. Northeast Asia, as Robert Scalapino correctly points out, is far too heterogeneous and too interrelated to nations elsewhere to permit domination by a single country.[43] The U.S. military presence will play the role of buffer, moderator, and power-balancer here.

NOTES
[1]Directory of Trade Statistics, Yearbook, 1989, IMF, Washington, D.C.
[2]"Asia 1991," *Far East Economic Review*.
[3]For arguments along this line, please see Selig S. Harrison and Clyde V. Prestowitz, Jr., "Pacific Agenda: Defense or Economics?" *Foreign Policy*, Summer,

1990, pp. 56-76; Joseph S. Nye, Jr., "Soft Power," *Foreign Policy*, Fall, 1990; pp. 153-171; and Richard Solomon, "Asian Security in the 1990s: Integration in Economics, Diversity in Defense," *Dispatch*, vol. 1, no. 10, United States Department of State.

[4]Yoshida, Shigedu, *The Yoshida Memoirs*, pp. 191-192, 266, 274-275; London: Heinemann, 1961.

[5]American aid to Japan totaled US$ 2.1 billion over the seven-year span of the occupation. See Kent Calder, "The United States and Japan: From Occupation to Global Partnership," in L. Carl Brown (ed), *American Diplomacy Since World War Two, 1990*.

[6]*Japan: An International Comparison*, 1989, Tokyo: Keizai Koho Center, 1989, p. 81.

[7]Sogoanzenhosho Kenyu Gurupu, *Sogoanzenhosho Senryaku* (Comprehensive Security Strategy), Tokyo: Okurasho Insatsukyoku, 1980, p. 7.

[8]*Ibid.*, pp. 7-8.

[9]Heiwamondai Kenkyukai, *Kokudaikokka Nihon no Sogo Anzenhosho Seisaku* (Comprehensive Security Policy of an International Japan), Tokyo: Okurasho Insatsukyoku, 1985, pp 24-9.

[10]These principles were presented in Takeshita's speech at the National Press Club in Washington on January 14, 1988. The speech is reproduced in full as "A Nation Contributing More to the World: Japan's Commitment to Global Prosperity," *Speaking of Japan*, vol. 9, no. 89, May 1988, pp. 27-32.

[11]Kuriyama, Takakazu, "New Directions for Japanese Foreign Policy in the Changing World of the 1990s: Making Active Contributions to the Creation of a New International Order," 1990, Tokyo, English version.

[12]See Kent Calder, "Japanese Foreign Economic Policy Formation: Explaining the Reactive State," *World Politics*, July 1988, vol. XL, no.4.

[13]Van Wolferen, "The Japan Problem," *Foreign Affairs*, Winter 1986-87, p. 289.

[14]Inoguchi, Takshi & Tomoaki Iwai, *Zoku Giin no Kenkyu* (Research on tribal dietmen), Tokyo: Nihon Keizai Shimbun Sha, 1987.

[15]Heiwamondai Kenkyukai, *Kokusai kokka nihon no sogo anzenhosho seisaku* (Comprehensive Security Policy for an International Japan) (Tokyo: Okurasho insatsukyoku, 1985). For an English-language discussion of Japanese comprehensive security, see Robert W. Barnett, *Beyond War: Japan's Concept of Comprehensive National Security* (Washington, D.C.: Pergmon-Brassey, 1984).

[16]"Gorbachev Goes to Tokyo: No Deal," *Newsweek*, Apr. 29, 1991, p. 40.

[17]Charles Smith, "Time to Compromise," *Far Eastern Economic Review*, Dec. 22, 1988, p. 28.

[18]"Arbatov Blasts Stance on Northern Islands," *Daily Yomiuri*, Sept. 19, 1989.

[19]A recent poll in Russia shows that more than 80% of those polled thought the Russian government should not return the Northern Islands to Japan. Data from Gennady Chufrin, presentation in "East Asia Transformed: An International Symposium," San Francisco, Sept. 1991.

[20]Andrei Piontkovsky, "Soviet-Japanese Relations and the Territorial Issue: Is a Solution Possible?" *Voennyi Vestnik*, June 1989, p. 3.

[21]"Gorbachev Goes to Tokyo: No Deal," *Newsweek*, April 29, 1991.

[22]A September 1990 World Opinion Poll shows that 61% of the Japanese felt hostility toward the Soviets, while only 1% polled felt very friendly. *World Opinion Update*, vol. XIV, issue 9, Sept. 1990.

[23] Private discussion with author. See also *Pacific Defence Report*, June 1989, p. 33.

[24] Alan Goodall,"Bird Diplomacy Thaws Japan's Icy Soviet Links," *Australian*, Dec. 19, 1988, p. 8.

[25] Segal, Gerald,"Quiet Progress on Ending the Japanese-Soviet Chill," *International Herald Tribune*, Mar. 18, 1989.

[26] Heiwamondai Kenkyukai, *Kokusaikokka Nihon no Sogo Anzenhosho Seisaku*, (Comprehensive Security Policy of an International Japan), Tokyo, Okurasho Insatsukyoku, 1985.

[27] *People's Daily* (foreign edition), May 20, 1991, p. 4.

[28] *New York Times*, Dec. 25, 1989 and *Financial Times*, Jan. 30, 1990.

[29] Masashi Nishihara, "Japan's Gradual Defense Buildup and Korean Security," *The Korean Journal of Defense Analysis*, vol. 1, no.1, Summer, 1989, p. 105.

[30] Kim, Chong whi, "Korea-Japan Relations and Japan's Security," in *Pacific Security Toward the Year 2000*, The 1987 Pacific Symposium, Dora Alves (ed), Washington, D.C.: National Defense University Press, 1988, p. 135.

[31] See "Media Sound 'shrill' Warning," FBIS-EAS-91-081, Apr. 26, 1991, p. 29.

[32] See, for example, Andrew Mack, "North Korea and the Bomb," *Foreign Policy*, 1991, pp. 87-104.

[33] Lane, Charles, "A Knock on the Nuclear Door?" *Newsweek*, Apr. 29, 1991, p. 39.

[34] *Ibid*.

[35] Shim Jae Hoon, "Pyongyang Paradox," *Far Eastern Economic Review*, Nov. 29, 1990, p. 28.

[36] Young Whan Kihl, "South Korea in 1990," *Asian Survey*, Jan. 1991.

[37] Cited in Ryozo Kato, "Present and Future Role and Missions of the Japanese 'Self Defense Forces'," in *The Pacific in the 1990s*, Janos Radvanyi (ed), 1990, University Press of America.

[38] For the Japanese view of the Japan-U.S. Security Treaty, see Takakazu Kuriyama, "New Directions for Japanese Foreign Policy in the Changing World of the 1990s: Making Active Contributions to the Creation of a New International Order," Tokyo, 1990.

[39] All trade data from the U.S. Commerce Department, *U.S. Foreign Trade Highlights*, 1988 and 1989.

[40] Kent E. Calder, "The United States and Japan: From Occupation to Global Partnership," in *American Diplomacy Since World War II*, L. Carl Brown (ed), pp. 279-304, 1989.

[41] *Ibid*.

[42] *Ibid*.

[43] Robert A. Scalapino, "The US-Japan Relationship—Looking Ahead," *CAPA Report*, no. 1, Apr. 1991.

CHAPTER 5

The Strategic Equilibrium on the Korean Peninsula in the 1990s

By Perry Wood

Background: The Crossroads of Northeast Asia

Korea is located at a strategic crossroads, both continental and maritime, where the interests of four major powers—the United States, the Soviet Union/Russia, China, and Japan—intersect. Historically, when one power has dominated the Korean peninsula, it has also dominated Northeast Asia. The arrangements at the end of World War II left the peninsula divided. Stalin's gamble at grabbing all of Korea, of course, led to war, and when it looked as if the United States would take the entire country, China entered the conflict. In the end, the peninsula remained divided. The partition of Korea has created a point of enormous military tension but also a source of regional stability.

Both the Republic of Korea (ROK) and the Democratic People's Republic of Korea (DPRK) have long sought to overcome the existing division. The end of the Cold War, political realignment in Europe, and a new Russian policy toward East Asia make that goal less of a distant future aspiration and more of a feasible goal than at any time in the past four decades.

The strategies of both Koreas are changing dramatically toward one another and in some regards toward the four major regional powers. Yet both countries' ties with their traditional allies remain significant constraints on their room for maneuver. Because the unification of Korea would portend major new strategic alignments, the central focus of this analysis will be on its prospects.

The Republic of Korea: Growing World Role
Introduction: A New Self-Confidence

South Korea has emerged as a significant independent actor on the international scene. It is a significant military power, and its economic

84   Trial After Triumph: East Asia After the Cold War

strength has won international recognition and bestowed it with growing regional influence. Economists have predicted that the South Korean economy will rival the major West European economies by early in the 21st century.[1] The South Korean economy has become a model for other Third World nations envious of the giant, efficient Korean *chaebol* business conglomerates which export and operate all over the world. South Korean foreign investment has become an important factor in the national economies of Southeast and South Asia, which are increasingly looking to Korea as an alternative source of technology and know-how. The growing economic and military power of South Korea is an unprecedented development which will have a critical impact on Northeast Asian security in the next decade.

South Koreans relish their newfound influence. There is a growing sense of self-confidence and aggressive nationalism in South Korea. This new feeling has been stimulated by a number of developments including South Korea's impressive economic growth, its successful, peaceful transition from authoritarian to democratic government, the international recognition won by hosting the 24th Summer Olympiad in 1988, the obvious political-economic decline of the South's rival in the north, the new policies of the Gorbachev government, and the great diplomatic successes of President Roh's "Nordpolitik" policies and the hopes they offer for Korean national reunification. Koreans have never been a shy people, and these developments have heightened their self-assurance enormously.

A Brief Overview of Foreign Policy During the Authoritarian Era

The new Korean assertiveness shocks Americans and Japanese because they have yet to adjust to the rapid transformation of Korea from a war-shattered, poverty-stricken nation into an economic giant. Surveys indicate that the American public's perception of Korea is largely identical with the image portrayed on the popular television show *M*A*S*H*: a poor, dirty, violent land. Even better-informed policymakers and opinion shapers remain influenced by their memories of the Korean war and their old postwar relationships.

In the 1950s, the nation was a virtual dependent of the United States. The country was among the world's poorest nations, dependent on American economic aid for its survival. South Korea's tie with the United States was not only its most important external relationship, it was virtually its only one. Formal diplomatic relations with Japan were not established until 1965. Given these facts, Syngman Rhee, South Korea's first postwar leader, pragmatically restrained his strong nationalism and accepted a virtual client relationship with the United States (although he was a prickly client).

The primary foreign-policy goals of the Syngman Rhee regime were national security (secured via the 1954 defense pact with the United States and the maintenance of the close U.S.-ROK security relationship) and international legitimacy. The Rhee government engaged the communist regime in Pyongyang in an unrelenting competition to secure international recognition over their archrival. South Korea adhered to the principle established in the Hallstein Doctrine, first enunciated by the Federal Republic of Germany to guide its competition with the communist German Democratic Republic. According to this doctrine, Seoul, like Bonn, refused to recognize any nation which established relations with North Korea (and broke relations with any nation that already had recognized the ROK).

The Park Chung Hee government brought some major changes to South Korea's international posture. Park came to power through a *coup d'etat* which overthrew Chang Myon and South Korea's first democratic government. The United States, although not enamored of Chang's government, supported the idea of a democratic South Korea and was embarrassed by Park's coup. Park reacted by asserting his independence from the United States, at least with regard to domestic policy. That was to prove characteristic of his regime.

Throughout his long rule, Park was an advocate of *chuch'e* (self-reliance), a concept which Kim Il Sung has elevated into an all-pervasive ideology in the north (*chuch'e sasang*). For Park the concept was more restricted and pragmatic, but still central to Korean national identity.[2] It lay at the core of his economic development program, by which he laid the foundation of South Korea's future international influence. It also lay behind his determination to normalize relations with Japan despite widespread popular opposition within South Korea. He recognized that Japanese foreign investment and technology were indispensable to his economic development program and that the establishment of bilateral relations would reduce South Korea's dependence on the United States. Of course, Park was careful to restore good relations with the United States as soon as possible after his coup and maintain them thereafter. Park's policies typically displayed a very pragmatic approach to self-reliance—guaranteeing South Korea's immediate security by relying on the United States, while laying the groundwork for its future independent role.

North and South Korea share a commitment to the idea of *chuch'e*. The enduring appeal of *chuch'e* in both nations stems from the fervid nationalism of the Korean people. As Byung Chul Koh has written, "The single most important ideological dimension for both Koreas is nationalism—the burning desire on the part of leaders and citizens alike to assert their national identity, to determine their own destiny, and to enhance their national prestige abroad in every conceivable way. The much-vaunted *chuch'e* idea is but a manifestation of this desire."[3]

Dr. Koh traces this fierce nationalism to the historical experiences of the Korean people—their long history of foreign invasion, domination, and Japanese colonial rule. Their experiences have also left the Korean people somewhat distrustful of foreigners and wary of excessive dependence on allied states. This latter characteristic is most evident in North Korea's relations with its communist allies, the U.S.S.R. and the PRC, neither of whom appears to be seen as truly reliable by the North Koreans. Indeed, Dr. Koh argues that Kim Il Sung's constant emphasis on *chuch'e* imparts the image of a "siege mentality" to the North Korean leadership.[4]

In the case of South Korea, this characteristic seems more restrained, although South Koreans clearly possess a deeply ingrained distrust of their old colonial subjugator, Japan. Until recently, the United States was an exception to this norm. The Korean War forged a unique bond between the two nations. As the war era fades into the past, South Koreans' growing doubts about the strength of the American commitment and suspicions regarding the motivations for American policy are now beginning to complicate the relationship. Even during the Park era, the President himself was very cautious in his dealings with the United States and the other great powers, however much he might have relied on their assistance. In the 1970s, for example, he wrote:

A multipolar world is certainly not a simple international environment. Unlike the Cold War days when dependence on the power of an ally was possible, we now carefully watch the moves of the United States, Japan, China, the Soviet Union and many other countries as well. This requires a high level of adaptability and creativeness.

Park went on to caution against the hazards of "the games that Big Powers play," in which "yesterday's friend can be abandoned without consideration, yesterday's adversary can be today's friend, and today's enemy can become tomorrow's negotiating partner." The principal lesson, according to Park, was that "we have only our own power to safeguard security and independence. Help is offered only when one helps oneself. . . . Our allies will begin to help us only after they are convinced that we, and not the North Korean communists, are overwhelmingly superior."[5]

Despite Park's strong anticommunism, his commitment to Korean nationalism and his foreign-policy pragmatism led him to establish the groundwork for President Roh's much-heralded "Northern policies." Throughout the 1960s, North Korea made considerable gains against the South in their mutual battle for international recognition, receiving the support of the Third World "Non-Aligned" bloc. As a fervid nationalist determined to expand South Korean international relations, Park could not accept any deterioration in South Korea's international position.[6] Accordingly, in January 1971, Park abandoned the nation's fervent anticommunist stance, scrapping the Hallstein Doctrine and announcing that his government would be willing to improve relations with "non-hostile" communist states.

Park then initiated a series of secret negotiations with Pyongyang, which resulted in the Joint Communiqué of July 4, 1972 urging the gradual reduction of tension between the two Koreas through a series of confidence-building measures. Park followed this success with his "Special Foreign Policy Statement Regarding Peace and Unification" on June 23, 1973. In this speech, Park stated that Seoul would no longer oppose Pyongyang's participation in international organizations, including the United Nations, and indeed proposed separate UN memberships for the ROK and the DPRK. He also extended his earlier opening to communist states by stating that the ROK would "open its door to all the nations of the world on the basis of the principles of reciprocity and equality."[7] Park's offer was immediately spurned by the North Koreans, but it set the future basis for South Korean policy toward its rival.

Park's domestic and foreign policies were interrelated, and were guided by his own fervent nationalistic ideals. His policies were directed at securing South Korean security, gaining international recognition and influence, and ultimately enabling South Korea to follow an independent path. The Chun Doo Hwan regime continued the basic trends of Park's foreign and domestic policies. Because the nonaligned movement had rejected the ROK's application for membership in 1973, the Chun government focused on strengthening South Korea's ties with Western Europe and attempting to develop economic and political relations with the Eastern bloc and, eventually, the Soviet Union and China. These policies built upon Park's initial efforts, and set the stage for President Roh's spectacularly successful efforts to improve South Korea's relations with the communist world. Indeed, it was Yi Pom-sok, Chun's foreign minister, who invented the term *pukbang chongch'aek* ("northern policy") in a speech at the National Defense Graduate School in June 1983.[8]

The Roh Era: Democracy and Foreign Policy Activism

Despite his foreign-policy innovations and his notable achievements in directing the South Korean economy, Chun suffered from weak legitimacy throughout his tenure. Almost from the moment he took office, Chun faced strong opposition which grew steadily. The era of military government was passing in South Korea. The collapse of Park's government had basically marked the end of the public's ready acceptance of military rule in the interests of economic development and national security.

By the end of Chun's term, massive public protests, American pressure, and the example of President Marcos' February 1986 overthrow in the Philippines convinced Roh Tae Woo, Chun's old KMA classmate and chosen successor, of the political necessity of compromise. Roh announced that he would recommend that Chun accept a direct presidential election and adopt a series of other "democratization" measures. Roh asserted that if Chun rejected these recommendations he would withdraw as a candidate and resign from public office. That action won Roh a public following, international stature, and a reputation for daring political initiative. It also led to the decision to implement direct Presidential elections in December 1987, which Roh won.[9]

Roh's successful election as the first President of a democratic South Korean government was followed rapidly by major advances in South Korea's relations with the communist nations. The catalyst for these gains was the 1988 Summer Olympics held in Seoul. The U.S.S.R., PRC, and Eastern European countries sent large contingents of athletes to the Games, along with trade and cultural delegations. Talks on trade, investment, and other forms of relations flowered. In the aftermath of the Games, Hungary became the first communist state to open diplomatic relations with the ROK, on February 1, 1989. Others quickly followed. In June 1990, Roh met with Gorbachev in San Francisco, which set the stage for Roh's ultimate achievement—the establishment of diplomatic relations between Moscow and Seoul on September 30, 1990. These stunning developments presaged Roh Tae Woo's historic three-day visit to Moscow for a meeting with Gorbachev and Gorbachev's own visit to the ROK on April 20, 1991, during which he offered a public endorsement of South Korea's recent decision to apply for UN membership.

Roh's successes can be traced to a combination of factors, including the new foreign-policy pragmatism initiated by Gorbachev, Roh's own status as the head of a new, democratic South Korea, the economic problems in the communist world and the ROK's economic power, problems in U.S.S.R.-Japan relations, and, of course, Roh's continued efforts to improve ROK-DPRK dialogue and Seoul's ties to the communist world. Before the opening of the Olympic Games, Roh made a special declaration (July 7, 1988) in which he pledged to abandon the traditional South Korean efforts to isolate the DPRK, announcing that Seoul would no longer oppose trade and other contacts between its allies and Pyongyang.

Roh's "Nordpolitik" policies[10] are based on the work of his predecessors but also reflect the impact of democratization on foreign policy. Improving relations with the communist world and reducing tensions with the North—while appearing to be forthcoming on the reunification question—strengthen Roh politically. Roh derives multiple benefits from these policies: he undercuts student radicals' attempts to appeal to the middle-class on the reunification issue; he might reduce the security threat faced by the ROK; he could gain expanded economic markets for South Korean products in a time of growing world protectionism; and he increases the ROK's world stature and legitimacy, undercuts the position of North Korea, demonstrates to the Korean people his commitment to national reunification, and increases his own international reputation and domestic popularity.

The impact of democratization on South Korean foreign policy has already created tensions with South Korea's old allies. As one analyst has written, "this is a heady period for South Korea. National pride and confidence are palpable. The country is feeling its oats."[11] These feelings are reflected in national policy. Roh's basic foreign-policy goals remain the promotion of the ROK's international legitimacy, preservation of the ROK's national security, and preservation and acceleration of the ROK's economic accomplishments. Roh, however, pursues these goals in a bolder, more independent fashion than his predecessors. His "Nordpolitik" policies have been undertaken at his own initiative, and, contrary to the expectation of many American policymakers, have led to impressive diplomatic coups for his government. Regionally, Roh's ROK has become one of the strongest proponents of the idea of Asia-Pacific economic cooperation embodied in the new Asia-Pacific Economic Council (APEC). South Korea's arrival on the world scene was truly heralded by the Roh government's bold decision to apply for UN membership this year.

Roh is actively attempting to carve out for his nation an independent international role commensurate with its rising economic and political prominence. While Roh attempts to improve ties with the ROK's old adversaries, he is also attempting to establish a more equal relationship with the United States and Japan. South Koreans believe that they have their own destiny to fulfill, and no longer wish to assume the compliant sidekick role traditionally accorded them by American and Japanese leaders. Many Americans and Japanese are uncertain as to how to respond to the ROK's transformation from a rabidly anticommunist "little buddy" into an independent-minded nation willing to open relations with every state. Inevitably, the growing assertiveness of the Koreans is leading to misunderstandings and generating tension with Korea's old friends. Managing these tensions is a major challenge for the Roh government. Roh wants an independent role for the ROK in world affairs, but he must preserve strong links to his old allies at the same time. The United States and Japan remain critical to South Korea's economic, political, and security interests. In particular, Roh needs to maintain secure and friendly relations between the ROK and the U.S.

Korea and the Great Powers
The United States

The ROK-U.S. relationship remains South Korea's most important external relationship. Despite the ROK's recent successes at expanding and diversifying its foreign export markets, the United States remains its most important market and also an important source of foreign investment and technology. Roh also requires American support for his international initiatives. The ROK application for UN membership is a good example. Reportedly, the ROK is depending heavily on American and Japanese support for its efforts to sway China and the Third World nations to support (or at least not oppose) its application. He also needs the United States to assist his initiatives toward North Korea by coordinating with the ROK its own policies toward Kim Il Sung's regime. Unilateral American policies toward the DPRK could have a deleterious effect on the Korean peoples' hopes for national reunification.

The United States remains the ultimate guarantor of South Korean security. Currently, the United States maintains about 40,000 troops in Korea (7,000 of which are scheduled to be removed over the next three years), including approximately 29,000 assigned to the Eighth U.S. Army (including the Second Infantry Division) and the 314th air division, which operates bases in Kunsan, Osan, Suwon, and Taegu. In conjunction with U.S. planes based in Japan and Okinawa, the 314th air division provides tactical support to both U.S. and ROK ground forces. The United States currently maintains no naval support facilities in South Korea because it has access to nearby Japanese facilities. South Korea has been mentioned, however, as an alternative to the U.S. naval and air bases in the Philippines.

Although the ROK military is becoming increasingly capable of defending the nation against its northern rival (see the section on the military balance later in this chapter), the U.S. security guarantee remains essential for three reasons. First, in the short to medium term, the threat of a DPRK attack remains high because of the DPRK's internal political dynamics and its declining military capabilities *vis-a-vis* the ROK.

Second, the U.S. security guarantee is a deterrent which the ROK military cannot match, ever. Although the ROK's military capabilities are rising, the balance between North and South will probably always remain tenuous. Accordingly, the DPRK leaders, given the political incentive or necessity, could always decide to risk an attack. Any attack, even if the ROK successfully blunted it, would devastate South Korea and destroy the economic and political achievements of the past three decades. The South Koreans believe that only the preservation of a strong U.S. security commitment to defend the ROK offers an adequate deterrence to potential North Korean adventurism.

Finally, in the long term, South Korean policymakers recognize that their nation remains surrounded by powerful, potentially hostile states: Japan, China, and the U.S.S.R. South Korea will never possess the economic, political, or military clout of these nations. A security link to a powerful, friendly, but distant state with vital interests in the region—such as the United States—enhances South Korea's strategic position significantly.

The preservation of close U.S.-ROK ties, however, will not be easy. Tensions clearly exist in U.S.-ROK relations today—the inevitable consequence of the need to restructure the relationship on a more equal basis. The U.S.-ROK economic relationship, for example, has become extremely conflictual—a source of tension which could sour general bilateral relations. Despite considerable Korean progress in opening up their economy in recent years, the United States continues to suffer large trade deficits in its bilateral trade account with Korea. American pressure on trade issues often creates deep resentment among the Korean populace, which perceives the United States as a rich bully in these matters. Such pressure fuels the rise of anti-Americanism. As a result, public American pressures are often counterproductive—making it more difficult for the ROK government to compromise on economic issues, while damaging overall bilateral relations. Trade issues will be on the front burner of U.S.-ROK relations for some time.

U.S. relations with North Korea are also likely to introduce considerable tension into the U.S.-ROK relationship. Although South Korea has eagerly sought to expand relations with its rival's communist allies, it has been wary of efforts by the United States and Japan to establish links with the North (despite Roh's recent policy statement indicating that he would no longer oppose such ties).

For these reasons, the South Koreans want the United States and Japan to consult fully with them on any changes in their policies toward the North. Ideally, the ROK would like to have the three allies pursue a coordinated policy toward the North, to avoid mutual misunderstandings and unforeseen complications for South Korean security and reunification goals.

To date, American policy has been supportive of South Korean concerns in its dealings with the North. The United States has taken four steps to initiate contact with the DPRK. First, the United States has increased diplomatic contact with North Korea, arranging eleven meetings between embassy political counselors in Beijing (from 1989 to July 1990). Second, the U.S. government has encouraged North Korean private citizens to visit the United States. Third, the U.S. allowed travel to the North by private Americans in January 1989. Fourth, the United States has allowed the limited export of American food and medical products to North Korea to "meet basic human needs." In 1989, these exports were valued at $8.4 million. At the same time, the Bush Administration has called upon North Korea to achieve "real progress" in North-South talks on confidence-building measures; to accept inspection of its nuclear plants and research facilities by international atomic energy agencies; officially to abandon its support of international terrorism; and to return the remains of Americans killed in the Korean War.[12]

The most troubling problem in ROK-U.S. relations is the visible increase in anti-Americanism in South Korea in recent years. Their recent emergence on the world scene has made the Koreans very proud. At the same time, their historical legacy of dependence on the United States and subjugation by foreign powers has created within many Koreans a feeling of insecurity. As one senior diplomat has stated: "The Koreans have come too far, too fast. They are still trying to catch up with themselves."[13] The combination of pride and insecurity can easily be mistaken for arrogance. It also accounts for the extreme importance attached to minor incidents. To the South Koreans, such incidents indicate a lack of respect for them and their nation by the United States and Americans. Fundamentally, South Koreans are now demanding that their old patron treat them with respect and as an equal. This attitude was exemplified by the comments of one young South Korean who was fulfilling his Korean military service as a *Katusas* (an acronym for Koreans serving in the U.S. army) on the U.S. army base in Seoul. He said, "Most of us Katusas are better educated than the GIs. It isn't the 1950s anymore. It's time for a change in our relations. It's time we had a Korean, not an American, in charge."[14]

Korean nationalism does not necessarily mean anti-Americanism. The assertion of Korean independence and national identity is not incompatible with Korea's friendship with the United States. Roh's initiatives demonstrate that an assertive South Korea is not necessarily harmful to U.S. interests.[15] There is no fundamental conflict between the two nations. Indeed, the United States and South Korea continue to share critical strategic, economic, and political interests. Assuming Korean and American leaders manage the evolution of the new relationship constructively, anti-Americanism will fade over time, as Koreans become more confident of their new role and assume greater responsibility for their own defense, and as the influence of the United States over internal Korean affairs declines and the presence and visibility of U.S. forces on the peninsula are reduced. On the other hand, if the relationship is allowed to deteriorate, it will be difficult to preserve close U.S.-ROK ties once the immediate threat from the DPRK declines.

Koreans see coordination in U.S.-ROK decision-making as vital. South Koreans will not respond well to American calls for increased burden-sharing, trade liberalization, or other reforms unless such proposals entail a willingness to practice increased "decision-sharing" as well.[16]

Japan

Japan has always regarded Korea as critical to its own security; it fought two wars, with China and Russia, to secure control over the peninsula in the early years of this century. The Koreans have not appreciated Japan's interest in their land. The era of Japanese colonial domination left deep-seated bitterness toward their colonial oppressor within the hearts of many Koreans. Today, South Korea and Japan are bound together by geography, economics, and mutual ties to the United States. Japanese trade, investment, and technology are vital to the South Korean economy. In turn, U.S. forces based in Japan are critical to South Korean security. But Japan and Korea remain uneasy associates rather than true allies.

Public opinion polls in both nations consistently indicate their peoples' mutual dislike. As noted in Chapter Four, Koreans rank Japan as one of the countries they like least, second only to North Korea; while Japanese rank South Korea third on their list of most-disliked nations, behind only the Soviet Union and North Korea. Koreans believe that the Japanese look down upon the Korean people and their culture, citing Japanese treatment of their own ethnic Korean population. Many Koreans are uncomfortable with their close economic links to Japan—fearing Japanese exploitation and manipulation.

They are also ambivalent about U.S. demands that Japan assume a larger security role in Northeast Asia. Although many Koreans have echoed American complaints regarding Japan's "free ride," they fear that any Japanese defense buildup will acquire its own momentum, transforming "pacifist" Japan and leading it once again to begin throwing its weight around the neighborhood.[17] For example, Japanese Prime Minister Kaifu's recent decision to placate the United States by sending minesweepers to the Persian Gulf prompted a firestorm of alarmism in the South Korean press, although the government adopted a measured, uncritical response.[18]

On the other hand, many Japanese perceive South Korea as more nationalistic and militaristic than Japan.[19] It would appear logical for some Japanese to be concerned that an increasingly powerful Korea could become something of a neighborhood bully itself. Such concerns are echoed by the views of one rising school of opinion in Japan, which sees Korea as an emergent economic competitor.

The depth of the two nations' mutual suspicions is easy for Americans to underestimate. Many Americans have argued for increased Korean and Japanese security cooperation. Because there is a clear interdependence between the U.S.-Japan security relationship and U.S.-ROK security ties, it would appear, on the surface, that increased bilateral defense cooperation between Japan and Korea—or even a trilateral defense arrangement involving Korea, Japan, and the United States—would offer an effective means of securing all three nations' interests.[20] In reality, however, such an arrangement is politically impractical.

The security interests of Korea and Japan are not identical. South Korea is primarily concerned with the threat posed by the North. South Koreans do not see the U.S.S.R. as a direct threat, but only as a secondary adversary (and now perhaps not even that)—an ally of their enemy. Indeed, in the absence of a threat from the north, it is more likely that Korean security concerns would focus on Japan rather than the Soviet Union, or now Russia. Japan, on the other hand, perceives the U.S.S.R., and probably its successor, Russia, as its primary direct threat. North Korea is not seen as a realistic independent threat to Japan.

South Korean strategy toward Japan is simple. The ROK government would like to continue to develop economic and political ties with Japan but avoid any security link. The ROK and Japan share many economic interests. Indeed, the two countries have cooperated in their efforts to promote enhanced Asia-Pacific economic cooperation. On the other hand, the ROK supports American efforts to pressure Japan to open its market to foreign goods. After all, it is likely that Korea would seize a larger share of the Japanese market than the United States would. At the same time, however, Koreans are disturbed by growing Japanese military power.

Japanese overtures to North Korea are an especially sensitive issue for South Koreans. They fear that Japan wishes to keep the peninsula divided. Indeed, South Koreans felt considerable consternation over the September 28, 1990 joint declaration signed by the representatives of Japan's leading political parties—the Liberal Democratic Party (LDP) and the Japan Socialist Party (JSP)—and the Korean Workers' Party (KWP) in Pyongyang, which urged the Japanese government to commence official negotiations to normalize Japan-DPRK relations.

South Korean concern focused on five issues. First, many South Koreans were disturbed by Japan's willingness to normalize relations with the DPRK without any preconditions, as well as by the "excessive speed" involved in the Japan-DPRK *rapprochement*. Second, South Koreans doubt the wisdom of Japan's efforts to normalize relations with the North at such a critical stage in North-South relations. Japanese normalization and economic assistance to the North could undermine the Roh government's efforts to pressure the DPRK to compromise in its negotiations with the South. Third, many Korean officials were also concerned by a provision in the joint declaration which begins with the phrase "Korea is one...." Since this is the basic premise of the North's reunification policies, that statement could be interpreted as indicating Japan's acquiescence to Pyongyang's unification policies. It also fails to recognize the existence of South Korea, which is North Korea's official position but certainly not Japan's. And it appears to contradict the 1965 ROK-Japan Basic Treaty, which clearly indicated that the ROK was "the only lawful" government of Korea according to the UN General Assembly resolution 195 (III) of 1948.

Fourth, the question of Japanese compensation to North Korea touched a sore nerve. When Park normalized relations with Japan in 1965, Tokyo agreed to pay compensation only for the period of Japanese colonial rule in Korea, not for the twenty years of abnormal relations between the two nations from 1945-65. In contrast, the joint Japan-DPRK declaration indicated that Japanese compensation would also cover the "losses inflicted upon the Korean people in the ensuing 45 years after the war." Japanese compensation money could provide Kim Il Sung with the ability to postpone reforms. Finally, South Koreans were also disturbed by Prime Minister Kaifu's apology to Kim Il Sung for Japan's colonial rule in Korea.

Originally, Japan had promised the Roh government that Kaifu would apologize to Kim simply as the LDP president, not in his official capacity as Prime Minister, since Japan still did not recognize the DPRK. As it happened, however, Kaifu used the phrase "he, as Prime Minister, . . ." in his remarks.[21]

Roh firmly expressed the ROK's position to Kanemaru Shin, the LDP representative at the talks with Kim Il Sung, in a meeting on October 8, 1990. While he reiterated the official ROK position that it does not oppose the establishment of Japan-DPRK relations, Roh stressed that such changes should not threaten "meaningful progress" in North-South relations, and requested that Japan consider the following five principles in negotiating with North Korea:
1. Japan should consult with Seoul before starting government-to-government talks with Pyongyang on normalizing bilateral ties.
2. Japan should urge North Korea to sign the nuclear safety agreement with the International Atomic Energy Agency (IAEA).
3. Japan should pay adequate attention to the state of North-South Korean dialogue.
4. Japan should withhold compensation or economic assistance to North Korea until formal diplomatic ties are established between the two countries, and it should ensure that any funds provided by Japan would not be used for upgrading North Korea's military capability.
5. Japan should take steps to prompt Pyongyang to move toward openness and reforms.[22]

These South Korean concerns were reportedly supported by the United States, which made similar requests to Japan in early October 1990.[23]

In Japan, by contrast, there appears to be emerging an attitude which favors "rescuing" Kim economically in the interests of preserving stability on the peninsula. The argument rests on the assumption that continued economic decline, coupled with international isolation, will lead Kim Il Sung to lash out at his old enemies while he still can. The common analogy is to a cornered rat. Wataru Kubo, a JSP MP involved in preparing the Kanemaru visit, argues, "Unless Japan normalizes relations, North Korea will feel threatened by a strong chain linking South Korea with Japan and the U.S." Not surprisingly, South Koreans see this Japanese argument as self-serving. The popular view in the south is that Japan wants to keep the peninsula divided to retard Korea's emergence as an economic rival, and for that reason is attempting to prop up Kim's "doomed" regime.[24]

The South Koreans were reported to be concerned that Japan, in deference to North Korea, would not support its current effort to enter the United Nations. The Japanese, however, have indicated publicly that they will support the ROK bid, and are reported to be working with the United States and South Korea to increase support among the nonaligned countries and convince China to abstain on the question. Japan's diplomatic efforts in this area should improve the atmosphere of ROK-Japan relations, but the future outlook for ROK-Japan relations suggests that continued bouts of tension are more likely than closer cooperation.

South Korea's ability to pursue successfully its strategy toward Japan depends heavily on the United States. Only U.S. cooperation can ensure that Japan does not shore up the DPRK and block eventual Korean unification on Seoul's terms.

The Soviet Union

Gorbachev's new policies toward the Asia-Pacific Region permitted South Korea to reverse its longstanding strategy of opposing Soviet influence in any form whatsoever. Although the Soviet Union had always been a secondary strategic concern for the ROK—behind North Korea— Moscow has suddenly become a primary means for weakening North Korea.

The Russians, like the Japanese and Chinese, have long sought to exert their influence over the Korean peninsula. In the postwar era, Soviet-Korean relations have until very recently meant Soviet-North Korean relations. The U.S.S.R. and the ROK had no diplomatic relations before last year. U.S.S.R.-DPRK relations have tended to fluctuate, because Kim Il Sung has attempted to maximize his bargaining position by shifting between the Soviets and the Chinese.

Generally, Kim has been closer to the Chinese politically, but always turned to the Soviets when he needed economic or technological infusions or military equipment which the Chinese could not supply. Soviet-North Korean relations, like Soviet-Vietnamese relations, have never been a love match. Mutual distrust has always colored the relationship. The Soviets resented what they saw as Korean ingratitude, and worried over Kim Il Sung's adventurist tendencies. The North Koreans were always convinced of the Soviets' desire to dominate and exploit them, and never truly believed that Moscow was a reliable ally.

From 1984 to 1989, Soviet-North Korean relations were on the upswing. Kim Il Sung visited Moscow in 1984, his first visit in 17 years, which was followed by yet another visit in 1986. During these years, Soviet-North Korean security ties grew much closer. Moscow helped Kim modernize his air force, providing him with Mig-23 and Su25 Frogfoot aircraft, as well as Mig-25s and SA-3 and SA-5 SAMs later. In October 1986, the two nations conducted their first joint military exercise, which has since become an annual event.[25] During the same period, U.S.S.R.-DPRK economic ties grew significantly. In 1988, for example, the Soviet Union accounted for over 50%

of North Korea's foreign trade (although trade with the DPRK accounts for only about 1% of Soviet trade). The Soviets also provided North Korea with large amounts of technological assistance during this period, building 70 industrial projects producing approximately one-quarter of the DPRK's gross output. The growing military-economic relationship between the DPRK and the U.S.S.R. greatly increased North Korean dependence on the Soviet Union during these years.[26]

Kim's increasing dependence on the Soviet Union was probably caused by his inability to obtain the economic aid and civilian and military technology he required from the Chinese. In addition, Deng's reform efforts would also have served to complicate PRC-DPRK relations during this period. In any case, it was a brief honeymoon. Soviet-North Korean relations began to suffer immediately after the Soviets began to develop ties with South Korea.

Gorbachev appears to have desired initially to limit Soviet-South Korean links to the economic sphere, while preserving Soviet-North Korean political and military links and using Soviet influence to pressure the North to undertake its own *perestroika*. Nevertheless, to gain South Korean economic support, Gorbachev was ultimately forced to cast aside his concern for North Korean opinion. In June 1990, President Roh met Gorbachev in San Francisco. Although Gorbachev implied at that time that full diplomatic relations were still very distant;[27] in fact, Moscow established relations with Seoul on September 30, 1990—only three months later. Not surprisingly, the decision did not please the North Koreans.

When Soviet Foreign Minister Shevardnadze visited Pyongyang to inform Kim that the U.S.S.R. would normalize relations with South Korea, Kim reportedly refused to meet with him. Following normalization, North Korea published an editorial entitled "Diplomatic Relations Bargained for Dollars," in which it characterized the Soviet decision as an act of betrayal, accusing the Soviets of having sold the dignity and honor of a Socialist state and the interests and faith of its loyal ally for South Korean economic aid. The North Koreans also stated that they had come to believe that the U.S.S.R. had joined with the United States to isolate North Korea and perpetuate the division of the peninsula.[28] Gorbachev's recent decision to support publicly the ROK's bid for UN membership was the ultimate insult to Kim Il Sung, and undoubtedly confirmed Kim's belief that Gorbachev had committed his government to supporting the continued division of the peninsula.

Gorbachev's decision to accelerate the development of U.S.S.R.-ROK ties can be traced to South Korea's refusal to provide significant economic aid and investment to the Soviet Union until Moscow normalized diplomatic relations, the Soviet Union's inability to gain significant Japanese aid, and the U.S.S.R.'s increasingly dire economic situation. Four months after normalization, on January 22, 1991, South Korea agreed to provide the

Soviet Union with a financial cooperation package valued at U.S. $3 billion over the next three years (including $1.5 billion in loans for purchasing Korean consumer products, $0.5 billion in trade credits for Korean capital goods, and $1 billion in commercial syndicate loans by Korean banks).[29]

South Korean interest in the Soviet Union--now Russia--has been primarily political, not economic. The ROK government wants to establish relations with Moscow for several reasons: to enhance its international legitimacy, to reduce the security threat posed by the DPRK by alienating it from its most important source of military support, and ultimately to promote Korean national reunification by weakening the DPRK and forcing it to negotiate on the ROK's terms. The Soviet Union's successor states also offer a new, potentially significant market for Korean exports and investment, but such benefits are less certain and of less importance.

The South Koreans surprised many Americans by their apparently warm feelings toward the Soviet Union. In part, Soviet-ROK normalization reflected the fact that South Korea did not perceive the U.S.S.R. to be a direct threat. In part, it reflected pride in being courted by a superpower. It also reflected a belief that the Soviet Union's new policies were helping the cause of Korean national reunification.

As long as the Soviet Union existed, it was unrealistic to expect South Korean-Soviet relations to blossom into a close relationship, at least in the near future. As Roh made clear to Gorbachev at their April 1991 meeting, South Korea remains wary of Moscow's collective-security schemes for Asia.[30] Furthermore, many outstanding tensions remain between the two countries. The shooting down of KAL 007 is one example. The March 1991 publication of the first photos of the undersea wreckage of the airplane (one of which showed a severed arm on the seabed) sent shock waves through Korea. Likewise, earlier reports from the U.S.S.R. that the pilot responsible for shooting down the plane was aware that he had fired on a civilian aircraft did not do much for the Soviet image. The families of the deceased have renewed pressure on the ROK Foreign Ministry to provide information on the incident and obtain the remains of those slain.[31]

Improvement in Russian-ROK relations seems likely to continue but remain relatively modest. South Korea's main benefit is in its competition with the DPRK. Aside from enhancing its leverage on the DPRK, Russia has little to offer the ROK, compared to the United States. Both countries could offer potential counters to Japan and China, but the U.S. is economically and militarily stronger, with closer historical and personal ties with the Korean leadership and people, and is much more distant geographically and therefore less threatening. Furthermore, close Russian-ROK ties would aggravate ROK-Japan relations and might encourage Japanese rearmament, while preservation of U.S.-ROK security bonds would not.

Russian-DPRK ties seem likely to continue to decline. Moscow's decision to put the two nations' bilateral trade on a hard-currency basis effective January 1991 has inevitably led to a decline in economic exchanges between them. For their part, the DPRK leadership will probably loathe Boris Yeltsin's Russian political and diplomatic policies more than it did Gorbachev's. Still, Kim Il Sung's distaste for the Russian leadership will probably be checked by his real economic dependence on Russia for oil and military supplies. The Chinese can offer only political aid and limited economic support. Unless Kim can open economic relations with Japan or other Western nations, he will have to suffer Russia's humiliations in order to gain whatever economic benefits he still can from the Moscow relationship. While Yeltsin's policies are not yet clear, they are likely, even in the best case for the DPRK, to be far less accommodating than the changed Soviet policies.

China

South Korea's strategy toward China has also changed considerably, and for the same reason as the change toward the U.S.S.R. and Russia—opportunities to isolate the DPRK. Seoul has had much less success, however, with Beijing. The ROK has offered economic ties in exchange for political help against North Korea, but has failed to get China to deal openly and normalize relations. The reasons are to be found in China's very different view of the Korean peninsula, and also in China's better access to the market economies on the Asian rimland.

Korea possesses greater strategic significance for the Chinese than for the Russians. The peninsula is adjacent to Manchuria—China's industrial heartland—which makes it a vital buffer between China and any outside power. For centuries, Chinese policy has been to prevent Korea from being dominated by any outside power. Since the end of the Korean War, the Chinese have carefully cultivated their relationship with North Korea, and have generally enjoyed better overall relations with the Kim Il Sung regime than have the Russians. Kim Il Sung appears to value his ties with China, as a source of both international political support and leverage on Moscow. Although the Chinese cannot match Moscow's military, economic, or technological gifts, Kim appears to trust the Chinese more than the Soviets, certainly more than the Russians. The Chinese, of course, have possessed cultural, historical, and personal advantages over the Soviets in their competition for influence in Pyongyang. The assistance of Chinese troops during the Korean War created a bond between the Chinese and North Korean leadership comparable to that between South Koreans and the United States and quite unlike the Soviet-North Korean relationship, which has always been based purely upon economic and military aid. In addition, the long historical and cultural ties between Korea and China make Koreans more comfortable with the Chinese than with the Russians. Finally, both leaderships share important experiences and perspectives: both have experienced the often-crushing embrace of the Soviet Union, both are divided nations, and both country's leaders still come from the revolutionary generation—unlike their Soviet counterparts.

Nonetheless, Chinese-North Korean relations have still suffered from considerable tension from time to time. Difficulties have stemmed from a variety of factors, including the DPRK's tendency to turn to Moscow for economic and military aid which China could not provide; Kim's refusal to spurn the U.S.S.R. and side entirely with China during the Sino-Soviet split; Chinese *rapprochement* with the United States and Japan, North Korea's chief enemies; and, of course, China's growing ties to South Korea.

Despite Chinese intervention during the Korean War, South Korea does not appear to have significant security concerns regarding China at this time. The South Korean perception of China contrasts sharply with popular views of Japan, and may be partially due to cultural links between the two nations and China's relative backwardness. Since the mid-1980s, China has maintained a nonpolitical trade relationship with South Korea; it has grown significantly over the years. In 1990, the two nations agreed to establish trade liaison offices in Seoul and Beijing. Nevertheless, official political contact between Seoul and Beijing has remained strictly limited.

South Korea would like to develop ties with China, like the links it established with the Soviet Union, to increase the pressure on the DPRK. Unlike Moscow, however, Beijing apparently remains solicitous of Pyongyang's concerns. In its contacts with the South, the PRC continues to exercise considerable circumspection. China continues to endorse Kim's demand for tripartite talks and the withdrawal of U.S. troops from the peninsula. China also continues to reject calls for cross-recognition and simultaneous UN membership for the two Koreas, a stance being overtaken by events.

Chinese-North Korean relations have grown closer since 1989 because of both nations' defensive reactions to the collapse of communist power in Eastern Europe and the Soviet *rapprochement* with South Korea. Given Chinese strategic concerns, it seems unlikely that China will willingly risk reducing its ties to Kim's regime. On the other hand, China has little to offer Kim in economic and military assistance with which to prop up his regime. Personal contacts and shared political perspectives appear to constitute the main basis for the relationship. Overall, DPRK-PRC relations will probably remain fairly static while the two nations' conservative, geriatric leaders still live. Meanwhile, ROK-PRC relations improved, despite DPRK objections, during the fall of 1991.

In the long term, Chinese-Korean relations could become tense. Korean unification would insure it. China has traditionally preferred to have weak, divided states on its borders—states over which it could expect to exercise considerable influence and from which it could expect to exclude undesirable foreign influences. Chinese policy in Indochina is a classic example of this strategy. Ideally, the Chinese would prefer to perpetuate the present arrangement, in which Korea is kept divided and weak and China exercises considerable influence over Korean affairs through its ties to Pyongyang (and its more-modest links to Seoul). Although an independent, unified Korea is better than a unified Korea under foreign influence (e.g., that of the U.S., Japan, or Russia), it is decidedly a second-best outcome for the Chinese.

At the same time, a unified Korean state is likely to feel more threatened by China than South Korea does today. A unified Korea could expect to face a significant Chinese military deployment on its borders. The recent rapid development of the Chinese Navy would also pose a challenge to Korean security planners who sit across the Yellow Sea from the Chinese North Sea Fleet.

North-South Relations in the 1990s
Overview

Since the 1970s, the two Koreas have engaged in an intermittent dialogue concerning confidence-building measures and unification. The principal motivations for South Korea to engage in this dialogue are to reduce the level of tension on the peninsula and the risk of war, to satisfy its American ally, to prevent the DPRK from gaining the diplomatic advantage it would if Seoul were to appear to be intransigent in the face of DPRK reasonableness, and, more recently, to take advantage of the favorable international environment to press for national unification on its own terms and increase domestic popular support for the government. The Roh government has pressed hard recently on inter-Korean relations, not only because of domestic political reasons and the new developments in the international environment but also because of a perception that compromise arrangements may be more feasible while Kim Il Sung is alive. There is concern that a Kim Jong Il regime (Kim's son and chosen successor) would be less able to compromise, because the younger Kim would be in a weaker political position.

Kim Il Sung's reasons for talking with his southern rivals are subject only to speculation. But they appear to include efforts to gain international advantage from the talks; use the talks to undermine domestic popular support for the ROK government; split the ROK-U.S. alliance and instigate the withdrawal of U.S. troops; and, of course, ultimately to promote reunification on North Korean terms.

Distrust has been the major characteristic of the talks, with the two sides typically talking past each other to a wider Korean and international audience. South Korea's basic position has been to recognize the reality of two existing regimes on the Korean peninsula and then work toward developing relations between the two regimes, leading ultimately to peaceful reunification. Since the 1970s, South Korea has maintained that cross-recognition of the two Koreas and simultaneous admission to the United Nations (similar to the German approach) should form the basis for peace on the peninsula. The North, however, has vigorously rejected this approach.

The North Koreans argue that simultaneous establishment of diplomatic relations and simultaneous admission to the UN would merely perpetuate the division between the two Koreas. They claim that the main obstacle to peace and reunification is the U.S. military presence on the peninsula. They maintain that if the U.S. military left the peninsula, a political federation between North and South Korea could be established and guarantee peace and eventual reunification. Despite much rhetoric, these two divergent positions have not changed significantly.

In reality, North-South relations are a diplomatic game in which each side attempts to gain the advantage of the other. Both sides are trying to use the negotiations to gain reunification on their own terms. Their respective approaches to the negotiations reflect their assessment of their relative strengths and weaknesses.[32]

South Korea, an open society with a strong economy and considerable international sophistication, believes that if it forces North Korea to open its closed, monolithic society, the North Korean people will learn the truth about their society and switch their allegiance to the ROK government, as the best hope for all Koreans. For this reason the South Korean strategy emphasizes societal integration prior to political unification. Most important, the South wants to avoid any action that could weaken the U.S.-ROK security alliance, which it believes deters North Korea from attacking. The South believes it has the advantage in the long-term political competition between the two Koreas, but remains at risk in the short term.

North Korea's strengths, by contrast, are its highly regimented party organization, its military power, and its propaganda apparatus. Kim's starting assumption appears to be that the ROK government is unpopular, and that, if he forces the United States to withdraw its troops, the weakened ROK government will be unable to suppress the activities of dissidents in the south. With his federation already in place, Kim can use a "United Front" strategy to disarm the ROK government, gain control of the federal government, and use its authority to order local authorities in the south to ease control over pro-DPRK forces there. These will then agitate for complete national reunification under Pyongyang's central authority. Above all, Kim wants to avoid opening North Korean society to outside influences as Seoul desires, because this threatens his personal political rule of the North itself. Recent events in East Germany have probably strengthened his determination in this regard.

North Korea: Domestic Decline and the Risk of International Isolation

North Korea is trapped in an economic vise which threatens the long-term survival of its political order. In 1989, North Korean GNP was estimated at $21.1 billion, and per capita GNP was $987. From 1987 to 1989, the country's economic growth averaged less than 3% per year.[33] Future growth is currently predicted at around 2% annually. Poor agricultural harvests have forced the government to reduce the already meager food rations. Nevertheless, military spending continues to absorb an estimated 24% of national GNP.[34]

South Korea, by contrast, continues to grow rapidly. In 1990, South Korean GNP grew by 9%, while current projections suggest 7% growth for 1991.[35] According to projections made by South Korean and Japanese analysts, the South Korean economy is currently about four-and-a-half times the size that of North Korea. Their projections indicate that this ratio will probably increase to at least 7:1 in favor of South Korea by the mid-1990s.[36] North Korean economic decline *vis-a-vis* the South not only poses serious problems for North Korea's military capabilities (to be discussed later), but also threatens the fundamental legitimacy of Kim Il Sung's government. The declining living standard undercuts Kim's claims that his *chuch'e* socialist system is superior to other systems, especially the South Korean capitalist system.

Evidence suggests that the economic decline has stimulated popular discontent. There have been reports of wall posters critical of the government's economic policies, of opposition slogans being painted on a Pyongyang railway station, of scattered industrial strikes, and even of some incidents of sabotage. Frequent visitors indicate that they now hear open criticisms of communist party cadres.[37] It would be a mistake to believe that these isolated incidents indicate that Kim Il Sung's rule is becoming tenuous, but they do indicate a radical change from the complete control his regime previously enjoyed.

To offset the economic decline, Kim launched a frantic "work-harder campaign" in 1990. No amount of hard work, however, can compensate for outmoded technology, inefficient plants, declining capital investment, and the limitations imposed by a small, overprotected, and uncompetitive domestic economy. North Korea needs to undertake radical economic reforms and open its economy to the outside world. Limited efforts in this direction have been made, but these changes amount to half-hearted gestures. Serious economic reform would fundamentally threaten the basis of the Kim regime, and significant reforms are extremely unlikely while he remains in power.

Still, the increasing impatience of Pyongyang's communist allies with North Korea's inefficiencies and boondoggles may ultimately leave the leadership with no choice. Despite his incessant harping upon *chuch'e*, or self-reliance, economic and military support from Moscow and Beijing have been indispensable to Kim's government. Without Russian and Chinese support Kim will be unable to sustain his economy and his high levels of military expenditure. Such assistance is costly for Kim's allies, however, and they no longer appear willing or able to sustain it. As indicated earlier, the Soviet Union placed its trade with North Korea on a hard-currency basis in January 1991. Trade between Pyongyang and its communist allies dropped by approximately 10% in 1989. The bottom line is that North Korea has little to sell and little with which to buy other nations' goods.[38]

Its deteriorating economic situation and declining support from its traditional allies account for the DPRK's decision to seek normalized relations with its old arch-enemy, Japan. "Anti-Japanism" has been one of the major themes of North Korean propaganda for more than 45 years. Park's move to normalize ROK-Japan relations was a target of venomous DPRK propaganda at the time. Kim's sudden decision to respond to Japanese overtures is a blatant effort to gain Japanese economic assistance for his dying economy. Japanese economic aid could allow him to put off significant economic and political reforms and preserve, at least temporarily, his political system. Successfully opening relations with Japan is essential to Kim's efforts to revive his economy. It is also an essential first step toward breaking out of North Korea's growing international isolation.

If North Korea fails to normalize relations with Japan and the United States, it will be increasingly isolated in the international arena. On the other hand, for North Korea to establish relations with South Korea's allies it will probably have to accept the South Korean unification formula of cross-recognition and confidence-building measures. Such an acceptance would also, however, constitute a long-term threat to the stability of the Kim Il Sung government. It would be starting down the road taken by East Germany. Ultimately, there may be no way for the DPRK to avoid this path, however. Unless the Japanese are willing to antagonize the United States and South Korea by following an independent path (which their support for the ROK's UN membership indicates is highly unlikely), North Korea will probably have to come to terms with the south to obtain significant economic support.

Therefore, the position of Kim Il Sung's regime is precarious. While it faces no immediate threat of revolt or collapse, its future looks increasingly bleak. The growing pressures on North Korea to undertake radical internal reforms and new foreign-policy initiatives have important implications for the succession to Kim Il Sung and the future security environment on the Korean peninsula.

North Korean Political Dynamics and the Prospects for Korean National Reunification

It would be wrong to draw a strong analogy between the political fragility that helped engender a rapid collapse of the regimes in East Europe, especially East Germany, and that of North Korea. The DPRK enjoys more legitimacy among the population, and it has no foreign troops on its soil to symbolize dependence. Although North Koreans may be unhappy with current economic conditions, they recognize Kim's success in raising the standard of living over that of the old days, and they appear to accept his nationalist credentials and the "myth" of his liberation of Korea.

They also have no reliable means of judging the regime's assertions. Unlike the Eastern European regimes, through its monopoly of the media the DPRK has been able to control virtually all access to information. North Koreans don't have shortwave radio receivers with which to listen to the BBC, the Voice of America, *et al.* Moreover, unlike the citizenries of most of the Eastern European nations, North Koreans have no close links to neighboring countries undergoing radical reforms.

Soviet political pressure could have stimulated North Korean reform as it did in Eastern Europe, but, unlike the Europeans, the DPRK could turn to the conservative Chinese to offset Soviet political pressure. Since Pyongyang believes that its *chuch'e* philosophy has transcended Marxism-Leninism at least as far back as the Sino-Soviet split in 1960, neither Eastern European nor Soviet ideological debates have had much impact on the North Koreans. The collapse of the Soviet Union, of course, merely vindicates Pyongyang's judgment that reform is a deadly path to be avoided.

The German model of unification is also unlikely to have any *immediate* relevance to North-South relations. Although North and South Korea began to negotiate in the early 1970s (the two German states signed their accord in 1972), their relations have not followed the German model. There are no communications, mail, media, personnel, or economic exchanges between the two states. North Koreans know very little about their neighbors to the south. The DPRK has deliberately rejected the East German approach, in the belief that it would undermine the communist political order. Indeed, it appears that they were right. The German example, as indicated earlier, will reinforce their determination to prevent significant social and economic interaction between the two nations prior to political unification.

The recent changes in Eastern Europe, therefore, have only indirect relevance to future events in North Korea. Change in North Korea will probably follow the post-Mao Chinese model, rather than the Eastern

European model. As in China, the main stimulants for change will probably be deteriorating economic conditions, a relative decline in the nation's international power position (in this case declining military capability vis-a-vis the South), factionalism within the leadership, rising popular political discontent amenable to manipulation by the competing leadership elites, and the nation's first leadership succession.

Significant change will have to wait until after Kim Il Sung leaves the scene. Kim will not undertake major reforms himself. Under Kim, reform efforts will be limited to tactical steps intended to offset the DPRK's decline, rather than initiatives that introduce fundamental changes to correct the inefficiencies in the North Korean economy and political system. Any such changes would undermine the basis for Kim's rule, so closely tied as it is to his *chuch'e* ideology and the current structure of North Korean society. Change is Kim's greatest enemy. Moreover, if Kim does not support reform, no other figure will be able to force through significant changes while he remains alive. He still dominates the system.

The most likely moment for change, therefore, is when Kim steps down and hands power to his chosen successor, his son, Kim Jong Il.[39] (Rumors indicate that Kim may step down next year in favor of his son; but, if he did, he would continue to wield real power behind the scenes. Real change will come only when he can no longer exercise power—that is, when he is dead or incapacitated.) Kim Jong Il (49 years old) is widely believed to lack his father's popular charisma, political skills, and carefully cultivated personal connections within the military, government, and party bureaucracies.

Kim Jong Il's only significant political asset is his legacy as the son and heir of the great leader, Kim Il Sung. The mantles of previous great communist leaders, however, have not proven particularly advantageous to their inheritors in other communist systems. Furthermore, Kim Jong Il's status as Kim Il Sung's son and successor generates potential opposition not only among opponents of his father's policies, but also among supporters of his father who do not want to establish an hereditary, dynastic mode of succession. This assumption is supported by the fact that although Kim Il Sung announced his succession plans at the fifth Central Committee meeting in 1974, he did not manage to obtain Kim Jong Il's formal appointment to senior Party status until 1980—six years which he apparently spent overcoming opposition to his son's succession.

There is strong evidence that various factions continue to contend for influence in North Korean politics and that not everyone supports Kim Jong Il's succession. Consistent reports indicate that there is opposition to the younger Kim within the military, the technocrats (educated in the U.S.S.R. and Eastern Europe), alienated leaders within the Party establishment, and even within Kim Il Sung's own family.[40] The DPRK government announced recently (February 7, 1991) that it had crushed a plot by "anti-revolutionary elements" opposed to Kim Jong Il's succession; this suggests that the opposition has not dissipated. Although it is unlikely that such a plot actually existed, the government clearly intended the announcement as a warning to any who harbored such ideas—a clear indication that the government believes that such opposition exists and is concerned about it as a threat to the stability of the succession.[41] Also, recent statements by South Korean officials have indicated their belief that there is within the North Korean leadership a moderate faction urging the government to undertake reform and openness in economics and technology.[42] Although these moderate factions are not necessarily identical with any groups opposed to Kim Jong Il, one can certainly assume (given the younger Kim's power base) that they do not support him.

As noted earlier, Kim Jong Il has not been associated with the tentative economic reforms of the last few years. A Kim Jong Il regime would not be in a position to implement wholesale changes in the DPRK's political-economic system. As his father's heir, Kim would have to preserve his legacy or undercut his own greatest source of legitimacy. Consequently, Kim Jong Il is not likely to instigate the much-needed reform of North Korean society.

Indeed, it is unlikely that a Kim Jong Il regime would be stable. He would probably face intensified economic problems with a weaker political base than his father. Assuming that he was able to consolidate his position immediately after his father's death (a very big assumption), it is highly likely that he would fall from power or become the powerless (and temporary) figurehead of a collective leadership shortly thereafter. In other words, he would probably face immediate arrest (the "Gang of Four" model) or medium-term political humiliation (like Hua Guo Feng).

The danger is that the younger Kim's technique for retaining his hold on power, and strengthening his weak base of support within the military, might be by following a path of military adventurism. He could use the DPRK's still-potent military power to attack the South and attempt to reverse the decline of North Korean fortunes on the battlefield.[43] The Japanese fear this possibility.

South Koreans are quite aware of the risks of continued North Korean isolation and decline. There is currently a debate within South Korean academic and political circles on this very question. Many Koreans worry that Roh's Nordpolitik, by isolating and destabilizing the DPRK regime, may actually undermine the goal of national reunification and risk a military attack.[44] Yang Sung Chol, a Kyunghee University professor, has made the point very simply: "A lean tiger is a mean tiger."[45] Therefore, some South Koreans—including opposition leader Kim Dae Jung—argue that the government should not try to pressure the DPRK but rather adopt a patient waiting game and allow the situation in the north to work itself out.[46]

The Roh government, however, clearly believes that progress on national reunification will be impossible without further pressure on the

DPRK government. It is a delicate path. The key is to preserve the U.S. security deterrent, which will make it absolutely clear to the North Korean military that an attack could not possibly succeed. For this reason, the Roh government places the highest premium on maintaining the U.S.-ROK security relationship.

Assuming, then, that the United States does not withdraw from the peninsula, the more likely outcome is the overthrow or eclipse of the Kim Jong Il regime by a coalition North Korean government consisting of a mixture of military officers, Soviet-trained technocrats, and disaffected leaders of the Party apparatus. The resulting regime would resemble the initial post-Maoist coalition of military officers and technocrats which coalesced around Deng Xiaoping and began the process of reform in China in the late 1970s and early 1980s. Like the early Dengist coalition, this new DPRK government would be a mixture of conservatives, concerned over the decay of internal political order and national power, and moderates dedicated to economic development. (Contrary to popular perception, so-called "liberal" forces did not become a significant factor in the Dengist government until the mid-1980s.)

This regime would begin the difficult process of economic reform and international initiatives. It would have to accept the ROK formula on unification. It would also have to develop economic and political relations not just with the United States and Japan but also South Korea. As reform proceeded, the new regime would be trapped in a time-compressed version of the East German experience. The East German regime remained stable for two decades after beginning to develop its relations with the West German government. A post-Kim Il Sung DPRK government would not enjoy such a long life. Expanding relations with the south would rapidly destabilize the government. The regime's claim to an independent identity would be undermined by the inevitable abandonment of Kim Il Sungism and *chuch'e*. The commitment of both North and South Koreans to a single national identity—coupled with the repudiation of Kim Il Sungism—would leave a reformist DPRK regime with little prospect of stability. Once the reform and opening process began, the political and economic dynamics would engender the inevitable absorption of the DPRK regime by the ROK. The main challenge would be to minimize the political and economic destabilization.

In the long term, the reunification of the Korean peninsula appears highly probable. While the old dictator should be able to preserve his *chuch'e* state as long as he lives, his successors will be forced to preside over the termination of the DPRK. Kim Il Sung's regime is caught in a dead end. Once he is gone, his successors will have to accept the necessity of reform. If they fail to do so, the DPRK will probably collapse within five years of Kim's death. If they attempt reform, they will be caught in the same process of political dissolution that eventually overcame the East German government, and they will thus face political absorption by the ROK within ten years of Kim's death.

This positive long-term prognosis, however, does not mean that the DPRK will disappear tomorrow, nor does it mean that the North Korean threat can be dismissed. Kim Il Sung should be able to maintain his government as long as he is able to function effectively, and his successors will not willingly abdicate their power to their hated rival in the south. Furthermore, in the short term, the risk of instability on the peninsula will grow—particularly in the immediate aftermath of Kim Il Sung's death or incapacitation. South Korea and its allies cannot afford to let down their guard.

Korean unification will have a revolutionary impact on the balance of power in Northeast Asia. The unification of Korea will create, for the first time in history, a powerful, united Korea capable of an independent role in Asian international affairs. Moreover, the stable diplomatic equilibrium that has existed since the end of the Korean War--with each rival power bloc possessing its own ally on that half of the peninsula most strategically vital to their concerns—will be terminated. As a result, the unification of Korea will also set the four great powers scrambling to compete for influence with the single, remaining Korean regime. The trend toward increasing multipolarity in the world and in Asia will intensify this competition. The United States, Japan, Russia, and China may all pursue their own policies toward Korea in varying degrees of competition with each other.[47] The situation will probably bear a closer resemblance to North Korean relations with its two communist allies than to traditional South Korean foreign policy, with its extremely close association with the United States. Nevertheless, if U.S.-ROK relations are managed effectively in the next decade, it seems likely that the U.S. will be the favored external power on the Korean peninsula.

NOTES

[1] Robert L. Pfaltzgraff, Jr., "Korea's Emerging Role in World Politics," *Korea and World Affairs*, vol. XI, no. 1, Spring 1987, p. 18.

[2] Park made frequent references to the concept of *chuch'e* and even used it to justify his effort to institutionalize his dictatorship via the "October Revitalizing Reforms" (*SiwolYusin*), which was inspired by the *Meiji Ishin* or Meiji Restoration period in Japanese history and which Park reportedly greatly admired. See Byung Chul Koh, *The Foreign Policy Systems of North and South Korea* (Berkeley: University of California Press, 1984), p. 17ff.

[3] Byung Chul Koh, *The Foreign Policy Systems of North and South Korea* (Berkeley: University of California Press, 1984), p. 235.

[4] *Ibid.*, p. 91.

⁵Park Chung Hee, *Korea Reborn: A Model for Development* (Englewood Cliffs, NJ: Prentice Hall, 1979), pp. 128-129, 132. Quoted in Byung Chul Koh, *The Foreign Policy Systems of North and South Korea* (Berkeley: University of California Press, 1984), p. 99.

⁶His actions were also undoubtedly influenced by the prevailing international trends of the time, which were embodied by the beginning of American withdrawal from Vietnam, Sino-American *rapprochement*, and Soviet-American détente.

⁷Quoted in B.C. Koh, "Seoul's 'Northern Policy' and Korean Security," *The Korean Journal of Defense Analysis*, vol. 1, no. 1, Summer 1989, p. 129.

⁸See B.C. Koh, *op. cit.*, p. 130.

⁹The South Korean transition to democracy is discussed in greater detail in Perry L. Wood, "South Korea: Towards Stable Democratic Government." HI-4048-P (Indianapolis, IN: Hudson Institute, December 1988).

¹⁰"Nordpolitik" is similar to the *Ostpolitik* popularized by Willy Brandt in the 1970s with reference to West Germany's relations with East Germany and its communist allies. The term has been used in South Korean academia to describe the ROK's policies toward the North and its communist allies since the Park era. Roh's "Nordpolitik" policy is defined by one South Korean academic ". . . as a diplomatic strategy to normalize relations with China, the Soviet Union and East Europe and through it to establish a mechanism for peaceful coexistence between South and North Korea." See Sang-Seek Park, "Northern Diplomacy and Inter-Korea Relations," *Korea and World Affairs*, vol. XII, no. 4, Winter 1988, p. 707.

¹¹Edward A. Olsen, "U.S.-ROK Relations: Common Issues and Uncommon Perceptions," *Korea and World Affairs*, vol. XIII, no. 1, Spring 1989, p. 43.

¹²More than 8,000 Americans are still listed as missing in action in Korea. See Daryl M. Plunk, "For the U.S.A. New Policy for Korean Reunification," *Asian Studies Center Backgrounder*, no. 107 (The Heritage Foundation: September 19, 1990), p. 12.

¹³Quoted in John McBeth, "Still a Hermit on the World Scene," *Far Eastern Economic Review*, Dec. 8, 1988, p. 24.

¹⁴Quoted in Susan Moffat, "Koreans See Need to Cut U.S. Military," *Asian Wall Street Journal*, Oct. 5, 1988.

¹⁵An assertive South Korea could become harmful to U.S. interests if it led to a serious, potentially destabilizing conflict between the ROK and Japan. But such a conflict is hardly inevitable. Indeed, the preservation of good U.S. relations with both nations will help to prevent any such eventuality. This is one argument for preserving the U.S.-ROK security tie once the immediate threat from the DPRK is past.

¹⁶ The term is from Byung-Joon Ahn. See his "Decision-Sharing in Korea-U.S. Relations," *Korea and World Affairs*, vol. XIV, no. 1, Spring 1990, pp. 5-15.

¹⁷Chong Whi Kim, "Korea-Japan Relations and Japan's Security," in *Pacific Security Toward the Year 2000*, The 1987 Pacific Symposium, Dora Alves (ed.), (Washington, DC: National Defense University Press, 1988), p. 135ff.

¹⁸The morning daily *Choson Ilbo* asked, "Why Japan? Why should Japan clear mines when it did not even fight during the Gulf War? Japan is an ex-convict. . . . It makes us uncomfortable to see an ex-convict pick up the sword again, even if it

is allegedly for peaceful purposes." See: "Media Sound 'Shrill' Warning," FBIS-EAS-91-081, Apr. 26, 1991. p. 29.

[19]Masashi Nishihara, "Japan's Gradual Defense Buildup and Korean Security," *The Korean Journal of Defense Analysis*, vol. 1, no. 1, Summer 1989, p. 105.

[20]See, for example, Edward A. Olsen, *U.S. Policy and the Two Koreas* (Boulder, CO: Westview Press, 1988).

[21]Hong Nack Kim, "The Normalization of North Korean-Japanese Diplomatic Relations: Problems and Prospects," *Korea and World Affairs*, vol. XIV, no. 4, Winter 1990, pp. 664-666.

[22]*Ibid.*, p. 667.

[23]*Ibid.*

[24]Shim Jae Hoon, "Pyongyang Paradox," *Far Eastern Economic Review*, Nov. 29, 1990, p. 28.

[25]Robert A. Manning, *Asian Policy: The New Soviet Challenge in the Pacific* (New York: Priority Press Publications, 1988), pp. 61-62.

[26]Byung-Joon Ahn, "South Korean-Soviet Relations: Issues and Prospects," *Korea and World Affairs*, vol. XIV, no. 4, Winter 1990, pp. 675-676.

[27]Gorbachev stated only that diplomatic relations "may arise as bilateral ties develop and in the context of the general improvement of the political situation in the region and on the Korean peninsula." See Sheldon W. Simon, "Security and Uncertainty in the North Pacific," *The Korean Journal of Defense Analysis*, vol. II, no. 2, Winter 1990, p. 89.

[28]Dae-Sook Suh, "Changes in North Korea and Inter-Korean Relations," *Korea and World Affairs*, vol. XIV, no. 4, Winter 1990, p. 616.

[29]"Korea's Economic Cooperation with the U.S.S.R.," Republic of Korea, Ministry of Finance, *MOF Bulletin*, no. 90, Jan. 1991, p. 10.

[30]*Ibid.*

[31]"Photographs of KAL 007 wreck shock South Korea," *Far Eastern Economic Review*, Apr. 11, 1991, p. 14.

[32]This analysis of South and North Korean strategies in their unification policies is derived from Rhee Sang-Woo, "North Korea in 1990: Lonesome Struggle to Keep *Chuch'e*," *Asian Survey* vol. XXXI, no. 1, Jan. 1991, p. 77.

[33]Rhee Sang-Woo, *op. cit.*, p. 72.

[34]Mark Clifford and Sophie Quinn-Judge, "Caught in a Vice," *Far Eastern Economic Review*, Nov. 29, 1990, p. 30.

[35]Damon Darlin, "Korean Economy Shows New Resilience," *The Asian Wall Street Journal*, Apr. 11, 1991, p. 1.

[36]Robert L. Pfaltzgraff, Jr., "Korea's Emerging Role in World Politics," *Korea and World Affairs*, vol. XI, no. 1, Spring 1987, p. 26.

[37]Norman D. Levin, "Global Détente and North Korea's Strategic Relations," *The Korean Journal of Defense Analysis*, vol. II, no. 1, Summer 1990, p. 37.

[38]Clifford and Quinn-Judge, *op. cit*, pp. 31-32.

[39]Of course, if conditions deteriorate past minimally acceptable levels before Kim dies (he is presently 79 years old), it is remotely possible that he could be removed from office by a coup. Given Kim's political dominance, his wily political acumen, and highly developed Party in-fighting skills, such a development must be classified as very unlikely. These are major incentives for opponents to avoid taking risks and postpone any action until the old man is dead or incapacitated.

[40]There are reports of conflict between Kim Jong Il and his stepmother, Kim Song-ae, and his uncle, Kim Young-ju (Kim Il Sung's younger brother). See Suk-Ryul Yu, "Political Succession and Policy Change in North Korea," *Korea and World Affairs*, vol. 10, no. 1, Spring 1986, p. 38.

[41]"Coup Talk in the Hermit Kingdom," *Asiaweek*, Feb. 22, 1991, p. 39.

[42]"'Moderate Faction' Reportedly Exists in North," FBIS-EAS-91075, Apr. 18, 1991, p. 33.

[43]The senior Kim would not be likely to undertake such an adventure. Since his personal political position would probably not be seriously challenged, such a dangerous action would not be worth the extreme risk entailed; and in any case, he has grown more cautious as he has grown older.

[44]See, for example: Sang-Seek Park, "Northern Diplomacy and Inter-Korea Relations," *Korea and World Affairs*, vol. XII, no. 4, Winter 1988, pp. 729-736.

[45]Quoted in Shim Jae Hoon, "Pyongyang Paradox," *Far Eastern Economic Review*, Nov. 29, 1990, p. 28.

[46]Shim Jae Hoon, "Pyongyang Paradox," p. 28.

[47]The degree of U.S.-Japan competition will, of course, depend on the degree of divergence that begins to occur between U.S. and Japanese foreign policy in the 1990s and beyond as Japan begins to assume a greater international role. U.S. and Japanese policies toward Korea could continue to be coordinated very closely, could diverge in limited areas, or could diverge significantly and compete directly.

CHAPTER 6

Conclusions

Our starting point for this study was a question: Is the strategic equilibrium that has characterized Northeast Asia for a decade or so transitory or stable? From the analyses of country strategies and foreign policies, one can readily see a number of dynamics—both in domestic politics and emerging state strategies—that threaten the equilibrium. Equally apparent are numerous stabilizing factors. To provide a cogent answer to the central question, we must try to understand how the factors of change interact and whether any of them promise to overcome the stabilizing elements in the strategic equation. All change, of course, need not be destabilizing. We must, therefore, also explore the prospects for a new equilibrium resulting from the regional dynamics.

To conceive the problem in this manner is to suggest a vector mechanics solution. Forces of change are colliding, and elements of stability stand in their way. The choice of this paramechanistic conceptualization is not accidental. It has the advantage of making us drop our American vantage point and forcing us to look at the numerous actors in the region, their aims, and the power they bring to achieving them. With that perspective, we can see more clearly how American power and alternative strategic choices are likely to affect the equation.

At the same time, we must be mindful of the dangers of overemphasizing the mechanical analogy. Northeast Asia, for example, is affected by many forces outside the region. The strategies of all the regional states deal as much with extraregional factors as with intraregional dynamics. The Soviet concept of the "Asia-Pacific Region" included Southeast Asia and South Asia, not to mention North America. Japan is centrally concerned with the greater Asian and Pacific region as well. And China uses its influence in Southeast Asia in the larger strategic game. Our analysis, therefore, has its limits in capturing all the dynamics bearing on Northeast Asia.

Equally troublesome is the number of intraregional factors, particularly domestic political and economic developments. We simply cannot capture them all. Eclecticism has its dangers, but we have tried to include all those that are sufficiently powerful to disturb the regional balance in the near future, the 1990s. Finally, politics and strategy are also matters of leaders' values, conceptual capacities, and choices. They can be highly variable and unpredictable. No analysis will capture them fully and accurately, particularly the voluntarist element of leadership. Leaders are also constrained by resources, geography, organization, alliances, and many things that the mechanics paradigm captures. As the study of each state's strategic outlook has revealed, the leaders' political and strategic choices are indeed constrained. They may surprise us with their future choices, but if our analysis has adequately exposed the structure of regional dynamics, we should be better able to understand both the motives and likely consequences of those new policy choices.

Major Structural Changes Deriving from States' Strategies

The present equilibrium, as noted in the introduction, derives from several structural conditions:
- The military weakness of Japan as a matter of Japanese choice
- The military weakness of China as a result of modern military technologies making the Chinese industrial base incapable of creating a modern military
- The large Soviet military threat directed toward China, Japan, the United States, and indirectly toward South Korea
- The stalemate between North and South Korea
- The U.S. military presence in the region, backed up by a capacity to reinforce it with large modern forces, which checked the Soviet military threat.

As a first step in identifying probable change, let us ask which of these conditions will endure and which are transitory. That should uncover the major potential sources of either destabilization or movement to a new equilibrium.

Soviet Strategy

The first and most striking change in these conditions was the new Soviet strategy. It produced a reduction of Soviet forces deployed against China. Although the CIS Pacific fleet remains essentially as it was—only slightly reduced—Gorbachev's "new thinking" in foreign policy moved military power to a new low in Soviet priority of strategic instrumentalities. In other words, the political rationale behind Soviet military power in the region was altered sharply from expansion to maintenance of the status quo. At the same time, the continuing deterioration of the Soviet, now Russian, economy promises to reduce industrial capacity for increasing and modernizing military forces in the Far East.

The collapse of the Soviet state and its military capabilities raises serious questions about the maintenance of the regional equilibrium. It appears to remove the most important and explicit rationale for the U.S. military presence. It would also seem to open the way to Russian-Japanese cooperation. This collapse has already brought a major improvement in Sino-Soviet relations, although they still face additional adjustment to the new Russian government. And it has brought normalization of South Korean-Soviet relations, relations Russia will continue to improve. (The warming between Seoul and Moscow, of course, tends to leave North Korea isolated, with its domestic ideology and foreign policy lacking the traditional Soviet support.)

This new Soviet strategy toward Northeast Asia, of course, had its parallel in Europe, and Soviet leaders apparently saw the parallel as important. They borrowed from their tactics in Europe—multilateral diplomacy in CSCE and regional arms-control proposals—in developing tactics for the Asia-Pacific Region.

This parallel naturally raises the analogy between a divided Germany and a divided Korea. Official Soviet policy on the reunification of Korea was unclear, but Soviet foreign-policy analysts have written about the issue, declaring it to be attainable and desirable. Moscow's formal recognition of South Korea and Seoul's grant of credits, of course, make reunification on the peninsula more than a mere future aspiration. Were it to transpire, another of the major stabilizing conditions in the region would be removed: the stalemate between North and South Korea. Soviet strategy was clearly intended to change the balance of power in the region. As several of its Soviet critics pointed out, that strategy might destabilize the area, particularly if it succeeded in weakening the U.S. military presence, and especially if it led to a break in the U.S.-Japanese security alliance. These Soviet critics did not, however, show the same awareness of the potential consequences of breaking the stalemate in Korea.

The End of the Korean Stalemate

Let us consider for a moment the likely dynamics of that event, because, of all the new developments in the region, it promises to create the most change in the near term. First, the old rationale for U.S. forces in Korea would disappear. Second, unification would probably take place on Seoul's terms, and the strong South Korean economy, like its West German counterpart, would be diverted to modernizing the newly acquired part of the country. Given South Korean military power, North Korea could hardly prevail if the U.S., China, and Russia stood aside. If North Korea set the terms and prevailed in the reunification process, it would destroy the economic base from which Moscow now seeks aid. It is difficult, therefore, to imagine how Pyongyang can prevail. Only one other regional power,

China, might prefer that outcome, but Beijing does not have the power to ensure it, particularly against U.S. and Russian desires. And Beijing would only prefer it if the new Korea were to be a Chinese client. Yet China already shows signs of preparing to accept what it cannot prevent by improving its ties to South Korea.

A united Korea under Seoul's leadership would eventually become a much stronger economic version of South Korea, a competitor to Japan, and, unlike Japan, a significant military power. The task of economic reconstruction of North Korea, however, is large, and it could not be completed quickly. Were South Korea to take over North Korea's nuclear program, it would soon become a nuclear power as well. Such a new Korea, with or without nuclear weapons, would indeed upset the regional equilibrium. Korea has never been able to maintain its autonomy in the past. China and Japan have never permitted that. The new Korea would have to find a major power to protect it, balancing the threat from China and Japan. The alternatives are limited—the United States and Russia are the only choices. That the Russian successor republic might fulfill this role should not be discounted. Its ground forces could check China, and the Russian fleet could protect Korea's coastline. Moscow, however, could only assume this balancing role at the cost of less-than-happy relations with China and Japan.

The Korean economy, however, might well provide enough aid to Moscow to compensate the loss. To be sure, Korea would certainly try to stay active in Western trading circles. Private capital could, in principle, ignore the tense political links created by this alignment. And it would be difficult for the United States and Japan to prevent such an arrangement unless Korea were to act aggressively enough to justify a trade embargo.

The alternative, the U.S. as strategic anchor for Korea, makes more sense. Moreover, as unification becomes more probable, South Korean leaders stress the importance of their country's military connection with the U.S. The military ties between the two nations are longstanding, and they would keep Korea's foreign security and economic relations in the same community. China could not easily challenge a Korea that has U.S. military support, nor could Russia. What about Japan? A strong U.S.-Korean security alliance should assure Japan. Moreover, it would be compatible with Japan's maintenance of its longstanding security alliance with the United States. This kind of post-unification arrangement makes a great deal of sense for all parties. It really does not threaten China or Russia; it places some restraints on Korean military power, especially acquisition of nuclear weapons; and it should allay Japanese fears. It looks so attractive that it would seem almost inexorable.

If a transition to this strategic configuration is possible, it certainly has the hallmarks of a new equilibrium. Getting there, however, is not simple. Consider some of the major hurdles.

Conclusions   117

First, Japan and China are already showing signs of trying to prevent Korean unification. The LDP delegation to Pyongyang appears to have been badly bungled, but it reveals the willingness of some in Japanese leadership circles to help North Korea avoid isolation. China shares that interest, and Beijing can be expected to keep the door open for Pyongyang, although it will probably try to avoid scuttling economic assistance from Seoul for Chinese modernization programs. South Korea has provided such assistance indirectly, apparently as part of its strategy for isolating North Korea. Finally, conservative domestic forces in Moscow, if they were to displace the Yeltsin government, would not like to see North Korea sold out to South Korea. North Korea, therefore, might prove too resilient for Seoul's present strategy.

Second, Korean nationalism could create a domestic political climate that makes the presence of U.S. forces impossible to maintain. The Russian connection does not require foreign forces on Korean soil. Similarly, Japanese nationalism, given a jolt by the change in Korea, could make it difficult to keep U.S. forces in Japan. Finally, domestic factors in U.S. politics—the declining Soviet threat, pressures to reduce the defense budget, Japan-bashing over trade issues, and calls for allies to share the defense burden—could make it increasingly difficult for a U.S. president to keep forces in Northeast Asia. Yet some ground-force presence in both Japan and Korea would be essential to underpinning confidence in this balancing role by the U.S.

These developments would bring the added danger of Korea acquiring nuclear weapons. With no U.S. military presence, the incentive for Korea to have its own nuclear capability would be strong. In turn, a Korean nuclear force would create an equally strong incentive for Japan to acquire one.

A third major problem is in finding a new threat rationale for the U.S. military presence. If the Soviet Union is no longer a problem, the publics in the United States, Japan, and Korea are sure to ask, why should U.S. forces not depart? The answer is easy: they keep peace between Korea and Japan and between Korea and China, and they limit Russian influence. Perhaps most important, they reduce the likelihood of Korea—and perhaps Japan in response—acquiring nuclear weapons. The easy answer, no matter how sound, may not be persuasive to taxpayers. Nor will all political leaders buy it. That will be true in all three countries. *Selling the military rationale of this new strategic configuration will probably be the most difficult step in creating it.*

Korean Strategies

The second-biggest source of potential change in the region is on the Korean peninsula. Both states seek to change the status quo. Neither state, however, can force change alone. The growing strength of the South Korean economy has not altered this reality, although it is becoming a more important factor. Acquiring nuclear weapons is clearly within the nation's industrial capability if it chooses to press forward and violate international controls. Moreover, the size of Korea's share of the international economy makes the country more important than it was two decades ago.

North Korea is struggling to acquire nuclear weapons, and it probably will succeed in the 1990s unless the regional powers make major efforts to prevent it. Its military power has peaked, but it still poses a serious threat to the south. At the same time, the North Korean economy is in serious trouble, with no prospect of realizing significant growth. In principle this should mean that the political system is fragile and subject to collapse. Here, however, the parallel with East Germany is interesting—not so much for analogies as for differences. There are no foreign troops in North Korea. Kim Il Sung's regime, therefore, has convincingly claimed the mantle of Korean nationalism. And the population is so isolated from knowledge of the economic prosperity of South Korea and the rest of the world that the political situation is quite different from the one in East Germany. Poverty does not weaken it in the same way economic privation undercut the Honecker regime. Moreover, the much larger potential costs of modernizing North Korea's economy will undoubtedly cause some South Koreans to pause before agreeing to pay them.

South Korea's strategy of isolating Pyongyang is militarily risky. Rather than go peacefully—at Moscow's direction—the way Honecker went, Kim Il Sung could decide to go down fighting. The South Koreans appear more sensitive to this prospect than most other states in the region, including the United States.

The critical variable for both Seoul and Pyongyang seems to be Kim Il Sung's life-expectancy. No one expects North Korea to collapse or yield to South Korea as long as he remains alive. After his death, however, the succession problem will introduce many new variables. Whether his son can succeed him is only one. Perhaps more important is how much of his father's image he can perpetuate. Clique struggles could unintentionally open up many political and economic questions in the public mind. Rigid bureaucracies and institutions could fracture. If Seoul has sufficiently isolated North Korea internationally, and if it has opened up better information channels to some strata of the North Korean society, the planned leadership transition might not occur, and the collapse of the system, therefore, cannot be ruled out.

Given the general collapse of Soviet-type political systems, why should North Korea not follow? It probably will, absent a global economic crisis for the West and a communist counterrevolution in Russia and Eastern Europe. The question is timing. Will it happen in the 1990s? Kim might well survive until the turn of the century, but the odds are against it. We must take the prospect of fundamental change on the Korean peninsula seriously, therefore, and we should be ready for it in the 1990s.

North Korea's strategy is to avoid isolation. We have already noted that Japan is ill-disposed to see Korea unified. China shares that view. This means that Pyongyang has genuine options. They might work for a time, but in the longer run they will require a political and economic transformation within North Korea. Can a more liberal and economically prosperous North Korea be possible without it giving way to forces for reunification? That cannot be ruled out, especially if Japan were to make DRPK stability a serious goal and support it with massive economic assistance. A post-Kim, highly dictatorial regime might follow the pattern we have seen in Taiwan. It might introduce a market under rigid political dictatorship, permitting a long-term pattern of economic growth, land reform, and, eventually, social and political change. Although China could hardly object to that development, it cannot sponsor it. It has neither the economic means nor the political disposition to do so. Japan, however, has good strategic reasons and adequate economic power.

The cost to Japan, of course, would be its relationship with South Korea. Although relations are cordial and cooperation exists in many fields, South Koreans, as noted in Chapter 5, consider the Japanese a much greater threat than the Russians. A Japanese strategy aimed at stabilizing the indefinite division of Korea would be bound to stimulate hostile public feelings in both Koreas and very hostile feelings in South Korean leadership circles.

Were Japan to pursue such a strategy, the United States would find itself caught in the middle. If relations were to deteriorate seriously, Washington might be forced to choose between its two allies. Whichever way it chose would open the door for Moscow, Beijing, or both to the country Washington chose to sacrifice.

In sum, a divided Korea—a stabilizing factor in the present strategic equilibrium—promises to become a destabilizing factor if Moscow's strategy continues on its present course while the economic disparities between the two Koreas continue to grow. A united Korea under Seoul's leadership, by contrast, could be a stabilizing factor. It depends on where that new Korea chooses to anchor itself strategically—in Washington or in Moscow. And if it chooses Washington, stability depends on the United States' capacity to maintain a significant military presence, not just naval—clearly the major element—but also a modicum of ground and air presence in both Korea and Japan. *Here we come back to the need for a new threat, a new military rationale for that presence in the post-Cold War era.*

Chinese Strategy

Chinese military weakness, of course, contributed centrally to the emergence of the presence regional equilibrium. China's strategy of "four modernizations" has been generally interpreted as putting military power at the lowest priority. That is probably a serious misreading, however. In the 1970s, Chinese leaders slowly came to recognize that their economy could not produce modern military weaponry in adequate variety and quantity to make China a military superpower. To have such a military sometime in the future, the fiscal resources for maintaining the present obsolete military forces would have to be reallocated to economic and scientific modernization. The four modernizations, therefore, probably reflect a long-term strategy for attaining military power.

The Soviet experience in the 1920s and 1930s is instructive in this regard. The Soviet Union virtually disbanded the Red Army in 1921-23—reducing it by 90%—and put all its emphasis on economic reconstruction, at first through a private agricultural and small commercial sector, and then, after 1927, through central planning and collectivized agriculture.

Although China has been unable to duplicate that experience—the People's Liberation Army, for example, successfully resisted such massive demobilization—it has tried. Some of the dangers that confronted Soviet leaders in the 1920s have also arisen in China. In the early 1920s, when peasants in Russia and the Ukraine found their products bringing lower and lower prices while state monopoly prices on industrial goods remained high, they responded by refusing to plant, which created a food crisis in the cities. The Bolsheviks saw this as not only an economic problem but also a serious political threat to their regime.

China has recently undergone similar behavior by its peasantry. In the industrial sector, however, the sequence is different because centralization had already been imposed there in the 1950s. Over the past decade, small commerce and industry create a diffusion of economic and political power similar to that engendered by private peasant farming. This is particularly true in Southern China under the influence of investment from Taiwan and Hong Kong. Regional government and party officials favor the diffusion, thereby creating a political problem for the central government and party. Added to this has been the more visible political dynamic of the pro-democracy student movement. In several of its manifestations, therefore, the Chinese experience is quite different from the Soviet experience in its first decades. Soviet industry was never decentralized, and no local areas had strong foreign assistance. The central political problem, however, is analogous. Decentralization of economic activity engenders a diffusion of political power, which threatens the communist party's monopoly on power. How far can the economic modernization process go without destroying the old political system?

As the chapter on China explains, Chinese leaders have had to turn inward. The dialectics of modernization and a central political monopoly have created massive domestic challenges for the old party leaders. China's weakness as a regional power, therefore, is likely to continue through the 1990s. This is not to say that Chinese power is trivial, or that China can be disregarded as an element in the equation. Quite the contrary: its mere size, aggregate human and economic resources, and military potential will give it a huge role. But it is not in China's interest to use its power to destabilize the region, to set in motion fundamental change.

Avoiding dramatic change seems to be China's major political and military goal while it strives to achieve major domestic change—change that could sweep away the regime and set China on a course toward regionalism and chaos.

If that is so, it might be asked, why did China normalize its relations with the Soviet Union? Was not the Soviet threat a stabilizing factor even for China? The answer is twofold. First, Moscow met all three of Beijing's longstanding conditions for normalization: reduction of Soviet forces on the Sino-Soviet border, withdrawal from Afghanistan, and Vietnamese withdrawal from Cambodia. Gorbachev simply removed all of China's excuses for not normalizing.

The second answer to why China normalized relations with the Soviets is in the changing character of the Moscow-Washington-Beijing Triangle. In the 1970s, Beijing and Washington were trying to play each other as "cards" in the game the triangle set in play. Washington wanted China to help balance Soviet power in the Far East, and China wanted to hold Washington's coat while Washington engaged in competition with Moscow. The collapse of Moscow's position in Central and Eastern Europe and Gorbachev's strategy for ending the East-West competition eliminated much of the strategic importance of the old "triangle" and the Chinese, American, and Soviet "cards" in the East-West game. By normalizing relations with Moscow, Beijing was trying to salvage some of that strategic importance and to prevent Washington from being the only winner in the game. The collapse of the Soviet regime, of course, has thrown the whole game into question, and its revival will depend on the kind of policies the new Russia develops in the years ahead.

Improved Sino-Soviet relations mark a major regional change, but they do not promise to affect the strategic equilibrium, even as Russia assumes the Soviet mantle. China is still weak militarily. Russia is less threatening militarily. Both sides have applauded each other and sought closer economic and scientific cooperation, but neither side can provide much help with the other's staggering economic problems. The South Korean offer of economic assistance, by comparison, has far greater strategic significance for Moscow than anything China can offer, and the same will be true for China if it can find a way to cooperate with South Korea. The strategic impact of Sino-Soviet normalization promised to be much greater outside Northeast Asia—for example, in Southeast Asia and South Asia. The demise of the Soviet Union has simply eclipsed the whole affair, leaving a number of new interregional relations to be worked out anew.

We have already considered China's strategy toward Korea. Beijing cannot be happy at the prospect of a unified Korea under southern rule, and although relations with Pyongyang have been troubled, North Korea can count on China for limited help against South Korea's strategy. The North Korean nuclear program, however, worries China, not just for its own sake but also because of the reactions it could set off in South Korea and Japan.

China has not considered Japan a central strategic problem in the postwar period. Lacking serious military power and very much under cover of U.S. military security, Japan has not drawn the kind of focus that fell on Moscow and Washington. Japan has more often been lumped together with the American problem. That situation, however, is changing for two reasons.

First, Japan's modern industrial base could support a major military buildup, one that China cannot possibly match in air and sea power. China's technological and industrial backwardness are simply not being overcome rapidly enough to engage Japan in military competition. Thus even the small but steady real increases in the Japanese military budget are a matter of growing concern for the Chinese. Unable to meet the challenge with its own military buildup, China has to look for other means of constraining Japan. Although Chinese public rhetoric sometimes suggests the contrary—such as supporting North Korean demands for U.S. military withdrawal—Chinese strategy undoubtedly counts the U.S. military presence in Japan and Korea as a positive factor. In the case of Taiwan, of course, the U.S. military shield is a negative factor, but China's strategy for regaining Taiwan has ruled out military action at least since U.S.-Chinese normalization in 1978.

Second, Japan's economic importance to China is growing. Heavily dependent on the United States for technology, China would like to diversify its sources, which would decrease the economic leverage that Washington could use in the political sphere. This, of course, became especially attractive to the Chinese after the events in Tiananmen Square in 1989. Japan has entered the breach, but not in the way China prefers. Japanese firms want to sell more than they want to invest, and they are reluctant to transfer leading-edge technology in the investments they do make.

The present strategic equilibrium, of course, depends on quiescence in the historical rivalry between China and Japan. The quickest way for the rivalry to be reactivated, on the other hand, is for Japan to continue its military programs. Japanese rearmament, to be sure, would remove one of the fundamental factors of regional stability, and although it is far from occurring, the modest Japanese military programs have already galvanized China's attention. In the economic sphere, Japanese policies may cause irritation, but they are not likely to upset the status quo if China finds other sources of foreign technology and capital.

Chinese strategy toward the United States has been critical to the regional balance of power, and it will remain so. Normalization between the two powers allowed China to make progress on several fronts. First, U.S. power did indeed check "Soviet hegemonism," causing Moscow to reverse its foreign and military strategy fundamentally. That reversal made possible Sino-Soviet normalization on Chinese terms. Second, normalization has afforded extensive Chinese access to modern technology and a new export market. Third, normalization still holds, at least in the Chinese view, prospects for a favorable resolution of the Taiwan issue. Thus far, Chinese strategy has contributed to stability, but its goals, if fully realized, would threaten the balance.

Keeping the U.S.-Chinese relationship on an even keel, however, has become increasingly difficult. The dynamics of Chinese domestic politics—that is, Beijing's struggle to keep the diffusion of economic power from destabilizing the communist regime—has created human-rights abuses and repressive domestic policies that offend American sensitivities. This problem is likely to become more serious, not less so, as long as the communists try to monopolize power. If they do not, on the other hand, China's domestic stability will be thrown into question.

In its efforts to earn hard currency from exports, China has not overlooked the Third World arms market. Sales of missiles and assistance to nuclear-weapons programs in several Third World states, therefore, has become another troublesome factor in U.S.-Chinese relations.

Although the U.S.-Chinese relationship may be managed successfully with some concessions on both sides—particularly, more Chinese cooperation in controlling arms flows and nuclear-weapons technology—let us suppose, for purposes of analysis, that the relationship will sour. Would it upset the Northeast Asian regional balance? Not in the 1990s. China's internal weakness denies it the means. Nor can China play the "Soviet card"—it no longer exists. Moreover, disturbing the equilibrium is not in China's own self-interest. In sum, in exacting compromises from China, the United States has more latitude than it has heretofore demanded.

Japanese Strategy

Japanese strategies are not like those of the other powers in the region. Chapter 4 described Japan as a "reactive" power. Japan has developed a very sophisticated economic strategy, but in the military and foreign-policy areas it has yet to develop new goals and tactics for achieving them. It has remained within the U.S. security sphere, and almost wholly dependent on it.

The structure of the Japanese government is an important cause of Japan's peculiar handling of strategy. Unlike the other states in the region, Japan does not have a centralized and highly coordinated national security apparatus. The Japanese Defense Agency is a very weak player, with little or no planning staff. The Foreign Ministry is more concerned with "reactive" diplomacy than with planning strategy. No significant intelligence organization exists. And the cabinet apparatus is wholly unequipped to conceive, staff, and implement a national strategy. In the first decades after the war, the Ministry of International Trade and Industry played a key role in developing an economic strategy. Some observers believe that it still does so, but others see Japanese economic strategy now as more diffused among the oligarchy of large business organizations.

As Japan has begun to play a major role in international economic assistance, the lack of adequate staff and analytical capacity to direct it has become a matter of concern, not only in Japan but also in the United States. Japan, through its banks and business circles, is quite good at dispersing "tied aid"—that is, capital tied to expenditures in Japan—but institutions for "untied" aid for political and economic development are very weak.

This particular structural condition of the Japanese government is a significant factor in moderating and constraining Japanese foreign policy and has had a positive effect on the regional equilibrium. At times in U.S.-Japanese relations, however, it has been a point of frustration on both sides. As Japan attempts to develop more foreign-policy autonomy, it will probably also improve its institutional capacity to design and implement it. If it does, we shall be dealing with a new factor, one Americans may learn to dislike more than the old "reactive" structure. Finally, the present situation forces the U.S. to infer Japanese strategy: to determine it objectively without depending much on explicit, official, Japanese policy statements and without much help from Japanese foreign policy analysts.

A number of pressures are pushing Japan to develop an "active" strategy and take its place as a new world power, standing on a more even military and political footing with the United States, Russia, and China.

The first pressure has been coming from the United States for more than a decade, in Washington's demand that Japan share more of the military burden in the region. Not only has the United States asked Japan to increase its armed forces, particularly its air and naval components, but it has also, as an incentive, initiated coproduction programs for weapons. Technology-sharing, however, has done more to create ill-will than to reduce the U.S.'s defense burden. To encourage an increased Japanese military effort made some sense when the Soviet military threat in the Far East was growing, but it also carried dangers that American policymakers tended to ignore. Once on the path to rearmament, why should Japan not go all the way? A rearmed Japan, of course, would remove yet another of the stabilizing factors in the present, remarkable equilibrium. And the adverse impact would not be limited to Northeast Asia. Most other states in the Pacific region would be highly disturbed by it. Now, with the decline of the

Soviet threat, Japanese rearmament has lost the little utility it once seemed to offer in spreading the U.S. defense burden.

Domestic pressures also push Japan to acquire an independent defense capability. These are indirect. Public anger at the way the United States led the offensive against Iraq in the Persian Gulf War has increased the influence of those Japanese elites who would like to reduce the country's security-dependence on the United States. The Gulf War episode alone will probably not push Japan into a serious military buildup, but it will make it a more legitimate public topic.

Events on the Korean peninsula probably place much more serious pressure on Japan to rearm. North Korean acquisition of nuclear weapons would disturb Japan deeply. Korean unification also would make Japan review its defense policy. As suggested above, how the unification takes place and the role of U.S. military power in a united Korea's security would be critical. Events could follow a course that left Japan satisfied with its present security arrangements, but they could also have the opposite effect.

In foreign policy toward the region, Japan's primary goal, judging by the public attention given to it, is regaining the Northern Territories, the several Kurile Islands now occupied by Russia. The significance of these islands is only marginally strategic; their real importance is to Japanese national pride. Russo-Japanese relations have never been good, and it takes little to stir up anti-Russian sentiment among the Japanese. Also, bashing Moscow over these islands probably mitigates the need to vent massive pent-up feelings of anger over their defeat in World War II. They cannot be discharged so vigorously against the United States or China, but Russia is fair game.

Although the economic promise of Japanese access to the Russian Far East has, at times, been judged great, in reality the return from capital invested there in extractive industries is bound to be small. Moreover, Japanese experience there in the 1970s showed mixed success at best. In sum, Japanese enthusiasm for improved relations with the Soviet Union, and now Russia, has no strong objective economic or military underpinning.

The Soviet Union, of course, based much of its new strategy toward the region on developing extensive economic interdependencies. As Gorbachev's visit to Japan in the spring of 1991 demonstrated, his strategy toward Japan made no appreciable progress. For his own domestic reasons, he was not really free to return the Northern Territories. And he came nowhere near to creating a market economy in the Soviet Union, a *sine qua non* for sustained economic interaction with Japan.

As the chapter on Soviet strategy shows, several Soviet critics accurately perceived the essence of the problem. Gorbachev's economic strategy toward Japan was up against a "great wall" that impedes interaction between market economies and their centrally planned counterparts. His strategy failed to overcome two causes of political paralysis in Moscow: between the central government and the Russian republic, which claimed it must have the final say on the Northern Territories; and between Gorbachev's foreign-policy liberals and the military and party conservatives who are still smarting about losing East Europe. How the new Russian government will deal with the problem is anyone's guess.

Even if the Northern Territories were returned and the Russian economy put on a market basis, the integration of the Soviet Far East into the Asian rimland economies, primarily Japan, would progress slowly. The capital requirements in this part of Russia are enormous, and profits on capital invested elsewhere are likely to be more attractive. For a long time, progress would depend not on market forces but on Japanese government policy.

What motives could Japan have for such large capital allocations? The only conceivable one is to make Russia a Japanese partner, to balance the Japanese dependency on the United States. Although the prospects for this alignment are not great, some Japanese military officers do talk about it. They remain a voice in the Japanese political wilderness, however, one unlikely to override Japanese business circles.

Japan's strategy toward China, if there is one, seems to be to take as much advantage of economic opportunities as possible without providing significant technological assistance. As the old Soviet military threat rapidly fades, Japan can afford to be dilatory in its policy toward Russia. China, however, is another matter. The author has tried to persuade several high-level Japanese officials to say which country poses the greatest strategic problem for Japan in the next decade or so. Most have refused to "speculate." A few Japanese general officers have been more forthcoming: China, without question. On the precise nature of the problem, however, they are without details. They seem rather to reflect a deep, subjective feeling based on a long history of competition and war. For the 1990s, the problem is likely to remain quiescent. The only potentially disruptive development seems to be Japanese rearmament.

Japanese strategy toward the United States is, of course, the most important of all Japan's relationships and among the most complicated. Japan's dependency on the U.S. security umbrella has been enormously advantageous, and not just in its military dimension. It brought Japan, shortly after its defeat in World War II, into the family of Western nations, opening the door to trade, technology, education, and cultural ties. To the extent that the Japanese government has a conscious strategy, it still appears largely "reactive," aimed at keeping the U.S. market open to Japanese business, meeting U.S. demands it cannot evade, and moderating domestic outrage at the "Japan bashing" that goes on in the United States.

Can the Japanese successfully make the transition to a less dependent relationship, as described in Chapter 4? The transition's basic dimension, of course, is diversification of its export markets. For the foreseeable future, it is difficult to see where Japan might find alternative markets for the 37% of its exports which now go to the United States. The Asian rimland economies are of increasing importance, but they cannot substitute for the U.S. market and access to the U.S. scientific and research communities.

Moreover, if Japan were to succeed in diversifying its markets, and then fell into an adversarial relationship with the United States, it would have to look after its own security. To rearm for that purpose would alienate most of the Asian rimland states where the diversification has to be achieved, thus defeating the purpose. Given the uncertainties in Korea, therefore, it would be very risky for Japan to let the U.S.-Japanese security alliance deteriorate.

For all the present public discussion in the United States about the growing threat from Japan, economic and security factors in the relationship are so interlocked that it is difficult to see how any self-interested Japanese leadership would want to provoke a break.

Is Japan likely to act in a way that upsets the present equilibrium in Northeast Asia? Tokyo can be a nuisance in some of its policies and behavior, but *the only serious disruption it could cause would be to rearm*. What are the prospects of that? A few domestic groups in Japan are so inclined, particularly in the Ground Self-Defense Forces, and perhaps some nationalist groups, but their political weight is minimal. The foreign factors include foremost the outcome in Korea: whether North Korea acquires nuclear weapons, whether Korea unites, and whether a united Korea seeks a major power patron in Washington or Moscow. Korea is the big potential security problem for Japan in the 1990s.

The only other stimulus for Japanese rearmament is the United States. Were the United States to decrease its forces to trivial levels and leave no ground forces in Korea and Japan, the Japanese government would have to consider rearmament seriously. It is not a foregone conclusion that the Japanese would rearm, however. The government would have to consider the problems it would create for Japanese trade relationships in East and Southeast Asia.

On the whole, Japan promises to play a highly stabilizing role in Northeast Asia in the 1990s. Only Korea and the United States are in a position to provoke it to do otherwise, and if either does, Japan certainly has the capacity to rearm and destabilize the region. Unlike China, Japan can make serious trouble.

Changes Not Intended by Policymakers

Thus far we have looked at what the leaders in the region apparently want to achieve, the changes they seek, and the constraints they face, and a few scenarios they could provoke in their interaction. What about other factors beyond the control of leaders and strategic planners?

The international economy, of course, is something policymakers try to control, but their degree of control is often limited and problematical. Moreover, they might misperceive its causal linkages and make it worse, not better.

A major world depression, of course, would affect Northeast Asia—primarily the market economies of Japan, South Korea, and the United States. The impact is impossible to anticipate accurately, but a number of factors affecting the strategic equilibrium are predictable, or at least worth worrying about.

First, a depression would seriously undermine U.S. military power in the region. The U.S. public would probably prove unwilling to pay the cost of maintaining forces there. Their withdrawal, of course, would probably set off a number of destabilizing events. South Korea's economy would also suffer, and North Korea might thereby be emboldened to attack. Japan would hardly stand by unarmed. Japanese rearmament might also be seen as a way to keep an industrial work force employed while world markets are weak or nonexistent. In light of our earlier analyses it is clear what some of the implications of these developments could be, and none of them portend a stable strategic equilibrium in the region.

Second, domestic political stability in some states in the region cannot be taken for granted. China, for example, could easily experience a collapse of the central government as it struggles toward economic modernization. As power shifted to the regions and local governments and as the central authorities failed to organize their peaceful transition to a new political system based on fundamentally different principles than Marxism-Leninism, the situation would become quite brittle. Even civil war cannot be ruled out.

Would this destabilize the region? If no other major changes—such as Japanese rearmament or Korean unification—occurred at the same time or before, the United States and Russia ought to be able to keep outside powers from intervening. The Taiwan factor might come into play, but the United States should be able to keep it from becoming serious. The regional balance would be shakier, and more vulnerable to a breakdown from other changes such as a crisis on the Korean peninsula, but it could be maintained, provided that the U.S., Japan, South Korea, and Russia cooperate. And they would have a strong interest to do so. Some increase in U.S. military presence might be required, particularly naval forces for the Taiwan Strait.

Politics in the former Soviet Union could also introduce a new factor. The demise of the Soviet Union has been accompanied by a peaceful transfer of power to the republics, leaving the Russian Republic as the new government concerned with Northeast Asia. That should not cause serious trouble. Civil war within and among the republics, however, or a somewhat later civil war within Russia, would add uncertainties. Even these events would probably not disturb the regional balance, however, unless China were to intervene, either in Central Asia or in the Russian Far East. North Korea might also intervene, and South Korea might well choose sides and offer supplies. Again, the United States ought to be able to stop most outside interference except from China and North Korea, and China might well be disposed to cooperate with the United States. Thus, stability in Northeast Asia outside of Russia could be maintained, essentially walled off from upheavals in the old Soviet territories.

We have already discussed the possible collapse of the North Korean regime. That would not be in the category of a "natural disaster," an unintended event. South Korea seeks it, and we have treated that scenario.

Two other political "natural disasters" are remote but worth thinking about. First, we consider Japan a remarkably stable country, a democracy, and likely to remain one. Not as a prediction but purely for analysis, however, let us challenge that assumption. Japan's Liberal Democratic Party has ruled continuously since 1955 without yielding power to an opposition party. Many political scientists consider a system fully democratic only after it has shown its capacity to allow an opposition party to win power, take office, and maintain the constitutional system. Japan has yet to meet this criterion. It is essentially a one-party system, and the structure of the opposition prevents a moderate alternative party from having a serious chance of unseating the LDP. The Socialists, the most likely candidate to do so, carry a lot of ideological baggage that makes much of the electorate nervous and prevents the emergence of leaders who can win at the national level.

Although the chapter on Japan does not delve deeply into Japanese domestic politics—strategy, not primarily domestic politics, is its central focus—we should nonetheless speculate on its potential dynamics. In a democracy, rigidities and weaknesses naturally grow over time. Corruption is one of their manifestations. The "throw them out" syndrome occasionally prevails in democracies where opposition parties are able to win, and a sense of renewal and cleansing occurs. Japan has not been able adequately to develop this aspect of democracy. At some point, however, such a renewal is bound to occur, and it might not be democratic if the system fails to allow for it. A rapidly declining world economy, led by the United States, could put enormous strain on the Japanese political system as export markets declined for Japanese industry. Resurgent nationalism would surely play a key role in such a crisis.

We know too little about Japanese nationalism: whether it is merely dormant but potentially explosive, or whether it has fundamentally matured. The Japanese are painfully aware that they are not liked in most of Asia, and increasingly they wonder about the United States. Such a sense of cultural rejection is not healthy for any nation.

We might also be overlooking economic rigidities in Japan. We see that country as an economic giant, a veritable superpower with a magic superiority on the one hand and a penchant for unfairness on the other. It wins by ability, but it also wins by cheating. Both of these views are partly inaccurate. The truth, if we really understood it, might well reveal a vulnerable economy on a special run of good luck and wit but in danger of serious disorders.

We also know too little about America's influence on Japan. Our social and cultural influence is enormous, and as the generations that knew World War II die out, the younger generations in Japan will make the weight of American influence even greater. Our "Japan bashing" also influences Japan, and the effect can hardly be positive. It may make some Americans feel good, but the price for the emotional relief it gives us could prove much higher than we really want to pay. For most of our charges of "unfairness," a countercharge of U.S. unfairness can also be made. For example, pressing Japan to import subsidized American rice in the name of free trade is the height of hypocrisy. The angels are not on our side in all the economic issues.

The point here is that we should not take Japan's domestic political system for granted. It could change, and a systemic change could indeed destabilize Northeast Asia. This is not to suggest that a Japanese domestic political crisis is probable, but it is to argue that, were a number of external developments to coincide for Japan, such a crisis is conceivable.

To sum up the potential for "natural disasters" not created by strategic intentions: most of the conceivable ones are manageable. Two, however, are not. First, a major, worldwide economic depression—which would particularly affect the United States, Japan, and South Korea—would probably ignite in Northeast Asia destabilizing events beyond the capacity of the regional powers to control. Second, although the prospect is improbable, a serious political crisis in Japan, one that undermined the present system, would be beyond the control of the regional powers. Unbridled U.S. political behavior would bear some of the responsibility for such a development, even if only as a minor contributor. The consequences would probably destabilize the region, or at least require major realignments to restore the balance.

As we noted earlier, this analysis of Northeast Asia is framed in a paramechanistic fashion. Our aim has been to set forth the goals and strategies of all the states in the region, and to view them as intersecting in many different ways and places. Such an approach runs the risk of overemphasizing some conflicts in goals and interests, but the analysis has also taken into account the power each state can commit to its aims. That gives a better sense of the probability that such conflicts will indeed destabilize the region. The advantage of this analytical approach is that it tends to identify more of the variables in the Northeast Asian equation.

Furthermore, it helps avoid a distorting, ethnocentric, American strategic viewpoint. To consider U.S. strategy, however, we must turn to a parochial American view which aims at advancing U.S. interests.

Strategic Options, Dangers, and Requirements for the U.S.

Thus far we have introduced the American variable only in a residual or secondary way in our analysis of the Northeast Asian balance of power. In exploring the strategies of all the other regional powers, however, the American factor has come up repeatedly. In the scenarios for Korean unification, the American factor is the major determinant of whether the change will produce a new equilibrium or send the region spinning into disorder. Soviet, now Russian, analysts see American power with ambivalence. On the one hand, they emphasize its strength—achieved through its compatibility with Japanese interests and the power of its ideological underpinnings—and the positive role of U.S. military power in East Asia. On the other hand, those who supported Gorbachev's new strategy urged diplomacy that would reduce the U.S. military presence and weaken the U.S.-Japanese relationship, and underestimated the critical role of the United States in preventing Korean unification from destabilizing the region. Likewise, for a decade or more Chinese strategy has exploited the United States' power to reach goals otherwise beyond Chinese means. Like their former Soviet counterparts, however, Chinese leaders and analysts show mixed feelings about the enormous U.S. role. Even North Korea has begun to court the United States to counter the South Korean strategy.

The U.S.'s allies in the region, Japan and South Korea, are conscious of their critical dependence on the U.S. military presence and the U.S. domestic market. Yet they too show ambivalence, not so much in government circles as in the anti-Americanism expressed by students and public groups.

The United States, therefore, has at its disposal a very large reservoir of strategic capital in the region, not just with its allies but also with its old adversaries. That means that U.S. strategic options are broader than in the past, but also more challenging to implement in the post-Cold War era. At the same time, the United States faces increasing demands on that capital, not only by the states in the region but also by domestic political forces. The hostile sentiments toward Japan—initially a response to the perception of unfair Japanese exploitation of the American market—seem to be acquiring a broader, less issue-specific, more subjective basis. Certainly the defense-burden issue has blurred into the economic issue in the minds of many Americans. This general American sentiment marks a danger for U.S. strategy. It not only threatens to undercut the power, particularly military power, available to the United States in the region but it also exacerbates some of the problems in the region. American jingoism that replaces the

Soviet Union with Japan as our major strategic adversary is hardly going to have a neutral impact on the Japanese. Equally troubling is the fact that such hostility can lead other states in the region to try to exploit the U.S.-Japanese tensions. China and eventually Russia might be tempted if we create openings for them.

Finally, let us consider strategic requirements for the United States. This process implies that we know our goals and strategy. For this analysis we make the following assumptions. First, in the post-Cold War era, the United States will reduce its forces in Northeast Asia but will by no means withdraw. Second, it will remain engaged, not to dominate the region but to play a balance-of-power role, seeking to perpetuate both the present strategic equilibrium and regional change that favors the interests of the United States and its allies. In other words, U.S. strategy will not be devoted entirely to maintenance of the status quo. It will promote some changes and oppose others, depending on how they affect our interests.

The primary requirement is a healthy global economy with the United States as its leader. A protectionist United States, even if reasonably prosperous, will be unable to play its old strategic role in Northeast Asia. This role includes, of course, keeping Japan heavily engaged with and dependent on the U.S. economy, and accepting growing dependence on the Japanese economy. Such interdependence is not bad; it is good and essential for our strategic power in that region. The reasons should be fairly obvious, but let us underscore some of the most important ones:

- Economic interdependence will make Japanese rearmament less likely.
- Economic interdependence is a major contributor to the economic boom on the Asian rimland.
- Economic interdependence will continue to constrain Japanese policy far more than it will constrain U.S. policy.
- Economic interdependence is increasingly important to the U.S. military-industrial base. The United States will not be able to fight future wars with U.S. economic autarky, as it did in World War II.[1] It will have to accept dependence on some foreign suppliers. Japan and Korea will be two of the three or four most important foreign suppliers.

Within U.S. national security policymaking circles, there are signs of confusion and ambivalence on the value of economic interdependence with Japan. (Korea is becoming part of the interdependency circle as well.) The United States must overcome these concerns. If our analysis is accurate, this ambivalence threatens U.S. interests in Northeast Asia. If it is wrong, the opposing case needs to be made cogently and accepted—and a different strategy formulated. We do not rule out that possibility, but we accord it very low probability. The arguments against interdependency are weak and the costs of autarky high.

The second strategic requirement—one highly dependent on the first—is an indefinite U.S. military presence in the region. The naval component should remain very large, and an operationally significant ground presence in Korea is also imperative. Ground forces are not only are more visibly reassuring; they also require interaction between the Korean and U.S. military staffs. The political value of that kind of connection should not be underestimated. It makes it far more difficult for either side to abandon the relationship abruptly and without consultation and thoughtful consideration. The U.S. naval and air presence in Japan provides the same kind of connection there without a significant ground-force presence. The small Japanese naval and air forces, working with their U.S. counterparts, provide an adequate U.S.-Japanese military tie. Over the past decade the Japanese Ground Self-Defense Force has been eager to increase its ties to the U.S. Army and the Marine Corps. There is no reason to discourage that connection, and good reasons to respond positively. Compared to Korea, however, where the army is such a dominant institution, a ground-force presence is much less important.

The third strategic requirement is a new and broadly accepted threat rationale for the U.S. military in the region. The Soviet threat, or a potential new Russian version of it, is no longer adequate either for military planning or for winning public support. The primary purpose of U.S. military power in Northeast Asia is to maintain good relations between Japan and South Korea, to help them cooperate despite their painful mutual experiences in the past. A secondary purpose is to slow or prevent Japanese rearmament and thereby allay Chinese fears of Japanese military power, and perhaps also similar Russian trepidations. Finally, the third purpose is to help manage a peaceful unification of Korea and retain its strong strategic dependency on the United States.

Some of the conditions sustaining the present regional balance have begun to change. First, the Soviet threat has vanished, and a successor Russian threat cannot emerge in the next several years, if it ever does. Second, the prospect of Korean unification is no longer fanciful. Both of these changes threaten to stimulate additional movement—Japanese rearmament, Japanese and Chinese efforts to block Korean unification, and U.S. military withdrawal from the region. Only the military weakness of China appears insulated from change once this sequence of reactions begins. Add nuclear proliferation to the equation and the outlook is deeply disturbing.

There are several scenarios that could produce this chain of events, but most of them are preventable if the United States meets the proposed strategic requirements—economic and military. The scenario that deserves fairly urgent attention, as our analysis has repeatedly emphasized, is an early reunification of Korea to which Japan and China remain opposed and from which the United States, either by choice or by force of events, stands aside. Although our analysis has been cast at a higher level of generality, let us descend for a moment to the particulars of how this outcome could be prevented. The exercise also serves the larger purpose of helping to shift American attention from the secondary to the primary issues in the region.

For several years now, American official and public attention has been directed toward U.S.-Japanese trade relations, at China's domestic politics and its trading practices, and at the prospects of U.S. military withdrawals from the region. More recently, the North Korean nuclear weapons program has galvanized some attention. If our analysis of the region demonstrates anything, it is that these focal points for U.S. policy reflect a woeful misunderstanding of the likely post-Cold War dynamics for Northeast Asia. More troubling, they not only keep American eyes off the key challenges for maintaining the regional balance; they can easily help upset the balance.

Every state in the region but North Korea desires the retention of a considerable U.S. military presence in Northeast Asia. Even China tacitly admits as much. Only a few Americans and many North Koreans are calling for its removal. The immediate reason for this remarkable consensus is deep concern over the impending changes in Korea. The larger concern is what those changes mean for Japanese rearmament.

If the United States focused its attention and energies on this issue, it could very probably manage the transition on the Korean peninsula in a way that leaves the regional balance undisturbed. The tactics of such a policy could vary widely, but some key parameters, if recognized early in the process, allow Washington to seize the initiative with a very strong gambit. First, the costs of rebuilding the North Korean economy will greatly exceed the means in South Korea if the process is to move speedily to a successful conclusion. By comparison with West Germany and East Germany, respectively, South Korea lacks economic power and North Korea is in much worse economic shape. Second, Japan could easily provide adequate capital to make this economic challenge manageable. Third, Japan is deeply concerned about Korea obtaining nuclear weapons. Fourth, South Korea neither wants a rearmed Japan nor an early American military withdrawal—although some Korean nationalists, certainly after reunification, would press for the expulsion of U.S. forces. These four realities offer the United States a great opportunity if it seeks the proper goals with timely initiative.

The goals of the U.S. strategy, of course, should be a reunified Korea that retains at least some U.S. forces, retention of U.S. forces in Japan, and good relations between Japan and Korea. These are the conditions for a new equilibrium in the region. Russia is likely to favor them. China cannot easily prevent them and may come to prefer them.

Now what is the process for getting to the goals? To begin, the United States should become more openly supportive of reunification on Seoul's terms and give that aim very high priority in U.S. policy toward the region, much higher than relations with China, for example. Next, to add specificity, Washington should begin laying the groundwork for a new relationship between Seoul and Tokyo based on the four parameters listed above. Its essence is a major Japanese-Korean-American deal over Korean reunification.

Japan should be encouraged to provide abundant capital assistance to Seoul when reunification eventually occurs. South Korean leaders, of course, will want the assistance, but they should not receive it without a *quid pro quo* consisting of two commitments to Japan and the United States. First, South Korea should foreswear all aspirations to acquire nuclear weapons, promising to dismantle Pyongyang's program if it falls into their hands. Second, the Korean leaders, including not only incumbents but also opposition political leaders to the extent possible, should commit themselves to indefinite maintenance of at least a modest U.S. military presence after unification. These two conditions should allay Japanese concerns about a reunified Korea. In addition to economic assistance for reconstruction in the north, Korea should also obtain a Japanese commitment to keep a significant U.S. military presence as well.

Such a three-way deal provides each state what it needs and demands from it what it is best able to give. Most important, it offers a route to a new and stable regional balance of power. Both Japan and a unified Korea would retain their strategic anchor with the United States, and they would be more dependent on each other in ways that would dampen mutual suspicions about Japanese rearmament and Korean military potential.

Given what our analysis tells us about the other powers in the region, namely China and Russia, they may not like all aspects of this deal, but their own interests in regional stability would be served by it, particularly hedging against Japanese rearmament and a Korean nuclear weapons capability. On the whole, they would probably welcome it. Only the Pyongyang regime loses from it, but the North Korean population would win handsomely.

This scheme is not the only way to lead the region through the post-Cold War dynamics to a new and stable power balance, but it demonstrates how the transition could be managed successfully. The critic, of course, will ask what is in it for the United States. Washington is left with its traditional military burden while everyone else seems to profit at the expense of the American taxpayer. The answer to this question raises the larger issue of the American role in the world, whether the United States can turn inward safely while making few or no investments in the maintenance of the old international security order, or whether a continued—although reduced—global engagement is required for both our military security and our economic well-being. Let us, therefore, end with some reflections on this central issue.

The Larger Strategic Meaning for the United States and the New World Order

The "new world order" is thrown around as a slogan without much content. If it is to have any content, some of it might be derived from our analysis of Northeast Asia. Consider its strategic meaning in historical perspective.

Like the emergence of German power in Europe, the emergence of Japanese power in East Asia has been among the most important political developments in this century. Japanese leaders proved remarkably inept in handling this process, but American leaders also acted with less-than-acute strategic insight. The result was fascism in Japan, and war with China, Korea, and the Soviet Union in the 1930s. Finally, Japan went to war against the United States.

The war did not solve the problem. It set it aside and gave the United States and Japan four decades of experience with a new relationship. Now, however, the old Japanese problem, like the German problem in Europe, is back on the agenda. The context is much changed, but the historical memories of the two nations are perhaps less so. That can make it difficult to advance solutions that presuppose fundamental changes.

One major change is that Korea is now wrapped up in the Japanese problem. To succeed in keeping the region stable, the United States must maintain effective strategic ties to both of these states despite the fact that they fear each other as much as any other regional power.

If the solution is to be reduced to its bare essentials, it must be based on this feature of the historical record: For most of the 20th century, the United States has had good relations with either China or Japan, but never with both. Only in the 1970s was it able to establish stable relations with both at the same time. Having good relations with both nations would make it much easier for the United States to balance the region. A corollary historical lesson is that strong U.S.-Japanese-Korean ties make a war in East Asia difficult to start. Indeed, whenever the United States has had poor or hostile relations with Japan, war has soon occurred in East Asia. The U.S. military connections to Japan and Korea, therefore, take on major significance for a "new world order" in Northeast Asia. Admittedly, they also depend on the economic connections.

Germany plays a similar role in its military alliance with the United States. While it remains in NATO it will remain the foundation of the Atlantic Alliance. NATO with Germany is the military element required for a "new world order" in Europe. The implications of its rupture are no less destabilizing for Europe than the consequences of a rupture of the U.S.-Japanese-Korean military connection would be for Northeast Asia. Also, to maintain both these sets of connections at the same time will require a new public rationale with which to replace the defunct Soviet threat. A formula for a "new world order" must include that rationale.

A strong world economy is as important for U.S. strategy toward Europe as for U.S. strategy in Northeast Asia. America's military power depends on it. The causal relationship is not unilateral, however. The four-decade postwar global economic boom was made possible by the security umbrella of U.S. military power in Europe and East Asia, and this protection was not just against the Soviet threat. Just as important was the fact that it allowed cooperation between old adversaries such as Korea and Japan. It enabled the members of EC—mostly longtime military adversaries—to risk unprecedented cooperation and mutual trust. The Western advanced industrial powers are unlikely to be able to manage the global economy successfully if the key Cold War alliance structures and military deployments cannot be maintained, albeit in somewhat modified form, in the decades ahead. Economic prosperity and military security have become highly interdependent in both Western Europe and Northeast Asia.

The most important point here is that our success in maintaining the strategic balance in Northeast Asia through changing times in the decade ahead will affect more than just that region. Failure to maintain that balance would also affect Europe and most of the U.S.'s alliance systems. The stakes are global. The challenges are not yet as conspicuous as those in Europe, but they can be expected to become as large; they will also be somewhat analogous, yet highly particular.

NOTES

[1] For an insightful analysis of this point, see Theodore H. Moran, "International Economics and National Security," *Foreign Affairs*, 69, Winter, 1990/91, pp. 74-90.

Bibliography

Ahn, Byung-Joon. "Decision-Sharing in Korea-U.S. Relations," *Korea and World Affairs*, Vol. XIV, no.1 (Spring 1990).

Ahn, Byung-Joon. "South Korean-Soviet Relations: Issues and Prospects," *Korea and World Affairs*, Vol.XIV, no.4 (Winter 1990).

Alagappa, Muthiah. "Japan's Political and Security Role in the Asia-Pacific Region," *Contemporary Southeast Asia*, Vol.10, no.1 (June 1988).

Aliyev, Rafik Shagi-Akzamovich. "The Soviet Union in East Asia: Reality and Problems," *Mirovaya ekonomika i mezhdunarodnye otnosheniya*, No.9 (September 1990).

Alves, Dora, ed. *Change, Interdependence and Security in the Pacific Basin. The 1990 Pacific Symposium*. Washington, DC: National Defense University Press, 1991.

Alves, Dora, ed. *Evolving Pacific Basin Strategies. The 1989 Pacific Symposium*. Washington, DC: National Defense University Press, 1990.

Alves, Dora, ed. *Cooperative Security in the Pacific Basin. The 1988 Pacific Symposium*. Washington, DC: National Defense University Press, 1990.

Alves, Dora, ed. *Pacific Security Toward the Year 2000. The 1987 Pacific Symposium*. Washington, DC: National Defense University Press, 1988.

AsiaWeek.

Asian Defence Journal.

Asian Wall Street Journal.

Barnett, A. Doak. *The Making of Foreign Policy in China: Structure and Process*. Boulder, CO: Westview Press, 1985.

Barnett, Robert W. *Beyond War: Japan's Concept of Comprehensive National Security*. Washington, DC: Pergamon Brassey, 1984.

Bean, R. Mark. *Cooperative Security in Northeast Asia: A China, Japan, South Korea Coalition Approach*. Washington, DC: National Defense University Press, 1990.

Calder, Kent E. "The United States and Japan: From Occupation to Global Partnership," in *American Diplomacy since World War II*. ed. L. Carl Brown. (1989).

Calder, Kent E. "Japanese Foreign Economic Policy Formation: Explaining the Reactive State," *World Politics*, Vol. XL, no.4 (July 1988).

Chen Yizi. *China: Ten Years Reform and the Democratic Movement in 1989*. Taipei, Taiwan, ROC: LianJin Press, 1990.

Cheng, Chu-yuan. *Behind the Tiananmen Massacre: Social, Political, and Economic Ferment in China*. Boulder, CO: Westview Press, 1990.

China, People's Republic of. Ministry of Foreign Economic Relations and Trade. *Almanac of China's Foreign Economic Relations and Trade.* (Beijing, 1990).

China, People's Republic of. National Statistics Bureau. *Annual Statistics of China, 1990.* (Beijing, 1990).

Chou, David S. "The Prospects for Peking-Seoul Relations: A Taiwan Perspective," *Issues and Studies* Vol.26, no.9 (September 1990).

Clough, Ralph N. *Embattled Korea: The Rivalry for International Support.* Boulder, CO: Westview Press, 1987.

Clyde, Paul H. and Beers, Burton F. *The Far East: A History of Western Impacts and Eastern Responses.* 6th ed. Englewood Cliffs, NJ: Prentice Hall, 1975.

Corning, Gregory P. "US-Japan Security Cooperation in the 1990s: The Promise of High-Tech Defense," *Asian Survey*, Vol.XXIX, no.3 (March 1989).

Council on Foreign Relations. *Korea at the Crossroads: Implications for American Policy.* New York, NY: Council on Foreign Relations and The Asia Society, 1987.

Crowe, William J., Jr. and Romberg, Alan D. "Rethinking Security in the Pacific," *Foreign Affairs*, Vol.70 (Spring 1991).

da Cunha, Derek. *Soviet Naval Power in the Pacific.* Boulder, CO: Lynne Rienner Publishers, 1990.

Dellios, Rosita. *Modern Chinese Defence Strategy: Present Developments, Future Directions.* New York: St. Martin's Press, 1990.

Dreyer, June Teufel. "Civil-Military Relations in the People's Republic of China," *Comparative Strategy*, Vol.5, no.1 (1985).

Drifte, Reihard. *Japan's Foreign Policy.* New York, NY: the Royal Institute of International Affairs. Council on Foreign Relations, 1990.

Ellison, H.J., ed. *Japan and the Pacific Quadrille: The Major Powers in East Asia.* Boulder, CO: Westview Press, 1987.

Ellison, Herbert J., ed. *The Sino-Soviet Conflict: A Global Perspective.* Seattle, WA: University of Washington Press, 1982.

Falkenheim, Victor C., ed. *Chinese Politics from Mao to Deng.* New York, NY: Paragon, 1989.

Falkenheim, Peggy L. "The Soviet Union, Japan, and East Asia: The Security Dimensions," *Journal of Northeast Asian Studies* (Winter 1984).

Falkenheim, Peggy L. "Moscow and Tokyo: Slow Thaw in Northeast Asia," *SAIS Review*, Vol.11, no.1 ( ).

Far Eastern Economic Review.

Fedulova, N.G. "USSR-US-PRC Relations and some Tendencies in International Developments," *Mirovaya ekonomika i mezhdunarodnye otnosheniya*, no.6 (June 1990).

Foreign Broadcast Information Service (FBIS). *East Asia.*

Garrett, Banning N. and Glaser, Bonnie S. "Chinese Assessments of Global Trends and the Emerging Era in International Relations," *Asian Survey*, Vol. XXIX, no.4 (April 1989).

Garrity, Patrick J.; Endicott, John E.; and Goetze, Richard B. *Regional Security Issues.* Washington, DC: National Defense University Press, 1991.

Ge, Gengfu. "Changes in the Development of Japan's Defence Policy and Defence Capacities," *Guoji wenti yanjiu*, no.1 (January 13, 1989).

Gorbachev, Mikhail S. *Perestroika: New Thinking for Our Country and the World.*

New York: Harper & Row, 1987.

Gordon, Bernard K. "The Asian-Pacific Rim," *Foreign Affairs* Vol.70, no.1 (1990/91).

Gregor, A. James. *Land of the Morning Calm: Korea and American Security*. Lanham, MD: University Press of America, 1990.

Gregor, A. James. *The People's Republic of China and the Security of East Asia*. Montclair, CA: The Claremont Institute, 1988.

Grinter, Lawrence E. and Kihl, Young Whan, ed. *East Asian Conflict Zones: Prospects for Regional Stability and Deescalation*. New York, NY: St. Martin's Press, 1987.

Hamrin, Carol Lee. *China and the Challenge of the Future: Changing Political Patterns*. Boulder, CO: Westview Press, 1990.

Harding, Harry. *China's Second Revolution: Reform After Mao*. Washington, DC: Brookings Institution, 1987.

Harrison, Selig S. and Prestowitz, Clyde V., Jr. "Pacific Agenda: Defense or Economics?" *Foreign Policy* (Summer 1990).

Hickey, Dennis Van Vranken. "America's Military Relations with the People's Republic of China: The Need for Reassessment," *Journal of Northeast Asian Studies*, Vol.VII, no.3 (Fall 1988).

Hinton, Harold C.; Kindermann, Gottfried-Karl; Lee, Chung Min; Lee, Jung Ha; Pfaltzgraff, Robert L.; and Zagoria, Donald. *The U.S.-Korean Security Relationship: Prospects and Challenges for the 1990s*. Washington, DC: Pergamon-Brassey's, 1988.

Hoffman, Stanley; Keohane, Robert O.; and Mearsheimer, John. "Back to the Future, Part II: International Relations Theory and Post-Cold War Europe." *International Security*, Vol.15 (Fall 1990).

Ikle, Fred and Nakanishi, Terumasa. "Japan's Grand Strategy," *Foreign Affairs*, Vol.69 (Summer 1990).

Inoguchi, Takshi and Iwai, Tomoaki. *Zoku Giin no Kenkyu (Research on tribal dietmen)*. Tokyo, Japan: Nihon Keizai Shimbun Sha, 1987.

Ivanov, V.I. "The Soviet Union and the Asia-Pacific Region: Evolution or Radical Change," *Mirovaya ekonomika i mezhdunarodnye otnosheniya*, no.9 (September 1990).

Jane's Information Group. *China in Crisis: The Role of the Military*. Surrey, UK: Jane's Defence Data, 1989.

Japan: An International Comparison, 1989. Tokyo: Keizei Koho Center, 1989.

Jencks, Harlan W. "The Military in China," *Current History*, Vol. 88, no. 539 (September 1989).

Jencks, Harlan W. *From Muskets to Missiles: Politics and Professionalism in the Chinese Army, 1945-1981*. Boulder, CO: Westview Press, 1982.

Jervis, Robert and Bialer, Seweryn, eds. *Soviet-American Relations after the Cold War*. Durham, NC: Duke University Press, 1991.

Joffe, Ellis. "People's War under Modern Conditions: A Doctrine for Modern War," *The China Quarterly*, no.112 (December 1987).

Johnson, LCDR Paul G., USN. "Japan: A True Partner in Defense," *US Naval Institute Proceedings* (March 1990).

Kane, Anthony J., ed. *China Briefing, 1990*. Boulder, CO: Westview Press, 1990.

Kaplan, Stephen S. *Diplomacy of Power*. Washington, DC: The Brookings

Institution, 1981.
Kato, Ryozo. "Present and Future Role and Missions of the Japanese Self-Defense Forces," in *The Pacific in the 1990s*, ed. Janos Radvanyi. Lanham, MD: University Press of America, 1990.
Kenkyukai, Heiwamondai. *Kokusai Kokka nihon no sogo anzenhosho seisaku (Comprehensive security policy for an international Japan)*. Tokyo: Okurasho Insatsukyoku, 1985.
Keohane, Robert O. *After Hegemony: Cooperation and Discord in the World Political Economy*. Princeton, NJ: Princeton University Press, 1984.
Kihl, Young Whan. *Politics and Policies in Divided Korea: Regimes in Contest*. Boulder, CO: Westview Press, 1984.
Kihl, Young Whan and Grinter, Lawrence E. *Security, Strategy, and Policy Responses in the Pacific Rim*. Boulder, CO: Lynne Rienner Publishers, 1989.
Kim, Hong Nack. "The Normalization of North Korean-Japanese Diplomatic Relations: Problems and Prospects," *Korea and World Affairs*, Vol.XIV, no.4 (Winter 1990).
Kim, Samuel. *China and the World: New Directions in Chinese Foreign Relations*. 2nd edition. Boulder, CO: Westview Press, 1989.
Kirichenko, Aleksei A. "Vladivostok 88: Hopes and Prospects," *Mirovaya ekonomika i mezhdunarodnye otnosheniya*, no.2 (February 1989).
Koh, B.C. "Seoul's `Northern Policy' and Korean Security," *The Korean Journal of Defense Analysis*, Vol. 1, no.1 (Summer 1989).
Koh, Byung Chul. *The Foreign Policy Systems of North and South Korea*. Berkley: University of California Press, 1984.
Korea, Republic of. Ministry of National Defense. *Defense White Paper 1990*.
Korea, Republic of. National Unification Board. *Overall Assessment of the North Korea Economic Situation for 1989*. (October 1989).
Kovalenko, I.I. "On a Complex Approach to the Problem of Asian Security," *Problemy dal'nego vostoka*, no.1 (January 1986).
Kunadze, G.F. "Soviet Union-Japan: How We See Each Other." *Mirovaya ekonomika i mezhdunarodnye otnosheniya*, no.3 (March 1990).
Kunadze, G.F. "New Thinking and Soviet Policy Regarding Japan." *Mirovaya ekonomika i mezhdunarodnye otnosheniya*, no.8 (August 1989).
Kunadze, G.F. "Reflecting on Soviet-Japanese Relations," *Mirovaya ekonomika i mezhdunarodnye otnosheniya*, no.5 (May 1989).
Kuriyama, Takakazu. "*New Directions for Japanese Foreign Policy in the Changing World of the 1990s: Making Active Contributions to the Creation of a New International Order*." (English language version) Tokyo (1990).
Laird, Robbin F., ed. Soviet Foreign Policy. Proceedings of the American Academy of Political Science, Vol.36, no.4 (New York, 1987).
Laird, Robbin F. and Hoffmann, Erik P., eds. *Soviet Foreign Policy in a Changing World*. New York: Aldine de Gruyter, 1986.
Lampton, David M., ed. *Policy Implementation in Post-Mao China*. Berkeley: University of California Press, 1987.
Lee, Sam K. "United States-Japan Security Relations: A Need for Realism," *Comparative Strategy*, Vol.9, no.2 (1990).
Lee, Ngok. *China's Defence Modernisation and Military Leadership*. Sydney: Australian National University Press, 1989.

Legvold, Robert. "The Revolution in Soviet Foreign Policy," *Foreign Affairs* Vol.68, no.1 (1988/89).
Levine, Norman D. "Global Detente and North Korea's Strategic Relations." *The Korean Journal of Defense Analysis*, Vol.II, no.1 (Summer 1990).
Levine, Steven I. "The Uncertain Future of Chinese Foreign Policy," *Current History*, Vol.88, no.539 (September 1989).
Lieberthal, Kenneth and Oksenberg, Michel. *Policy Making in China: Leaders, Structures, and Processes*. Princeton, NJ: Princeton University Press, 1988.
Lincoln, Edward J. "Japan's Role in Asia-Pacific Cooperation: Dimensions, Prospects, and Problems." *Journal of Northeast Asian Studies*, Vol. VIII, no.4 (Winter 1989).
Lugovskoi, Yu. "The Krasnoyarsk Initiatives and Security of the APR." *Azii i afriki cegodnya*, no.2 (February 1989).
Machado, Kit G. "Japanese Transnational Corporations in Malaysia's State Sponsored Heavy Industrialization Drive: The HICOM Automobile and Steel Projects," *Pacific Affairs*, Vol.62, no.4 (Winter 1989-90).
Making, John H. and Hellmann, Donald C., eds. *Sharing World Leadership?: A New Era for America and Japan*. Washington, DC: American Enterprise Institute, 1989.
Manning, Robert A. *Asian Policy: The New Soviet Challenge in the Pacific*. New York: Priority Press Publications, 1988.
MccGwire, Michael. *Military Objectives in Soviet Foreign Policy*. Washington, DC: The Brookings Institution, 1987.
Mearsheimer, John J. "Back to the Future: Instability in Europe after the Cold War." *International Security*, Vol.15 (Summer 1990).
Menon, Rajan. "Gorbachev's Japan Policy." *Survival* Vol.32 (March/April).
Mikheyev, Vasili. "The Korean Problem in the Future," *International Affairs*, Vol.9 (1989), pp.138-47.
Mills, William de B. "Gorbachev and the Future of Sino-Soviet Relations," *Political Science Quarterly*, Vol.101, no.4 (1986).
Nishihara, Masashi. "Japan's Gradual Defense Buildup and Korean Security," *The Korean Journal of Defense Analysis*, Vol. 1, no.1 (Summer 1989).
Olsen, Edward A. "U.S.-ROK Relations: Common Issues and Uncommon Perceptions," *Korea and World Affairs*, Vol. XIII, no.1 (Spring 1989).
Olsen, Edward A. *U.S. Policy and the Two Koreas*. Boulder, CO: Westview Press, 1988.
Olsen, Edward A. and Jurika, Stephen, eds. *The Armed Forces in Contemporary Asian Societies*. Boulder, CO: Westview Press, 1986.
Orr, Robert M., Jr. "Collaboration or Conflict?: Foreign Aid and U.S.-Japan Relations," *Pacific Affairs*, Vol.62, no.4 (Winter 1989-90).
Pacific Defence Reporter.
Pacific Regional Security: The 1985 Pacific Symposium. Washington, DC: National Defense University Press, 1988.
Park Chung Hee. *Korea Reborn: A Model for Development*. Englewood Cliffs, NJ: Prentice-Hall, 1979.
Park, Sang-Seek. "Northern Diplomacy and Inter-Korea Relations," *Korea and World Affairs*, Vol. XII, no.4 (Winter 1988).
Pfaltzgraff, Jr., Robert L. "Korea's Emerging Role in World Politics," *Korea and*

World Affairs, Vol. XI, no.1 (Spring 1987).
Pi, Ying-hsien. "Peking-Moscow Relations as seen from Li Peng's Visit to the Soviet Union." *Issues and Studies*, Vol.26, no.9 (September 1990).
Polomka, Peter. "Towards a Pacific House," *Survival* 33 (March/April 1991).
Pye, Lucian W. *Asian Power and Politics: The Cultural Dimensions of Authority.* Cambridge, MA: Harvard University Press, 1985.
Rhee Sang-Woo. "North Korea in 1990: Lonesome Struggle to Keep Chuch'e," *Asian Survey*, Vol. XXXI, no.1 (January 1991).
Rix, Alan. "Japan's Foreign Aid Policy: A Capacity for Leadership?" *Pacific Affairs*, Vol.62, no.4 (Winter 1989-90).
Russett, Bruce M.; Risse-Kappen, Thomas; and Mearsheimer, John J. "Back to the Future, Part II: Realism and the Realities of European Security." *International Security*, Vol.15 (Winter 1990/91).
Saito, Shiro. *Japan at the Summit: Its Role in the Western Alliance and in Asian Pacific Cooperation*. London: Routledge, 1990.
Scalapino, Robert A.; Sato, Seizaburo; Wanandi, Jusuf; and Han, Sung-Joo, eds. *Regional Dynamics: Security, Political, and Economic Issues in the Asia-Pacific Region.* Jakarta, Indonesia: Centre for Strategic and International Studies, 1990.
Schwartz, Benjamin. "The Chinese Perceptions of World Order, Past and Present," in *The Chinese World Order: Traditional China's Foreign Relations*. ed. John K. Fairbank. Cambridge, MA: Harvard University Press, 1968.
Shaw, Yu-ming. *Power and Policy in the PRC.* Boulder, CO: Westview Press, 1985.
Shevarnadze, E.A. "ATP: Dialog, Peace, and Collaboration." *Mezhdunarodnaya zhizn'*, No.10 (1990).
Simon, Sheldon W. "Security and Uncertainty in the North Pacific," *The Korean Journal of Defense Analysis*, Vol.II, no.2 (Winter 1990).
Singh, Bilveer. "The Asia-Pacific in the Era of Reduced Soviet Military Presence." *Issues and Studies*, Vol.26, no.9 (September 1990).
Solomon, Richard. "Asian Security in the 1990s: Integration in Economics, Diversity in Defense." *Dispatch*, Vol.1, no.10 United States Department of State.
Sogoanzenhosho Kenyu Gurupu. *Sogoanzenhosho Senryaku (Comprehensive Security Strategy).* Tokyo: Okurasho Insatsukyokyu, 1980.
Stephen, John J. "Asia in the Soviet Conception," in *Soviet Policy in Asia*. ed. Donald S. Zagoria. New Haven: Yale University Press, 1982.
Suh, Dae-Sook. "Changes in North Korea and Inter-Korean Relations," *Korea and World Affairs*, Vol. XIV, no.4 (Winter 1990).
Swaine, Michael D. "China Faces the 1990s: A System in Crisis." *Problems of Communism*, Vol. XXXIX, no.3 (May-June 1990).
Thambipillai, Pushpa and Matuszewski, Daniel C., eds. *The Soviet Union and the Asia-Pacific Region: Views from the Region.* New York, NY: Praeger, 1989.
Tikhonov, V.D.; Chufrin, G.I.; and Sulitskaya, T.I., eds. *Mezhdunarodnye otnosheniya y yugo-vostochnoi asii v sovremennom etape*. Moscow: Nauka, 1988.
Tsvetsov, P. "New Thinking in the APR," *Aziya i Afrika cegodnya*, no.12 (December 1988).
van Wolferen, Karel. "The Japan Problem," *Foreign Affairs* (Winter 1986-87).
Voronstov, V. and Muradyan, A. "APR Security: Concepts and Reality," *Far*

Bibliography 145

Eastern Affairs, no.1 (January 1990).
Waltz, Kenneth N. *Theory of International Politics*. New York: Random House, 1979.
Waltz, Kenneth N. *Man, the State, and War: A Theoretical Analysis*. New York: Columbia University Press, 1959.
Weinstein, Franklin B. and Kamiya, Fuji. *The Security of Korea: U.S. and Japanese Perspectives on the 1980s*. Boulder, CO: Westview Press, 1980.
Weinstein, Martin E. "Trade Problems and U.S.-Japan Security Cooperation," *The Washington Quarterly*, Vol. 11, no.1 (Winter 1988).
Wheeler, J.W. "The Transformation of Japanese Foreign and Defense Policy: The Impact of Domestic Politics." HI-4014. Indianapolis, IN: Hudson Institute, October 1990.
Whiting, Allen S. *Siberian Development and East Asia: Threat or Promise?* Stanford, CA: Stanford University Press, 1981.
Whiting, Allen S. and Xin Jianfei. "Sino-Japanese Relations: Pragmatism and Passion." *World Policy Journal*
Wolf, Charles; Henry, Donald P.; Yeh, K.C.; Hayes, James H.; Schank, John; and Sneider, Richard L. *The Changing Balance: South and North Korean Capabilities for Long-Term Military Competition*. Santa Monica, CA: RAND, December 1985.
Wood, Perry L. and Naomuhan Bayat. "Chinese Politics and Chinese Defense Policy: Implications for the PLAN and Chinese Maritime Power in the 1990s." HI-4013. Indianapolis, IN: Hudson Institute, October 1990.
Wood, Perry L. "South Korea: Towards Stable Democratic Government." HI-4048-P. Indianapolis, IN: Hudson Institute, December 1988.
Wood, Perry L. and Kearney, Adrienne A. "South Korea: The Politicization of Trade Policy." HI-3836-P. Indianapolis, IN: Hudson Institute, May 1986.
Woon, Eden Y. "Chinese Arms Sales and US-China Military Relations," in *Essays on Strategy VII*, ed. Thomas C. Gill. Washington, DC: National Defense University Press, 1990.
Wortzel, Larry M., ed. *China's Military Modernization: International Implications*. New York, NY: Greenwood Press, 1988.
Xi, Zhihao. "Japan is Stepping up Arms Expansion." *Jiefangjun bao (Liberation Army Daily)* (August 28, 1989).
Xiang, Huang. "Sino-US Relations over the Past Year," *Beijing Review* (February 15-28, 1988).
Xu, Kui. "The Prospects of Sino-Soviet Relations." *Foreign Affairs Journal* (Beijing). (June 1989).
Yang, Richard H., ed. *China's Military: The PLA in 1990/91*. Kaohsiung, Taiwan, ROC: National Sun Yat-sen University, 1991.
Yang, Richard H., ed. *SCPS Yearbook on PLA Affairs 1988/89*. Kaohsiung, Taiwan, ROC: National Sun Yat-sen University, 1989.
Yang, Richard H., ed. *SCPS Yearbook on PLA Affairs 1987*. Kaohsiung, Taiwan, ROC: National Sun Yat-sen University, 1988.
Yasutomo, Dennis T. "Why Aid?: Japan as an `Aid Great Power.'" *Pacific Affairs*, Vol.62, no.4 (Winter 1989-90).
Yim, Yong Soon. "The Impact of Change in Eastern Europe on the Korean Peninsula." *Korea and World Affairs*, Vol.14, no.3 (Fall 1990).

Yoshida, Shigedu. *The Yoshida Memoirs*. London: Heinemann, 1961.
Yu, Suk-Ryul. "Political Succession and Policy Change in North Korea," *Korea and World Affairs*, Vol. 10, no.1 (Spring 1986).
Zagoria, Donald S. "The Moscow-Beijing Detente," *Foreign Affairs*, Vol.61 (Spring 1983).
Zagoria, Donald S., ed. *Soviet Policy in East Asia*. New Haven: Yale University Press, 1982.
Zagoria, Donald S. *Vietnam Triangle: Moscow, Peking, Hanoi*. New York: Pegasus, 1967.

Index

Abe, Shintaro, 67
Afghanistan, 15, 18
Ahn, Byung-Joon, 110 n.16, 111 n.26
Albania, 1
Aliyev, Rafik Shagi-Akzamovich, 15-16, 22-23, 30 n.11
Anti-Americanism in South Korea, 91-92
Arbartov, Georgi, 66
Asia-Pacific Economic Council (APEC), 89
"Asia-Pacific-Region"(APR), 14, 17, 23, 115
Asian Games in Beijing, (1990), 46
"Asian Security System," 8-9

Bandung Principles, 12, 18
Beijing Summit with Gorbachev, (1989), 18-19
Breslauer, George W., 6 n.4
Brezhnev, Leonid, 8-9, 12
Bush, George, 91

Calder, Kent E., 12, 81 n.5, 82 n.40-42
Cambodia, 12
Carter, Jimmy, 60
Chaebol business conglomerates, 84
Chen, Yizi, 39-40, 55 n.13
China, 2, 4; as arms seller, 52; challenge to international order, 33, 35; Cultural Revolution, 48, 49; leadership, 39; Deng Xiaoping, 35-36; domestic issues, 36-40; foreign trade, 40; GNP, 37, 71; historical legacy in Northeast Asia, 33-36; "inward-looking," 53, 120-21; leadership, 39; Maoist rule, 34; military, 2, 36, 51-52; modernization, 71; nationalism, 33, 53-54; nuclear forces, 8; participation in world system, 36; politics, 53; reform process, 36-37; Sino-centric period, 33; society and state conflict, 39; and Soviet Bloc, 1; victimization period, 33-35
China: economic issues, 37-39, 40, 53, 71-72; Japan, 45
China: foreign policy, 32-36, 54, 69-70; Japan, 43-46, 122; Korean reunification, 26, 46, 100-101, 117; North Korea, 35, 47-49, 100, 122; Northeast Asia, 31-36, 40-41, 52-54, 119-23; South Korea, 35, 46-49, 99-101, 122; Soviet Union, 3, 18-20, 34, 41-43, 52-54, 121; Taiwan, 18, 35, 51; United States, 34-35, 49-52, 123
Chinese Communist Party (CCP), 7, 33-34
Chinese Nationalists, 7
Chollima, 48
Chong Whi Kim, 110 n.17
Chuch'e (self-reliance), 85, 103
Chun Doo Hwan, 87
Clifford, Mark, 38, 111 n.34
Clines, Francis X., 17, 30 n.12
Cold War end, 1-2, 5-6
Comprehensive Security foreign policy plan, 65
Czechoslovakia, 1, 24

Darlin, Damon, 111 n.35
"Deideologization," 15-16, 23, 27
Democratic People's Republic of Korea

(DPRK). See North Korea
Democratic Russia party, 24
Deng Xiaoping, 35, 39, 51, 108

Engles, F., 54 n.1
Europe versus Northeast Asia, impact of Cold War, 2

Federation of Economic Organizations, 68
Fedulaova, N.G., 19

Ge Gengfu, 55 n.26
German model of reunification, 105
Glasnost, 9
"Global partnership" of United States and Japan, 65
Goodall, Alan, 82 n.24
Gorbachev, Mikhail, 1-2, 14-17, 23-25, 97
Gurupu, Sogoanzenhosho Kenyu, 81 n.7-8

Hallstein Doctrine, 85, 86
Harrison, Selig S., 80 n.3
Heiwamondai Kenkyukai, 15, 81 n.9, 82 n.26
"Hermit kingdom" of North Korea, 48
Hiraiwa, Gaishi, 68
Ho Chi Minh, 12
Hoffmann, Stanley, 2, 6 n.3
Hong Kong, 71
Hong Nack Kim, 111 n.21-23
Huang Xiang, 55 n.38
"Humankind interests," 14
Hungary, 1, 24, 88

IMEMO (Institute for Economics and International Affairs), 22
"Imperialist camp," 11
India, 13, 18
Indian Ocean "zone of peace," 15
Inooguchi, Takshi, 81 n.14
"International buffer zone," 69
International economy, 128
Iranian hostage crisis, 60
Ishihara, Shintaro, 62
Ivanov, V.I., 19
Iwai, Tomoaki, 81 n.14

Japan, 12; defense effort, 44-45, 93; demilitarization, 58; domestic issues, 44-45, 62-65, 123-24, 129-30; "economic miracle," 59-60; government-business relationship, 64; interest-group pressures, 64; military, 2, 68, 76, 80, 127; nationalism, 62, 129; Official Development Assistance program, 57; power emergence in East Asia, 136; security, 1; social structure, 63
Japan: economic issues, 59-60, 64, 123; China, 70-71; Northeast Asia, 56; South Korea, 72; United States, 4, 6, 59, 77-79, 132
Japan: foreign policy, 2, 57-64, 65, 68, 76, 79, 123-27, 136; China, 45, 69-72, 126; North Korea, 73, 74-75, 80, 94; Northeast Asia, 65-66; reactive, 62-64; Russia, 68-69; South Korea, 72-73, 75, 92-96 ; Soviet Union, 10, 66-69, 76-77, 125-26; United States, 3, 10, 21-22, 58, 65, 75-79, 126
"Japan-bashing," 79, 130
Japan Socialist Party (JSP), 94
The Japan That Can Say No (Ishihara), 62
Japanese Defense Agency, 124
Japanese Diet, 64, 76
Japanese Socialist Party (JSP), 62
Japanese-Soviet summit in Tokyo, 20
Jiang Zemin, 18

Kaifu, Toshiki, 64, 67, 73
Kaplan, Stephen S., 6 n.4
Kato, Ryozo, 82 n.37
Katusas, 92
Khrushchev, Nikita, 3; Third World policy, 12
Kim Chang Soon, 74
Kim Chong Whi, 82 n.30
Kim Dae Jung, 107
Kim Il Sung, 85, 94-95, 118; "work-harder campaign"
Kim Jong Il, 106-107
Kirichenko, Aleksei A., 30 n.28
Koh, Byung Chul, 85, 109 n.2-5, 110 n.7-8
Korean Peninsula. See North Korea;

Index 149

South Korea
Korean reunification, 25-27, 74-75, 83, 105-109, 119; China, 26, 46, 100-101, 117; Japan, 117, 135; South Korea, 107-108, 115-16; Soviet Union, 25-26, 115, 117; United States, 26-27, 134-35
Korean War, 7, 48, 86
Korean Workers' Party (KWP), 94
Krasnoyarsk speech, 14-15, 22
Kubo, Wataru, 95
Kunadze, G.F., 5, 7, 9, 10, 13, 20-21, 29 n.2, 30 n.3
Kurile Islands, 67
Kuriyama, Takakazu, 62, 81 n.11, 82 n.38

Lane, Charles, 82 n.33
Laos, 12
Lenin, Vladimir, 1, 11-12
Levin, Norman D., 111 n.37
Liberal Democratic Party (LDP), 58, 59, 62, 64, 94, 129
Lugovskoi, Yu, 30 n. 27

Mack, Andrew, 82 n.32
Makoto, Tanabe, 75
Manning, Robert A., 111 n.25
Mao Tsung, 7, 32, 35-36
Marxist-Leninism: class struggle, 9-10; ideology, 32, 48
McBeth, John, 110 n.13
Mearsheimer, John, 2, 6 n.1
Media control, 105
Menon, Rajan, 30 n.19-21
Mikheyev, Vasili, 24, 30 n.24
Moffat, Susan, 110 n.14
Moran, Theodore H., 137 n.1
Morita, Akio, 62

Nakasone, Yasuhiro, 58, 60, 61, 70
National Unification Board, 55 n.33
"New thinking," 12, 14-17, 21, 23, 114
"New world order," 50, 136-37
1952 San Francisco Peace Treaty, 59
Nishihara, Masashi, 82 n.29, 111 n.19
Nixon, Richard M., 60
"Nordpolitik," 84, 88-89

North Atlantic Treaty Organization (NATO), 1
North Korea, 11, 12, 83; chuch'e, 86; control of media, 105; domestic issues, 103, 105-109; economic issues, 48, 74, 103-104; GNP, 73; isolationism, 48, 102, 119; military spending, 73-74; nationalism, 85-86, 117; nuclear weapons, 74, 118; opportunity for change, 106
North Korea: foreign policy, 48-49, 84-87, 104; China, 99-100; Japan, 104; South Korea, 101-102, 105; Soviet Union, 96; United States, 91
Northeast Asia: balance of power, 3-4; equilibrium, 2-3; versus Europe on impact of Cold War, 2; intraregional factors, 113-14; strategic equilibrium, 113; U.S. military presence, 3
Northern Territories, 9-10, 12, 20, 22, 24, 27, 66-69, 125-26
Nuclear forces: China, 8; and Khrushchev, 12; North Korea, 74, 118

Official Development Assistance (ODA), 65
Ohira, Masayoshi, 61, 65
Olsen, Edward A., 110 n.11, 111 n.20
Ozawa, Ichiro, 64

Pakistan, 13
Park Chung Hee, 85-87, 110 n.5
Park Sang-Seek, 110 n.10, 112 n.44
"Peaceful coexistence," 12, 14-17
People's Liberation Army, 120
Perestroika, 16-17, 68
Persian Gulf War, 50, 73, 74
Pfaltzgraff, Jr., Robert L., 109 n.1, 111 n.36
Piontkovsky, Andrei, 67, 81 n.20
Plunk, Daryl M., 110 n.12
Poland, 1, 24
Policy Affairs Research Council, 64
PRC (People's Republic of China). See China
Prestowitz, Jr., Clyde V., 80 n.3
Quinn-Judge, Sophie, 38, 111 n.34

Reagan, Ronald, 60
Red Army, 120
Republic of Korea (ROK). See South Korea
Rhee, Syngman, 84-85
Rhee Sang-Woo, 111 n.32-33
Rogachev, Ivan, 20
Roh Tae Woo, 86-89, 95
ROK-Japan Basic Treaty, (1965), 94
Russia: foreign policy: Japan, 20; North Korea, 98-99; South Korea, 98. See also Soviet Union: foreign policy

Sato, Katsumi, 74
Scalapino, Robert A., 82 n.43
Sea of Okhotsk, 67
"Second image," 3
Segal, Gerald, 82 n.25
Shevardnadze, Eduard, 20, 23
Shiina, Motoo, 76
Shim Jae Hoon, 82 n.35, 111 n.24, 112 n.46
Shin, Kanemaru, 75, 95
Siberian boom, 68
Simon, Sheldon W., 111 n.27
Smith, Charles, 81 n.17
"Socialist camp," 11
South Korea, 2-4, 11, 12, 83, 86; democratization, 88-89; GNP, 73; military, 73-74; nationalism, 73, 85-86, 92, 117; Northern policies, 86-87; Park Chung Hee government, 85; presidential elections, 87-88; Rhee, Syngman, 84-85; Roh era, 87-89; 1950's, 84-85; United Nations, 88-90 South Korea's economic issues, 73, 84, 103; China, 100; Soviet Union, 97-98
South Korea: foreign policy, 83-87; China, 100; East Europe, 24; Japan, 85, 93, 94, 96; North Korea, 95, 102, 107, 118; Soviet Union, 25, 96-99; United States, 3, 89-91
Soviet Bloc, 1, 11
Soviet Far East, 16
Soviet hegemony, 1, 123
Soviet Union: Cold War, 1; collapse of state, 115, 128-29; collective-security schemes for Asia, 98; invasion of Afghanistan, 9; military, 1, 3, 8, 12, 18; "new thinking," 10, 18; World War II, 7
Soviet Union: domestic issues, 3, 23-24; Japan, 20-21
Soviet Union: economic issues: Japan, 22; North Korea, 97
Soviet Union: foreign policy, 12-17, 28-29, 114-15; China, 8-10, 18-20, 28; East Asia, 7; Japan, 9-10, 20-24, 56-57; Korean reunification, 25-26, 115, 117; North Korea, 11-14, 26-27, 96, 97; Northeast Asia, 12-14, 28-29; South Korea, 11-14, 24-25, 28, 96-99; United States in Asia, 13, 27-28
Stalin, Joseph, 1, 7, 11
States: leaders' intentions, 4; strategies, structural changes, 114
Structural Impediment Initiative (SII), 79
Suh, Dae-Sook, 111 n.28
Summer Olympics in Seoul, (1988), 88

Taiwan, 13, 51, 52
Takeshita, Noboru, 61
"Third image" dynamics among states, 2
Third World policy, 12
Tiananmen Square, 18, 19, 33, 36, 37, 49

United Nations, 88-89, 94, 102
United States: economic issues, 132; Japan, 61
United States: foreign policy, 131-35; China, 10, 13, 60; Japan, 9-10, 13, 56, 60; North Korea, 91; Northeast Asia, 5, 7, 131-35; South Korea, 3, 13, 90; Taiwan, 13
United States: military, 117; bases in Japan, 59; buildup under Reagan, 60; Northeast Asia, 3, 133-34; power in region, 128; South Korea, 90
U.S.-Japan Security Treaty, 56, 76, 77
U.S.S.R. See Soviet Union, Russia
Utsumi, Makato, 79
Van Wolferen, Karel, 63, 81 n.13
Vietnam, 8, 12

Vladivostok principles, 14, 22, 27

Waltz, Kenneth, 2, 3-4, 6 n.2
"Western alliance," 60
Wood, Perry L., 110 n.9
World economy, 128, 130, 137

Xi Zhihao, 55 n.27
Xu Kui, 55 n.15

Yakovlev, Alexander, 18
Yang Sung Chol, 107
Yeltsin, Boris, 20, 24
Yi Pom-sok, 87
Yoshida, Shigeru, 58, 81 n.4
"Yoshida strategy," 58
Young Whan Kihl, 82 n.36
Yu, Suk-Ryul, 112 n.40

About the Author

Lieutenant General William E. Odom, USA (Ret.), is Director of National Security Studies for Hudson Institute and an adjunct professor at Yale University. He is stationed in the Washington office of the Indianapolis-based Institute. In 1988, General Odom retired from the Army after 34 years of service. At the time of his retirement, General Odom was Director of the National Security Agency and Chief, Central Security Service, at Fort George Meade, Maryland.

As Director of the National Security Agency from 1985 to 1988, General Odom was responsible for the agency's work in signals intelligence and communications security, and was the principal SIGINT advisor to the Secretary of Defense, the Director of Central Intelligence, and the Joint Chiefs of Staff.

From 1981 to 1985, General Odom served as Deputy Assistant and then Assistant Chief of Staff for Intelligence, responsible for all Army intelligence operations. During the Carter Administration, from 1977 to 1981, General Odom was a senior member of the National Security Council Staff and military assistant to the President's Assistant for National Security Affairs, Zbigniew Brzezinski.

General Odom graduated from the United States Military Academy in 1954. He received an M.A. in Political Science from Columbia University in 1962, and a Ph.D. in 1970. He also attended the Army Language School and the U.S. Army Russian Institute. His military education includes the Armor Officer's Advanced Course, Airborne School, Ranger School, and the Command and General Staff College.

His previous books include *The Soviet Volunteers*, from Princeton University Press, and *On Internal War*, from Duke University Press.

General Odom is a member of the Council on Foreign Relations, the International Institute for Strategic Studies, the American Political Science Association, and the American Association for the Advancement of Slavic Studies. He holds an honorary degree from Middlebury College.

About the Contributors

Perry Wood

Perry Wood, a Hudson Institute Research Fellow, is a political scientist who specializes in developing-country politics and economic policy, with particular expertise on the trade and investment environments of East and Southeast Asia, Latin America, and the Caribbean. Mr. Wood's writings include the book *Beyond Recrimination: Perspectives on U.S.-Taiwan Trade Tensions* and the monograph *ASEAN in the 1990s: New Challenges, New Directions*. He is a member of The American Political Science Association, The American Association for Chinese Studies, The United States Naval Institute, and Phi Beta Kappa.

Andy Yan

Andy Yan is a Research Fellow in the Washington office of Hudson Institute. Mr. Yan's background includes experience with The World Bank, Policy and Planning Division, Department of Population and Human Resources. He also served as a Research Fellow at the State Council of China Institute for Economic System Reform, and The Chinese Social Science Academy of Anhui Province.

About the Hudson Institute

Hudson Institute is a private, not-for-profit research organization, founded in 1961 by the late Herman Kahn. Hudson analyzes and makes recommendations about public policy for business and government executives, as well as for the public at large. It does not advocate an express ideology or political position. However, more than thirty years of work on the most important issues of the day has forged a viewpoint that embodies skepticism about the conventional wisdom, optimism about solving problems, a commitment to free institutions and individual responsibility, an appreciation of the crucial role of technology in achieving progress, and an abiding respect for the importance of values, culture, and religion in human affairs.

Since 1984, Hudson has been headquartered in Indianapolis, Indiana. It also maintains offices in Washington, D.C.; Montreal, Canada; and Brussels, Belgium.